Change and Renewal in
Children's Literature

Recent Titles in
Contributions to the Study of World Literature

Change and Renewal in Children's Literature

Edited by
Thomas van der Walt

Assisted by
Felicité Fairer-Wessels and
Judith Inggs

Published under the auspices of the International
Research Society for Children's Literature

Contributions to the Study of World Literature, Number 126

Westport, Connecticut
London

Library of Congress Cataloging-in-Publication Data

Change and renewal in children's literature / edited by Thomas van der
Walt ; assisted by Felicité Fairer-Wessels and Judith Inggs.
     p. cm. — (Contributions to the study of world literature, ISSN 0738–9345 ; no. 126)
    Includes bibliographical references and index.
    ISBN 0–275–98185–1 (alk. paper)
    1. Children's literature—History and criticism. I. Van der Walt, Thomas.
II. Fairer-Wessels, Felicité. III. Inggs, Judith. IV. Series.
PN1009.A1C4928   2004
809′.89282—dc22   2003062251

British Library Cataloguing in Publication Data is available.

Library of Congress Catalog Card Number: 2003062251
ISBN: 0–275–98185–1
ISSN: 0738–9345

First published in 2004

Praeger Publishers, 88 Post Road West, Westport, CT 06881
An imprint of Greenwood Publishing Group, Inc.
www.praeger.com

Printed in the United States of America

The paper used in this book complies with the
Permanent Paper Standard issued by the National
Information Standards Organization (Z39.48–1984).

10 9 8 7 6 5 4 3 2 1

Every reasonable effort has been made to trace the owners of copyright materials in this book,
but in some instances this has proven impossible. The author and publisher will be glad to
receive information leading to more complete acknowledgments in subsequent printings of the
book and in the meantime extend their apologies for any omissions.

Contents

Introduction

Thomas van der Walt

Literary critics agree that over the past number of years, children's literature has evolved into a genre with greater complexity and sophistication. Changes taking place are causing children's literature to move closer to so-called mainstream literature, and Nikolajeva (1996: 8) speaks of a contemporary evolution. Quite a number of books are being published that are crossing the borders to mainstream literature.

Not only is the literature itself changing, but so too is the study of this literature. According to critics, these two aspects cannot be separated. In her contribution to this book, Johnston (chapter 1) states that discussions of change and renewal in children's literature can refer as much to the role of critics, teachers, and researchers as to the actual literature itself. Nikolajeva (1996: 7) adds to this: "Once children's literature had been established as a special literary system, the system started to be questioned by most radically minded children's writers. Instead of writing within a given genre, they began to write against the genre, thus changing and renewing it."

With these changes in the approach of literary critics and theorists toward children's literature came a disregard of, and attack on, previous methods of study of children's literature. Established ideas have been challenged, "criticism [has become] more critical, less pedagogical, more sophisticated, less concerned with ideas of literature as life enhancement and more concerned with literary and ideological concerns" (Johnston chapter 1). The question arises as to what extent this challenge is the result of an endeavor to establish children's literature as study-object with status in the broader field of literature

2 Change and Renewal in Children's Literature

and, in the process, to disregard other critical perspectives—pedagogical, moral, religious, sociocultural, psychological—as being of lesser importance.

One sometimes reads about the "emancipation of children's literature," because children's literature is now regarded as part of "mainstream literature": as an interaction between texts and inherent features of texts themselves. This "discovery" of children's literature by critics and theorists and their critical commentary and theoretical analysis has led to the writing of children's books that are "deliberately more experimental, metafictive, intertextual and creative" (Johnston chapter 1). There have, however, always been certain children's books that have stood the test of any literary analysis—and have also, for decades, stood the test of the child reader. One must, therefore, be wary of a one-sided perspective that children's literature has been emancipated due to certain types of children's books that have been published, whereas it may rather be the result of how certain literary theorists have linked emancipation to the manner in which they approach the field of study. The part of children's literature that these theorists often regard as "quality literature" (Nikolajeva 1996: 206) and that has passed the test of emancipation is minor, however. It is known that more adults are reading young adult books and that publishers are satisfying this need. However, the mere publication of the books should not be seen as a reason to refer to children's literature as emancipated. In 1996, Roderick McGillis (17) argued that "the audience for critical readings of and approaches to children's books is, generally, other critical readers: in other words, professional 'book people.' . . . Critics speak to critics and not to the people directly involved in childrens' books: teachers, librarians, parents. . . . In the middle, the children's literature critics speak among themselves, more often than not forgetting the children who are the impetus for the enterprise in the first place."

The changes that have taken place in children's literature, the challenging of established ideas, and the fact that children's literature is seen today from a much wider perspective, are exciting and can only enhance the field of study. One must, however, be wary not to emphasize the divide between practitioners (teachers, librarians) and theoreticians. The emancipation of children's literature must not be seen at the expense of practitioners. Even the use of the term "practitioners" can be seen as derogatory. The approach of these so-called practitioners toward childrens' literature may differ from that of the literary critics, but this does not imply that their work is inferior. The fact that they have a different perspective, and probably consider the reader before the text, does not classify their work as "pre-evolutionary" within the context of children's literature. In the aspiration to negotiate an equal status or position for children's literature within the broader field of literature, one must not throw out the baby with the bathwater—and here the reference is to the works that children actually read, the real stuff, the true children's literature, in the words of Peter Hunt (1991: 14) and also the work of people who endeavor to bring children and literature together.

Although the issue of renewal and change in children's literature—with regard to pure literature and to the study thereof—has been debated for some time, it remains a topical subject. This is the reason why the board of the International Research Society for Children's Literature decided on this theme for its biennial congress held in South Africa in 2001. A selection of the papers delivered at the conference appears in this volume.

Children's literature is involved in a continuing and irreversible process of change and modernization. This, of course, starts the moment the recipient is exposed to, and comes in contact with, a narrative. As Doderer (chapter 17) phrases it in his contribution to this book: "Each recipient will accept the forms, contents, and messages of the text in her or his own way. It is therefore not possible to present a children's story, poem, or play without giving a new version or sometimes a new interpretation of the original."

The chapters in this volume deal with various aspects of renewal and change in children's literature: changes in the handling of certain subjects, changes with regard to a particular type of style, changes in the perception of certain texts of an author's work, and changes that have taken place when a particular work has been reworked in another genre. However, these changes always contain references to aspects that remain the same—that serve as the basis for remittal. As McGillis (1996: 25) points out: "because narrative feeds on narrative, because all forms of imaginative thinking partake of previous constructions of the human imagination, knowledge of the past and its cultural products is formative."

Clare Bradford, for example, discusses how texts produced by Aboriginal children renew and change through the strategies by which they address tradition, history, and political and cultural questions in contemporary Australia. In what is regarded as the politics of renewal, the Renaissance of Aboriginal culture, and specifically of Aboriginal children's literature, they aspire (and successfully manage) to overcome the effect of colonial rule on the Aboriginal population by means of recovery, rewriting, and collaboration.

Political change and its impact on children's literature is also the topic of Judith Inggs's chapter. She analyzes the reconstruction of the child, in relation to both the physical and mental space occupied by the characters, in the new and changing environment in South Africa.

Maria Lassén-Seger approaches renewal and change by analyzing a particular motif, namely metamorphosis. In her chapter, she indicates the major changes that have occurred in the use of child-animal metamorphosis. Although the popularity of animal characters in children's literature is always seen as evidence of a special connection between children and animals and refers to the connection between the universal state of childhood innocence and animalism, changes in criticism have indicated that the image of childhood as social, cultural, and historical construction is not static, and that the preoccupation with animals and metamorphosis is probably rather a reflection of an adult preoccupation that regards child and animal as interchangeable.

The prevalence of animals in children's literature is also the topic of Darja Mazi-Leskovar's chapter. Her focus is on the way in which authors succeed in presenting the fictional "animal mind"; the animal in its animal nature, but as an identifiable character. However, this has also changed as a result of authors' changing suppositions about the readers' expectations about the world—about nature and a particular species, the society and the child, the adult who enters into a relationship with the animal, changes in the point of view, and so forth.

In contrast to animal characters and stories that deal with animals, topics dealing with sexuality, homosexuality, and immorality have long been regarded as unsuitable for younger readers. Irrespective of the association that cross-dressing has with these taboo themes, there has always been an abundance of children's narratives with elements of cross-dressing. In her contribution, Victoria Flanagan indicates the changes that have taken place in stories that portray cross-dressing as a harmless act of childish experimentation and imagination. It is seen as nonsexual and temporary and there has been a proliferation of literature "which has demonstrated an unprecedented willingness to embrace adult concepts previously considered off limits to younger readers" (Flanagan chapter 6).

Margot Hillel's chapter follows suit, dealing with the eroticized figure in Australian books for teenagers. She shows how the figurative expression of the eroticized child figure has long been a part of children's literature, but how this earlier eroticized figure of the innocent child has been frequently supplanted in contemporary literature by the eroticizing of the teenage figure linked with pubescent sexuality. The last decades of the twentieth century, however, saw a clear renewal in the depiction of the erotic child.

Eva-Maria Metcalf addresses the way in which the importance of democratic structures and procedures has been reflected, and how these structures and procedures have shifted focus in children's literature during the past few decades. Paying specific attention to German and Scandinavian children's books, she argues that children's books published since the 1970s have implicitly and explicitly contributed to the formation of a democratic mind-set and have propagated more democratic child-adult interactions.

Changes evident in childhood and the portrayal of change and renewal in children's books over the years is a binding thread in Helene Høyrup's chapter. She focuses on the historic concepts of childhood as they appear in Hans Christian Andersen's work and states that "studying Andersen's view of childhood is like reading a story of cultural perspectives at war with themselves" (Høyrup chapter 9). Anna Karlskov Skyggebjerg, however, addresses a totally different aspect of Danish children's literature—namely, how recent Danish fantasy tales belong to an established genre tradition with canonized works, but also how the same stories challenge and renew the genre tradition. In her discussion of the works of Louis Jensen and Knud Holten, she indicates how, on the one hand, they draw on the legacy of E.T.A. Hoffmann and Lewis

Carroll, but, on the other hand, how they represent originality and innovation in the genre.

Other contributions to this volume deal with change and renewal that occur in a particular author's work over a period of time. David Rudd, for example, indicates how the work of Enid Blyton has withstood the test of time—going through a number of transformations. These transformations derive partly from Blyton's own reconstruction of herself, and partly from critical reactions to her work. In addition to showing this process of change and renewal in action, Rudd points out that it might well have been at the expense of some of Blyton's original appeal. The result of the constant reworking and retouching of her original stories in different styles, the writing of prequels and sequels, and the customizing of her work for different nationalities may be that her work could "become ephemeral in a more final sense" (Rudd chapter 11).

Another author whose work is often seen as ephemeral but has withstood the test of time is Edgar Rice Burroughs's novel, *Tarzan of the Apes*. Rolf Romören discusses the treatment of different motifs in retellings of the novel and indicates how some recent Scandinavian contributions show a changing perspective on the Tarzan mythology.

Then there is Roald Dahl. Eileen Donaldson states that Dahl, in contrast to the popular view that fantasy is merely escapist and thus bad, uses fantasy to enable his readers to transcend their realities. By injecting magic into their worlds, Dahl binds the children into new, loving familial relationships. Because Dahl concentrates on the possibilities that fantasy can bring to the "real" world, his fantasy does not necessarily encourage escapism but rather satisfies the "desire for a better, more complete, unified reality" (Donaldson chapter 13).

Rosemary Johnston's contribution to this volume has already been referred to; she discusses the effect that change has had on the study of children's literature, and on the divide between practitioners (teachers) and theoreticians. The various changes in the study of children's literature have also been responsible for exciting changes in literature itself. She refers to children's literature as a creative art, and by viewing it as such, broadens not only critical perspectives but also includes everyone involved with literature—academics; researchers; educationalists; and, to use her term, practitioners. She indicates how artistic practices, processes, and paradigms of the creative arts provide another live viewing area from which we can actively observe and comment. This makes it possible for researchers in the field of children's literature to also play an intrinsically creative role.

Tove Jansson is one children's book author who has stood the test of time. Long before there was talk of "emancipation" or "evolution" of children's literature, she wrote books that were valued and admired by both literary critics and theorists, and by so-called "practitioners." It is fitting that at least one chapter in this volume covers her work. Sirke Happonen explores the spatial representation of the tension between solitude and togetherness, the individual and the others, in one of Jansson's illustrated short stories, "The

Hemulen Who Loved Silence." She illustrates how Jansson spins complex existential and social ideas in the reshaping movement and form of the merry-go-round (a central idea in Jansson's production)—a metonym of interpersonal patterns and distances—and how it is shaped by different voices and views that are representations of various character and narrator worldviews.

Anne de Vries's approach to change and renewal in children's literature takes the reader back to the beginning—to lullabies, the first literature most people encounter. This primal source of literature [McGillis (1996: 9) says that all literature is the ghost of an oral form] has many expected universal characteristics. A basic foundation or framework has remained the same through the ages; but, on the other hand, changes have taken place that show that even the universal elements have cultural differences, as de Vries illustrates in his examples of recorded lullabies.

Obvious examples of the changing (and renewing) of children's literature are translations and reworkings into other genres and media. As Riitta Oittinen indicates, translations are never the same as their originals; they always take on a new language, a new culture, new readers, and a new point of view. In the case of translations of picture books, whole situations—including the words, the illustrations, and the whole (imagined) reading-aloud situation—are translated, and changed to a lesser degree.

The reworking of a book to film—specifically, *Emil und die Detektive*—is the subject of Klaus Doderer's chapter. Doderer, however, places this reworking into a broader perspective, by describing how the reworking of texts for children is often focused on "preserving culture and on reproducing conservative outcomes" (Stephens and McCullum 1998: x).

In a truly international conversation about youth literature—and that is what this volume, with its contributions from academics from various parts of the world, constitutes—one can, as Nancy Huse (chapter 18) states, "expect that regional patterns, various kinds of group diaspora, and the migrating identities of readers would produce a multiply intersecting set of discourses, splendid and intriguing, empowering and puzzling." The interaction among academics—especially as is the case in this volume, in which chapters have been based on papers delivered at an international conference—should result in work about generation, reproduction, and the newness of cooperation and community. Huse indicates the important role of "play" in this regard. For many of us, children's literature constitutes a cultural text that demonstrates the "work" of "play." However, that very paradox complicates the production of knowledge in the field and unfortunately very often nothing much comes of newness and the result of scholarly work. Whether it is papers delivered at conferences or chapters in volumes, there is a definite sameness according to Huse. One trusts that this is not the case with this volume, which aspires to give new voices the opportunity to address new topics within the broader field of change and renewal in children's literature. Hopefully, this volume will lead to further renewal in the field of study, while also bringing about a change in the barrier that exists between the various "camps" that all work toward a common goal—the study of children's literature.

BIBLIOGRAPHY

Hunt, P. 1991. *Criticism, Theory, and Children's Literature*. Oxford, UK: Blackwell.

McGillis, R. 1996. *The Nimble Reader: Literary Theory and Children's Literature*. London: Prentice Hall.

Nikolajeva, M. 1996. *Children's Literature Comes of Age: Toward a New Aesthetic*. New York: Garland.

Stephens, J., and R. McCullum. 1998. *Retelling Stories, Framing Culture: Traditional Story and Metanarratives in Children's Literature*. New York: Garland.

CHAPTER 1

Renewing Stories of Childhood: Children's Literature as a Creative Art

Rosemary Johnston

Discussions of change and renewal in children's literature can refer as much to our role as teachers and researchers as to the actual literature itself. Different critical perspectives—literary, pedagogical, moral, religious, and socio-cultural—initiate different discourses and can challenge established ideas. Thus, as children's literature came into the academe, there was a significant change in how it was talked about: criticism became more critical, less pedagogical, more sophisticated, less concerned with ideas of literature as life enhancement, and more concerned with literary and ideological concerns. The result of this has been, on the one hand, problematical, with a clear divide emerging between practitioners (teachers) and theoreticians; and, on the other hand, exciting, with the literature itself—in verbal and visual text—reflecting the results of the critical commentary, and becoming more deliberately experimental, metafictive, intertextual, and creative. Indeed, children's literature is a creative art, and viewing it as such not only enlarges critical perspectives but also engages us—as teachers, educators, academics, and researchers—in that creative process.

The term "creative arts" is not, as some curricula suggest, limited to only art, drama, and music; rather, it refers to the many ways in which and through which humans create linguistic, visual, and aural stories and images of who and what they are. Thus, it includes literature, design, and dance. Further, the "creative arts" are not only product; they are also a range of artistic practices, processes, and paradigms that provide another live viewing area from which we can actively observe and comment, opening to us, as researchers, an intrinsically creative role as well. If we look at literature through the optic of dance and drama theory, and, for example, Laban's basic movement theory, it is clear that his description of the relationship between *movement* and *emo-*

tion; his theory of eight working actions (wringing, slashing, pressing, punching, floating, gliding, dabbing, and flicking); and his concept of the motion factors of weight, space, time, and flow all can expand how we think about the illustrations of picture books and provide the theoretical tools—and languages—to make creative connections. For example, in considering the exuberance of an illustration in *Papa Lucky's Shadow* (Daly 1992), we can move beyond the formal terms of conventional art criticism (pertaining to line, form, shape, and color), and even beyond the wonderful medieval idea of the simultaneous principle. We can consider this illustration in terms of the *dynamic factor of weight*—distribution of lightness and strongness; we can discuss how the figures intersect in different *planes of space;* we can note the pictorial depiction of the rhythmic factor of *time* (the intuitive distinctions between past and future, sustained and quick); and we can contemplate the idea of *flow* of time—the cyclic nature of movement, and its freedom or degree of impediment.

I am particularly interested in the creative representation of *time,* and in the significance of time and complex time perspectives as the pivotal element in stories of real childhoods renewed as picture book texts. These retellings of childhood are artistically mediated retrospectives: the re-creation of lived experience as autobiographies of adults presented in children's book form. Here, indeed, as a preliminary to our discussions, is the intuitive application of the simultaneous principle: authors renewing their childhoods in the present, pulling back and unraveling time, and recreating and shaping the children they once were, but doing so from the simultaneous moment of an older perspective. Cassirer (1996: 83) notes that part of the complexity of *space* is its representation of objects of "see ability"; many of these autobiographies succeed spectacularly in making past time and the passing of time—"seeable," not just as effect (although that is part of it) but more in a Foucauldian sense of "layers of an ever-accumulating past." As part of their drawing up of past time into present, or reaching out from present time to past, these texts also make seeable other, equally complex abstractions, such as nostalgia, regret, hope, yearning, and sorrow; all of which are related to time and its immutability.

The challenge for us as researchers is to explore how this process works, and to describe it creatively. Laban's theories lead to Jean Sabatine's idea of "essence theory." Essence theory emerges from Sabatine's jazz choreography, and refers to the physicalization of the image in dance. In drama, it has been adapted to train actors to conceptualize *essence* (intrinsic) rather than appearance (extrinsic): don't try to express what a tree *looks like,* but what a tree *is*—the strength of its roots, the roughness and layerness of its bark, the softness and movement of its leaves.

This suggests that picture books make the abstract seeable by describing or depicting its essence—the impression of the deeply innate informs the more superficial "reality." For example, the passing of time is made seeable in the Swedish text, *Jag såg, jag ser* (Jaensson and Grähs 1997), not only by the appearance of the effects of the passing of time, but also by the impression/ expression of the *essence* of the passing of time: change. Time, this text shows, changes not only what we see but how we see it. With change can come grief, loss, mortality, and absence rather than presence—absence "traced" by presence in a photograph. In a very simple format—the juxtapositions of past and present tense in the verbal text, and of past and present focalizations in the visual text—time and its inexorability and "sad mortality" are made seeable. The passing of time is expressed phenomenologically, in terms of perceptions, and ontologically, in terms of being and beingness. Time is perceived in relation to being and in relation to past and present worlds. The passing of childhood is the passing of more than a way of life; it is the passing of life itself. What was, no longer can be. It is also a prescient view into the future— the baby who sees itself in the reflection of the last page will similarly change: what is seen now will be what was. This sparse little book makes grief—as well as humor—seeable. The first picture of the mother's face shows not only the significance of mother in a child's world, but also the smallness of the world, seen from inside the containment of the pram. Jaensson and Grähs have not only caught the essence of babyhood—helplessness, dependence, love, containment, smallness, and boundedness—but in this retrospective have transcribed it into the essence of humanness. The frames may change, but the dilemma does not. We live on the edge of loss.

Bakhtin's idea of the chronotope offers another way of considering this process of see ability. The word "chronotope" *(xronotop)* was not invented by him, but his application of it to literature—specifically the novel—has led to new ways of considering relationships in narrative between people and events on the one hand and time and space on the other. The term (from *chronos*, time, and *topos*, place) was a mathematical one relating to Einstein's theory of relativity, which redescribed time not as the objective absolute of Newtonian physics, but rather as subjective, changeable, multiple, and dependent on the position of the observer. The appropriation of the chronotope as a literary descriptor has provided us with an important critical tool; in Holquist's words (1981: 425–26), it gives us "an optic for reading texts as x-rays of the forces at work in the culture system from which they spring."

Extending this idea into a concept of the visual chronotope (Johnston 2001: 408)—that is, the visual depiction in narrative of the relationships of time and space to people and events—becomes particularly significant in representations of the renewal of lived childhood that is autobiography. The essence of Bakhtinian theory is what he called *napravlennost* (the "impulse that reaches out beyond the word"). The impulse that reaches out beyond the words of the two Australian texts *A Is for Aunty* (Russell 2000) and *Do Not Go around the Edges* (Utemorrah and Torres 1990) is overtly subjective and autobiographical: the authors want to retell the experience of their childhoods. In *A Is for Aunty*, the essence of the remembered experience is expressed in two chronotopes: the verbal text expressing the author's past, and the visual text expressing a sense of time beyond the lifetime of the actual author. In *Do Not Go around the Edges*, there are three intersecting chronotopes: one (the prose of the autobiography) expressing past experience, one expressing the ramifications of the past in the present (the poetry), and one joining both past and present into a sort of present continuous (the illustrations).

Ricoeur (1988: 271) has described at length the complexity of time in narrative and of what he calls the "limit experiences" depicted by fiction. *A Is for Aunty* by Elaine Russell (2000) delimits time in a naive—naïf—but powerful way. Russell uses the genre of the alphabet book and the sequential letters of the alphabet to give narrative shape to her memories of an indigenous childhood. In the *words* of the text, people and events are related to time and space through the normal chronology of the narrator's lifetime: "M is for Mission. The mission where I lived as a child was like a small suburb outside the main town, in the bush near a river." Each letter of the alphabet stimulates a memory of the past: "I is for Inspection Day. The manager's wife visited each house on the mission to make sure our homes were clean and tidy—which they were!"

The past, which is clearly expressed in words, is the remembered past of an older person looking back, the past of an individual lifetime. However, something more than an individual lifetime is being made seeable in this book. Using the research optic of the visual chronotope, we can compare and contrast how people and events are drawn in relation to time and space in the *pictures* of the text with how people and events are described in relation to time and space in the *words* of the text. These are two differing chronotopes. The verbal text draws the individual within the mortal constraints of an individual lifetime. The visual text draws the individual in a time and space that is far beyond that of the individual lifetime. The past expressed in the illustrations is unbound by the restrictions of personal event and experience; it is a dense cultural past/present that could be called a type of Dreaming chronotope. Ricoeur's (1988) idea of past as "Other" is not appropriate here. This is a notion of past as present continuous, of relationships between people and events and time and space that have been, that will be, that *are*. The pictures construct multiple references—to totemic figures; to the circles of sites, camps, waterholes, and campfires; in fact, to physical and spiritual maps that represent the essence of indigenous beings. The roads present an imagery of paths and movement, while the river that dominates most of the illustrations is a reminder of Water Dreamings, and of a snake or Rainbow serpent; it is a type of genesis, life-giving and connecting.

In prose (without its pictures), this is a twentieth-century story told in a warm but matter-of-fact way; it is a charming story of random memories, with a deep but not bitter subtext implicating sociocultural attitudes, practices, and policies in relation to indigenous people. In pictures (without its prose), this is a story that, in depicting a "modern" Australia, reaches back into a land and a way of life that existed centuries before white settlement. In the form of a picture book, with both prose and pictures as carriers of narrative that come together to jointly form "story," the visual chronotope amplifies the verbal chronotope to a landscape/mindscape of time and space beyond the individual experience of it. This does not devalue individual life experience; it expands it. The relationship of people to the time-spaces of the illustrations is different than the relationship of people to the time-spaces of the verbal narrative, and the effect of this difference is to transpose *A Is for Aunty* into a "seeable" representation of an abstract and complex temporal and spatial dimension.

Do Not Go around the Edges is a trifurcated narrative, with, first, a simple line of autobiography (old Daisy renewing her life story in picture book text); second, a poetic response that is triggered out of present wisdom, knowledge, and disappointment as the author confronts in memory the events of the past; and third, a visual response—the art work of Utemorrah's niece, Pat Torres, that is fiercely protective of indigenous heritage, infills current space with dreaming, and is another version of the Dreaming chronotope.

The essence of these two texts is that, through the use of two different chronotopes (those of the words and the pictures), they are representing a sense of time that cannot be contained in any one person's lifetime; it is a sense of what Bakhtin (1986: 1–9, 84) calls *Great Time*—the perspectives of centuries. This is a "fullness of time" (1986: 42): time and space beyond the personal, but made personal through the experience of it. The deep structure of these texts is configured with a gathering of multiple times and spaces, and interconnecting relationships that are at once personal and *present*, and communal and continuous.

The two books mentioned above invoke a sense of Great Time that pertains to Australian indigenous perspectives, but the idea of Great Time is not limited to such texts, although they provide telling examples of it. There are, for example, a number of picture books about childhood wartime experiences in which Great Time is evoked through the noncoincidental intersections of visual and verbal narratives. The two Japanese texts, *My Hiroshima*, by Junko Morimoto (1987) and *The Bracelet* by Yoshiko Uchida (1976); and the American text, *All Those Secrets of the World*, by Jane Yolan and L. Baker (1991), are retellings of everyday childhoods shocked out of the everyday by the horrors of war. *My Hiroshima* is the remembering—from a long way off in both space and time—of one of the most terrible moments in human history; *The Bracelet* tells a story of the pain of internment, of loss of identity, and of "essence"— in this case, not only the essence of self but the material and immaterial essence of friendship that the bracelet represents. *All Those Secrets of the World* is overtly about perspectives—things far away are smaller—but the shadow of ships that appear small on the horizon loom large in the children's lives, and push Yolan's story about loss and parting into a Great Time that includes millions of war dead.

In theoretical terms, the idea of Great Time implies that narrative time space can represent both the present—as a series of moments that contains specific, "essential" meanings that are absolutely held within that particular fusion of time and space (cultural, social, historical, who is present, who is speaking and listening, how they feel toward each other, what has just happened, time of day, weather, and so on)—and, simultaneously, a sense of past/present/future that is an accumulation of meanings that is not limited to specific presentness, and includes the utterances of others. Picture book autobiography is a dual-media genre that uses both words and pictures to renew and represent personal histories, and thus can depict two sorts of pastness, two sorts of presentness, and two sorts of memory.

Bakhtin (1981: 254) notes that texts are continually renewed through the creative perception of listeners and readers. I would also add "researchers." Our role is a creative one too, as we open up debates and set up new platforms for discussion. In discussions about intelligence, Gardner (1984: 240) notes the significance of interpersonal intelligence that has, as its core capacity, *"the ability to access one's own feeling life"* (my italics). These writers have not only accessed their own "feeling life" (i.e., the life of one's feelings), but, visually and verbally, laid it out for others to access, "read," and renew. There is a shared intimacy in this, a creative bond across time and space, across generations. Picture book autobiographies, in renewing stories of particular childhoods, make seeable not only the essence of those childhoods, but also something of the essence of a larger time-space beyond personal presentness. Thus, they extend the critical mindscape of children—and, dare I say, of us as well.

BIBLIOGRAPHY

Bakhtin, M. M. 1981. *The Dialogic Imagination*, ed. Michael Holquist, trans. Caryl Emerson and Michael Holquist. Austin: University of Texas Press.

Bakhtin, M. M. 1986. *Speech Genres and Other Late Essays.* Austin: University of Texas Press.

Cassirer, E. 1996. *The Philosophy of Symbolic Forms.* New Haven, Conn.: Yale University Press.

Daly, N. 1992. *Papa Lucky's Shadow.* Claremont, South Africa: Songololo Books.

Featherstone, M., ed. 1992. *Cultural Theory and Cultural Change.* London: Sage Publications.

Gardner, H. 1984. *Frames of Mind: The Theory of Multiple Intelligences.* London: Fontana.

Holquist, M. 1981. "Glossary." In *The Dialogic Imagination*, ed. M. M. Bakhtin, 425–27. Austin: University of Texas Press.

Jaensson, H., and G. Grähs. 1997. *Jag såg, jag ser.* Stockholm: Alfabeta Bokförlag.

Johnston, R. R. 2001. "Children's Literature." In *Literacy: Reading, Writing and Children's Literature* by G. Winch et al. Melbourne: Oxford University Press.

Morimoto, J. 1987. *My Hiroshima.* Sydney: William Collins.

Morson, G. S., and C. Emerson. 1990. *Mikhail Bakhtin: Creation of a Prosaics.* Stanford, Calif.: Stanford University Press.

Ricoeur, P. 1988. *Time and Narrative*. Vol. 3. Chicago: University of Chicago Press.
Russell, E. 2000. *A Is for Aunty*. Sydney: ABC Books.
Sabatine, J. 1995. *Movement Training for the Stage and Screen: The Organic Connection between Mind, Spirit and Body*. New York: Back Stage Books.
Uchida, Y. 1976. *The Bracelet*. New York: Philomel Books.
Utemorrah, D., and P. Torres. 1990. *Do Not Go around the Edges*. Broome, Australia: Magabala Books Aboriginal Corporation.
Yolan, J., and L. Baker. 1991. *All Those Secrets of the World*. Boston: Little, Brown and Co.

CHAPTER 2

When Everything Old Is New Again: Aboriginal Texts and the Politics of Renewal

Clare Bradford

When the British invaded Australia in 1788, there were probably around a million Aboriginal people spread unevenly across the continent, speaking well over 200 languages and affiliated into several hundred groupings. Their belief systems were based on the Dreaming, which in the words of the anthropologist William Stanner (1979: 24) is "a kind of logos or principle of order" instituted when creative beings walked about the universe and produced landforms, animal and plant species, and humankind. Not only this, but they created the Law that governs relationships between the constituent parts of the universe, and ensures that balance is preserved. It should not be imagined that Aboriginal cultures prior to 1788 were static or impervious to change, because over a span of perhaps sixty thousand years, Aborigines witnessed dramatic changes in the land and its inhabitants, described by the archaeologist John Mulvaney (1989: xvi) as follows: "In the face of fluctuating climates, contrasting environments, creative insights and cultural innovations, populations increased, people shifted residence and countless meetings occurred between groups of people when ideas or goods were exchanged." Such environmental and cultural shifts were managed and accommodated within rituals and practices that referred to and enacted the Law as established in the Dreaming.

The colonial relations that operated after 1788 effected a massive assault on Aboriginal cultures as the land was occupied and gradually appropriated. The starkest indicator of the effects of colonial rule is the fact that from 1788 to 1901, the Aboriginal population decreased from around a million to something like 66,000. Entire clans were wiped out, languages became extinct, and ritual practices and narratives died with them. Throughout the colonial period and for much of the twentieth century, the doomed race theory held sway,

until by the 1940s it became evident that Aboriginal cultures stubbornly refused to die out, despite the effects of colonialism and assimilationist policies.
The renaissance of Aboriginal culture that occurred in the 1970s was marked
by a sharp increase in cultural production by Aboriginal artists and authors,
whose work reflected and produced meanings around political issues such as
the struggle for land rights.

Within the field of children's literature, another renaissance has been unfolding over the last decade, and in this chapter I consider some recent children's texts produced by Aborigines and through the collaboration between
indigenous and nonindigenous Australians. These texts relate to the theme of
change and renewal through the strategies by which they address tradition,
history, and political and cultural questions alive in contemporary Australia.
Their agendas can be summarized as follows:

Recovery and retelling of traditional narratives.

Recovery and deployment of Aboriginal languages, including Aboriginal English.

Rewriting of historical narratives from the point of view of indigenous people.

Narratives featuring the experience of Aboriginal people in urban settings.

Engagement with contemporary cultural and political questions.

Production of hybrid texts incorporating indigenous and nonindigenous traditions.

New forms of collaboration between Aboriginal and non-Aboriginal people.

The texts I discuss have been produced by indigenous publishers and, in
one case, by a TAFE college; that is, an institution for vocational training.
They emerge at a time when relations between indigenous and nonindigenous
Australians are marked by contradictory and opposing discourses. To sketch
some of these contradictions: a series of reconciliation marches in major cities
during 2000 attracted many thousands of Australians. At the same time, the
conservative Howard government had wound back the processes whereby
Aboriginal clans could seek the restitution of ancestral land. A far-right backlash against Aborigines manifested during the late 1990s in what Gelder and
Jacobs (1998: 65) called "postcolonial racism," the effect that occurs when
non-Aboriginal people who feel themselves to be disadvantaged blame Aborigines for having too much, in the form of government programs, land
rights, and even attention and sympathy. Aboriginality has never been more
important to Australian self-representation, at the same time that Aboriginal
people are massively overrepresented in all the markers of poverty and social
disadvantage: low life expectancy, high infant mortality, rates of incarceration
out of all proportion to their population, and appallingly high rates of youth
suicide.

As a solution to these problems, the Howard government proposes what it
calls "practical reconciliation"—that is, the provision of health and welfare
services to Aboriginal people. On the surface, these seem like commonsense

measures, but they address only the symptoms of postcolonial unease. The priorities of Aboriginal communities typically have to do with the reclamation of culture and the re-establishment of associations with the land. The recovery of traditional stories is central to these priorities, because narratives derive from and are enacted on particular stretches of country. The story *Kupi-Kupi and the Girl* (2000), written by Daphne Punytjina Burton and illustrated by Carolyn Windy, originates from Areyonga in the Northern Territory and was published as a dual-language text (Pitjantjajtara and English) by the indigenous publishing company, Magabala Books.

Earlier versions of traditional stories typically recast them into Western genres such as the *pourquoi* tale, the hero legend, or the fairy tale. In contrast, *Kupi-Kupi and the Girl* is situated within its country (that is, the region in which it is told) through peritextual information, which includes a map of language and cultural groupings and a guide to the pronunciation and orthography of the Pitjantjatjara language. In other respects too, *Kupi-Kupi and the Girl* makes a claim for a set of traditions and cultural meanings particular to its origins. The girl of the title is taken by the *kupi-kupi*, a sudden wind that "sucked her up and took her a long way across the country to another place" (Burton and Windy 2000: 7). Finally, it throws her into a waterhole, where she is taken captive by the *wanampi* or watersnake that inhabits the waterhole. She is rescued by a witchdoctor who carries her on his back away from the waterhole; but the *wanampi* is angry and sends a flood over the country to look for her. The flood cannot find her, and returns to the waterhole; the witchdoctor restores the girl to her parents, she marries him, and they live happily together.

It is easy enough to imagine how such a story might have been recast into a Cinderella schema within assimilationist publishing practices, but Burton's retelling foregrounds the significance of a number of elements particular to Pitjantjatjara traditions. The first of these is the reaction of the girl's parents to their loss: "Because they were unhappy they left their home and went to a different country to live with some other people"; to leave one's country is the most extreme way possible to demonstrate grief, because it involves a loss of identity. Secondly, the witchdoctor's rescue of the girl is constituted by her restoration to her parents, a move that reinstates her as a member of the clan and therefore as a person. Finally, the girl's marriage to the witchdoctor adheres to a highly complex set of traditions that define rights to a country and rules concerning relatedness. Carolyn Windy's collage illustration of the episode when the witchdoctor carries the girl back to her parents dramatizes the fissure between Western paradigms of romantic love, and marriage practices that are retained in many Aboriginal communities, as the young (that is, prepubescent) girl of the story is carried to her country by the man who is to be her marriage partner.

If *Kupi Kupi and the Girl* recuperates an ancient story for a contemporary audience, Pat Lowe and Jimmy Pike's *Desert Cowboy* (2000) writes back to colonial first-contact texts, which invariably privilege the perspectives of white children observing Aborigines who are represented as primitives or savages. The focal character in *Desert Cowboy* is Yinti, a young boy whose family is among the last of the desert people to "come out" of their ancestral homelands in order to live and work on cattle stations in Western Australia. In fact, Jimmy Pike and his family were among the last of the Walmajarri people to leave the Great Sandy Desert when Pike was an adolescent, and in this sense *Desert Cowboy* conforms with the category of text known in Kriol as *trustori*, an account of events authorized by someone who was present when they occurred.[1] *Desert Cowboy* is the product of collaboration between Pike and his non-Aboriginal partner Pat Lowe, and exemplifies a new wave of intercultural production.

Lowe and Pike defamiliarize Western practices by representing them from the point of view of Aboriginal people. For instance, a story in *Desert Cowboy* (2000) about kangaroo hunting begins with these words: "The kartiya people at Wynyard Station didn't like kangaroos. They didn't hunt them and eat their meat. Instead they ate the meat of their own sheep" (83). To Yinti, then, it seems extraordinarily wasteful to take the trouble to introduce animals only to kill and eat them, when there are abundant native animals to be used as food. Western practices such as wearing clothes, working for money, and betting on horse races are made strange as they are observed in relation to Yinti's knowledge of life in the desert.

What the anthropologist Deborah Bird Rose says about the stories of the Yarralin people in the Northern Territory is true of Aboriginal narratives more generally: that they "bring past and present, specific and general, individual and collective into a shared matrix" (Rose 2000: 30). In *Desert Cowboy*, Lowe and Pike maintain the narrative practice in which a story gathers meaning in relation to others, in a chain of signification. One sequence of stories concerns colonial violence and its repercussions in the time of the book's narrative. The first story in the sequence celebrates practices usually invisible to non-Aboriginal people, when Western modes of thought and behavior are subjected to parodic mimicry. Yinti and his companions are working on a large cattle station called Fairvale, where the manager and his wife are unkind and demanding. Every morning when the young men leave to round up cattle, the manager's wife reminds them that they must work hard if they expect to be fed:

Danny, one of the Fairvale boys, made fun of the boss's wife.
"Remember, boys," he'd say in an artificial kartiya voice, "Plenty cattle, plenty food; not much cattle, not much food!"
This had the other stockmen falling about in their saddles with laughter. (103)

The comedy of this episode lies in Danny's mockery not merely of the meanness of the boss's wife, but of her bad impersonation of Aboriginal English. Following this parodic narrative, Yinti is told a story whose function is to remind him (and readers) of a more sinister history of relations between Aboriginal and white people. The story is about a particular hill, the site of a colonial massacre:

> "That's a bad place, boy," [Danny] said. "Lot of black people were killed over there."
> "What for?" asked Yinti. Danny shrugged.
> "Might be they were spearing cattle. Might be for nothing. Kartiya used to kill a lot of blackfellas in the early days." (103)

Danny's bald and evasive telling refers to, but does not explain, this incident of colonial violence. Deborah Bird Rose (2000: 29), describing her experience of living with the Yarralin, explains that "verbal learning, although it may seem straightforward, is often opaque to the newcomer," because to understand one story it is necessary to be familiar with others, and with broader social processes. In *Desert Cowboy*, Yinti is observed undergoing such verbal learning, which must be informed by the reading of country and of the physical traces of the past.

In the third story, the manager gives Yinti a gun to kill a rogue bull, and, having carried out his task, he visits the hill that Danny has shown him. As he reads the contours of the land, he can tell that people once dug for water at a waterhole, which is now dried up. On the red sand are white fragments, neither wood nor stone, and when Yinti picks some up he realizes that they are shards of bone. He replaces them on the sand so as not to disturb the ground, and returns to the homestead. The fourth story gathers up the previous three although in an indirect and allusive way; in it, Yinti returns to the homestead with the manager's gun. It is dark and he looks inside the house to where the manager and his wife sit at the kitchen table after their meal. Yinti lifts the gun to his shoulder and aims first at the manager, then at his wife. He stands for a long time in this posture, but does not press the trigger. Then he lowers the rifle, hangs it in the rack, and returns to the camp.

Beneath the deceptive simplicity of this sequence lies a set of complex meanings, encompassing colonial relations, the need for reticence in referring to events like the massacre, the connections between the past and the present, and questions of retribution and of compensation. Similarly, Pike's illustration of the homestead story, with its emphasis on the figure of Yinti and the possibilities open to him, locates the key players against a ground suggesting country, the site of personal and collective identity, but a version of country in which the homestead, the windmill, the farm shed, and the utility iconically represent the pastoral industry and refer to the colonial appropriation that transformed country into bundles of land owned by white people. The collaborative work of Lowe and Pike, like that of Boori Pryor and Meme McDonald, produces narratives that "reclaim the past in order to liberate the present" (Rose 2000: 234) and model new forms of engagement between cultures.

Finally, I want to refer to texts produced by Aboriginal students: a set of books, under the general title "Once Upon a Koori Time," produced by Aboriginal tertiary students in Mildura, in northern Victoria; and *Goanna Jumps High*, a book created and illustrated by primary school children at Urandangi on the border between Queensland and the Northern Territory. The six "Once Upon a Koori Time" titles come from a region where pastoralism had an early and drastic effect on Aboriginal people, resulting in rapid depopulation. The Aborigines who now live in and around Mildura generally come from other places, so that several of these stories are tales of migration, loss of homelands, and the formation of Aboriginal subjectivities forged between traditional and new associations. Thus, the story *My New Home*, by Kylie Atley, compares two experiences of swimming: "When it is hot we go swimming in the brown Murray River, and I miss the clear blue sea. The Murray River is only very small compared to the sea" (Atley 2000: 10). Here, the conjunction of place and identity is complicated by the overlay of memory on the experience of life in new country. The split of subjectivity dramatized through Atley's representation of the two stretches of water is balanced by the rueful smile of the narrator as she swims in the brown river and dreams of the blue sea. Elsewhere, the narrative alludes more directly to an identity formation wrought between places and people: "At my new home in Mildura, Aboriginal people call themselves Koories. In Tasmania we call ourselves Palawa people. I don't know much about my mob but I am learning more each day" (Atley 2000: 7). Aboriginal children are trained in knowledge of country and kin, these being the two axes around which identities are formed; and *My New Home* argues that contemporary Aboriginal children undergo training in the same fields of knowledge, although in forms complicated by colonial history.

Aborigines are, as I have noted, essential to Australian self-definition, because "their art, their archaeological remains, their concepts of the sacred, and their physical presence are appropriated to fuel images of national identity" (Rose 2000: 2). Allan Harris's book, *My Olympics* (2000), inverts this relationship by Aboriginalizing the Olympics. The crowd scenes show a mix of ethnicities with an Aboriginal flag displayed alongside other national flags and near a sign proclaiming "Oi Oi Oi," the chant deployed by Australian crowds at sporting fixtures. Native animals (identified by their names in the Wiradjuri language) are seen winning various events, as in the following two examples: "The barrandharr won the rowing. The dhanguurr won the fifty-meter freestyle swimming" (4–5); and the climactic moment of the narrative occurs when "I danced in the Corroboree" (11). The global significances of the Olympics are here reconfigured into a view from within Aboriginal culture, which incorporates Australianness into its production of identities. The chant that precedes "Oi Oi Oi" is always "Aussie Aussie Aussie"; thus, what

My Olympics imagines is a claim to identity going far beyond the tokenistic deployment of Aboriginal culture at public events.

The text *Goanna Jumps High* was produced through funding by the State and Federal Governments for remote country areas. The program makes it possible for artists and authors to visit schools in such areas and to enable children to produce texts that are normally printed as in-house reading material, because English is a second language to children in remote communities. The eight children named as the book's authors and illustrators ranged in age from 6 to 17; all were Aboriginal except for one boy, the publican's grandson. Daryll Bellingham, a white storyteller, and the white artist Narelle Oliver worked with the children to develop the narrative and a sequence of illustrations produced as linocuts. The narrative concerns a goanna, a large lizard described as follows:

Now a goanna's not a very handsome sort of animal. It's got a tail, four legs, a belly and back, a head with a wicked-looking mouth, two eyes and a long tongue. . . . It can eat grasshoppers as fast as you blink, but it couldn't jump to save its life. One year though, the kids at Urandangi proved all the experts wrong. (3)

In the narrative that follows, the Urandangi kids train a goanna to jump by feeding it grasshoppers until "it start[s] to jump like one" (9). The goanna wins the high jump event in the regional school sports, beating the kangaroo entered by the children of Dajarra school. After the goanna appears on local television, "someone down in Brisbane" sends a fax to Urandangi asking the children and their goanna to appear on national television. The children train the goanna to jump over the smoke stack in Mt Isa, the mining town. It succeeds in this feat, but at a cost.

What is most striking about this narrative, and especially its ending, is that its style and content are so clearly congruent with traditions of Australian bush narrative: the understated, wry tone; the emphasis on action; the combination of the tall tale and a schema in which country people go to the city (always a site for comedic comparisons). To some degree, this can be explained by Daryll Bellingham's influence on the development of the narrative; but there are more complex cultural moves going on in this story. The last sentence of the narrative, "At least we can have a good feed of goanna," was contributed by one of the youngest of the Urandangi children.[2] In its shift from the fantastic to the mundane, and its humorous undercutting of the dramatic moment, it dramatizes the interplay of traditions and the effects of Aboriginal modes of thought and expression on cultural formations.

In his essay, "The Local and the Global: Globalization and Ethnicity," Stuart Hall reflects on what he terms "the return to the local," and the "struggle of the margins to come into representation" (1997: 183). Contemporary Aboriginal textuality fits within his description of the "new subjects, new genders, new ethnicities, new regions, and new communities [that] have emerged and acquired through struggle, sometimes in very marginalized ways, the means to speak for themselves for the first time" (1997: 183). The children's texts I have described do not evoke a return to an imagined utopia prior to colonization, but make a claim for Aboriginal subjectivities formed in the spaces between languages and cultures, and through new forms of cross-cultural collaboration that emphasize reciprocity and mutuality. In doing so, they formulate cultural meanings capable of contributing to the processes of decolonization that will address the "historical imbalances and cultural in-equalities produced by the colonial encounter" (Gandhi 1998: 176).

NOTES

1. Kriol is an English-based creole language used by Aboriginal communities in the northern regions of Australia.

2. Bellingham, Daryll. 2001. Telephone interview by author. Melbourne, 7 August.

BIBLIOGRAPHY

Atley, Kylie. 2000. *My New Home*. Mildura, Australia: Sunraysia Institute of TAFE.
Burton, Daphne Punytjina, and Carolyn Windy. 2000. *Kupi-Kupi and the Girl*. Broome, Australia: Magabala Books.
Gandhi, Leela. 1998. *Postcolonial Theory: A Critical Introduction*. St Leonards, NSW: Allen & Unwin.
Gelder, Ken, and Jane M. Jacobs. 1998. *Uncanny Australia: Sacredness and Identity in a Postcolonial Nation*. Carlton South, Australia: Melbourne University Press.
Hall, Stuart. 1997. "The Local and the Global: Globalization and Ethnicity." In *Dangerous Liaisons: Gender, Nation, and Postcolonial Perspectives*, eds. Anne McClintock, Aamir Mufti, and Ella Shohat, 173–87. Minneapolis: University of Minnesota Press.
Harris, Allan. 2000. *My Olympics*. Mildura, Australia: Sunraysia Institute of TAFE.
Lowe, Pat, and Jimmy Pike. 2000. *Desert Cowboy*. Broome, Australia: Magabala Books.
McDonald, Meme, and Boori Pryor. 1998. *My Girragundji*. Sydney: Allen & Unwin.
Mulvaney, D. J. 1989. *Encounters in Place: Outsiders and Aboriginal Australians 1606–1985*. St Lucia Old, Australia: University of Queensland Press.
Rose, Deborah Bird. 2000. *Dingo Makes Us Human: Life and Land in an Australian Aboriginal Culture*. Cambridge: Cambridge University Press.
Stanner, William. 1979. *White Man Got No Dreaming*. Canberra: Australian National University Press.
Urandangi State School. 1999. *Goanna Jumps High*. Broome, Australia: Magabala Books.

CHAPTER 3

Space and Race in Contemporary South African English Youth Literature

Judith Inggs

Change and renewal in South African society has meant a reconstruction of the child in children's fiction. In reality, as well as in fiction, the South African child—and especially the young person—is challenged with redefining his or her identity in relation to a new environment. This new environment is both physical and cultural—who is the child in relation to the surroundings, and who is the child in relation to others? These are common themes in youth literature all over the world, but they are of particular interest in the case of South Africa over the last decade in the context of a new and changing society. This chapter analyzes this reconstruction of the child in the "new South Africa" in relation to both the physical and mental space occupied by the characters.

The question of space in relation to race is of central importance in South Africa, with its history of apartheid and separate development. Very few works prior to the 1990s were able to realistically depict children of different races moving in the same space. If writers wished to portray contact between different races, they tended to set their stories in rural areas, or on farms, where contact was more usual. This situation has changed gradually over the last decade, and works have increasingly reflected the ways in which writers have portrayed this new reality.

There are several configurations of the interaction between characters and the space around them. There is, for example, a contrast between the physical and mental space experienced by the characters, between rural and urban space, and between an alienation from and a sense of belonging to a particular space. These oppositions are explored in the characters' search for identity and efforts to define themselves in relation to their environment. In addition, the landscape and the weather are frequently used as a means of reflecting and influencing the mood and mental attitude of the characters. Earlier works are generally set in a single space. For example, *My Father and I* (Williams 1989) focuses on a young girl's quest to find out the truth about her father's death and to answer questions about her own identity. Her space is clearly identified as an area of Johannesburg in the 1930s. When Penny finally discovers the identity of her biological father and mother, and comes to understand the role played by her "real" mother, her newly regained identity is confirmed by her surroundings, and specifically by the onset of the rainy season.

It was raining. People cheered. The drought was breaking. Within a few moments the rain was falling in sheets and the noise under the iron roof had become deafening. . . . She dragged her mother out onto the street, with all the other people from Jeppes Town, into the pelting, driving, reviving rain. (Williams 1989: 103)

Other works focus on a sharp division of space along racial lines, a movement from one space to another, or a meeting of characters in a neutral space. Dianne Case's *92 Queen's Road* (1991), set in Woodstock (Cape Town) in the 1960s, reflects the harsh effects of apartheid on young people at the time. When chased away from his children by an irate white father, Kathy learns abruptly why she is not allowed to play with them:

"What's coloured?" I asked. She ran her forefinger along the outer length of my arm, from my shoulder to my finger tips. "This," she said, "is coloured. This brown skin is coloured. Those people are white, that is why they have a better beach than we do. We, on this side, we are all coloureds." A wave of repulsion swept over me. I felt dirty. (Case 1991: 46)

Along with the division of space, there is an alienation and absence of identity. Kathy's uncle tells her: "We don't belong here. This is not our country" (Case 1991: 48). Eventually, Kathy's uncle and aunt decide to cross permanently into that other space and "become white," losing their own identity within their family. Kathy's grandmother disowns her son, and, later, when Kathy passes one of her cousins in the street, he ignores her completely (100–101).

Other novels of the same period grapple with the issues around this division of space, some dealing with relationships between teenagers of different colors. Lawrence Bransby's *Down Street* (1989) tells the story of a developing romance between two young people. The illogicality of the apartheid classification system is revealed when Christina tells Ted she is actually colored. His shock is tangible: "I was holding the hands, my flesh touching hers, of a colored girl—somebody officially classified as not white. I felt my flesh creep at the idea" (Bransby 1989: 56).

The onset of apartness, otherness, in contrast with the growing closeness portrayed in the first half of the novel is striking. Ted does attempt to cross into Christina's space by going to church with her, but he becomes immediately aware of "not belonging . . . of not being wanted" (Bransby 1989: 77). This physical transgression results in him being beaten up by several colored boys, and subsequently punished both by the white authorities of his school and his parents. The impossibility of such a relationship is also stated quite clearly by Christina's father: "It must end, and it must end now, today" (91).

Bransby's novel was one of the first to attempt to present a fresh perspective on South African society and the difficulties young people were experiencing in making sense of it. Such works increased in number after the official end of apartheid when writers turned to issues arising from the profound reconstruction of society. The previously marked division of space was increasingly blurred. Movement between spaces took different forms. For example, in *Dark Waters*, by Jenny Robson (1995), the central theme is that of a perceived invasion of "white" space by people of other races. Zack's parents feel that they themselves have to move in turn to a "safer" space. By the end of the story, however, they become reconciled with their new neighbors, discovering similarity rather than distance between them. The perceived invasion instead becomes a merging.

Several novels dealing with space reflect this preoccupation in their titles. Bransby's *Outside the Walls* (1995b), deals with a search for identity by teenagers struggling to make sense of the confusion and violence around them during the run-up to the first democratic elections in South Africa. Feeling isolated in their own homes, their search takes them into the living space of the poor, black squatters on the outskirts of the town:

Gweneth and I seemed to be isolated, halfway between our own world and the world of the squatters. We didn't know where we belonged any more or whether what we were doing was right. . . .

Philip's shack became our hideout, our cave in the wilderness. . . . We ate putu with our fingers and samp and beans with the same spoon and heard about the killings in the rural areas, the attacks of ANC and Inkatha hit squads which everyone claimed didn't exist. (Bransby 1995b: 104–5)

Both change and renewal are reflected in the way in which characters increasingly seek answers in the space traditionally belonging to others. In *Into the Valley* (Williams 1990), which is also set during the period prior to the 1994 elections, Walter, a teenage white boy, moves out of his own urban surroundings and "into the valley," in an attempt to make sense of his own life and of his brother's accidental death. He travels to a strife-ridden area of KwaZulu-Natal, where he has heard of a 17-year-old so-called "General Gadaffi," fighting against local vigilante groups. When he finally manages to meet Gadaffi, he is blindfolded for the journey, denied the opportunity to belong to or to recognize his surroundings, excluded from the group of Zulu

boys, and clearly identified as having crossed the boundary into space belonging to others. Both *Outside the Walls* and *Into the Valley* end with the
characters returning to their own environment with a changed and revitalized
understanding of the society they live in.

Moving into other space is also the focus in Elana Bregin's *The Boy from
the Other Side* (1992), again reflected in the title. Space *belongs* to one or
another kind of people. Lora shouts: "You shouldn't be here! This isn't your
place!" (Bregin 1992: 2). A river symbolizes the barrier between the two
spaces:

> The river made a natural border between the two worlds, dividing them as surely as
> if they were separate countries. Not too far away from the shacks was a bridge across
> the water. But Lora would no more have thought of crossing that bridge than she
> would have thought of going to school in her pajamas. (3)

Crime and danger is identified with the space across the river, underlining
a potential invasion of space such as that described in Jenny Robson's *Dark
Waters*. Lora's mother states firmly, "I wish they'd go back to wherever they
came from, and leave us decent people to get on with their lives in peace"
(Bregin 1992: 13).

The "other side" is known as Nomansland, where Lora eventually meets
Gabriel, the boy from the other side. He represents a freedom expressed
directly in a crossing of boundaries—"being with him was like stepping over
a magic threshold" (Bregin 1992: 26). At the end of this novel, in contrast to
those discussed above, Gabriel moves in with Lora's family, where he can take
advantage of the opportunities available to him. Thus, he crosses the barrier
and takes up a new position in a new space.

All of the stories mentioned above involve individuals seeking answers by
crossing into other spaces. Later works involve the parallel existence of apparently separate worlds that are in a process of moving together and apart
again, as if sliding over each like fluid Venn diagrams. In *The Boy Who Counted
to a Million* (Bransby 1995a), the white protagonist observes that it is "as if
South Africa was made up of two worlds: one where certain things happen to
white people and another where different things happen to black people" (21).

He later wonders, however, "What would happen if the two worlds over-
lapped and mixed—not just an occasional bump?" Bransby has moved on in
his works from a world in which overlap was expressly forbidden, to a world
in which overlapping is a real option for the future. By juxtaposing images
from the First World War, through the eyes of Matthew's great-grandfather,
with images of violence in KwaZulu-Natal in the early nineties, Bransby
brings Matthew toward an understanding of the reality of violence and division, and an optimistic belief that the two spaces may eventually merge.
Change is tangibly possible.

In several of the novels mentioned above, rural landscapes are the scene of strife. More commonly, however, the calming effect of the rural landscape is contrasted with the alienation of the urban environment. Two of Bransby's works illustrate this contrast. In *Homeward Bound* (Bransby 1990), the city is the space in which Jason feels alienation from his family and his surroundings—his parents are fighting, the weather is bad—"it blew easterly for five out of the ten days" (81). At school in the country, his mental state changes, as does the weather:

It's good to be back in the gentle green hills of the country. I looked out from my window this evening and watched the sun set red against the mist, the plantations black patches amidst the green farmland. Peaceful. (Bransby 1990: 83)

Similarly, in *A Mountaintop Experience* (Bransby 1992), Kat experiences the urban environment in which she lives as alienating and claustrophobic. She seeks to escape to what she perceives as the freedom of open country and mountains: "I wish I could see a *real* mountain, Kat often thought," and "get . . . away from the streets and the blocks of flats and the traffic and the people" (Bransby 1992: 2).

The rural landscape is also often a symbol of unity; a space where there is a greater chance that different characters can share the same land. In 1990, one of Williams's characters wonders: "Gogo says we're all sons and daughters of the soil, but what if the wind drives us against one another?" (Williams 1990: 2). By 1996, a more positive situation is reflected at the end of *All Anna's Children* by Shelley Davidow (1996: 111):

The truth is that in some way or another, even if only for a short time, Sipho, Joey and I were all Anna's children, and I know that her love, this magic, will carry each of us forward, help us on our way as we grow up under these deep, wide, blue African skies.

In Slingsby's *The Joining* (1996), the physical space of the story serves both as a focus of shared identity for the characters and as a symbol of continuity and potential renewal. The story is essentially a time-shift story. The children from the present and the /Xam of several thousand years before both recognize the same mountains and hills, providing a powerful sense of the continuity of the landscape. Seeing this space through the eyes of another people, Jeremy perceives the harmony lacking in his own urban home in Cape Town and comes to identify himself with his surroundings:

Jeremy gasped. He had never thought of himself being in Africa very much before. The views he'd seen had always been framed by the mountains or the sea. Now there was this view, this enormous, never-ending landscape that stretched unbroken to the horizon. "Africa!" he whispered. (Slingsby 1996: 117)

By the end of the novel, Jeremy and the other characters undergo a change in their understanding of their own, different historical origins, and also acquire an understanding of their essential unity, in that they all belong to the same space. Jeremy realizes that, "We are all people, we are all /Xam. We need to make a joining, if the next hundred thousand years are to be ours" (Slingsby 1996: 153).

However, several of the characters choose to remain in the other time, and move permanently into the past. This negates the sense of optimism that is characteristic of the majority of other works. There is no positive sense in this work of belonging in a new country and sharing a new identity, which is the focus of other works discussed below, such as *Crocodile Burning* and *The Secret Song*.

Crocodile Burning (Williams 1998) is an example of circular movement, beginning with alienation from one's own surroundings and the leaving of those surroundings, culminating in a process of re-identification. Alienated from his family and his home, Seraki dreams of a future home—a house, painted white, with water and electricity, and a real roof with a TV antenna, and a garden and a car. The simplicity of his dream stresses the harshness of his own environment. He addresses his own father as Mr. Nzule, and the town is described as belonging to the criminals: "the Naughty Boys own the street" (Williams 1998: 24). For Seraki, the key to escape lies in music—"this music has a place for me within it" (17). The show in which he performs goes to New York, where the change in landscape results in a clear sense of displacement. As the months pass, the place that they were so glad to leave becomes more and more enticing. The father of one of the children is killed, and a video is sent of the funeral: "I catch glimpses of Soweto, the African veld, and the wide blue sky of home" (170). Williams uses Mandela's release as a trigger for his characters to find a new identity as South Africans in a new society. Seraki realizes that "a new world has started there today, and I am here" (174). When he does return, the alienation is gone, and the identification strong. The story ends: "I punch my fist into the African sky and sing to my family, to my brother, to the new man that I am, and to the new South Africa that is my home" (208).

Escape from one's surroundings is less conventional in another, more complex work by Williams. In *The Genuine Half-Moon Kid* (Williams 1992), Jay's sense of self-worth and identity is seriously threatened after his father leaves with another woman, and he has to deal with his mother's boyfriend. His escape is found by submerging himself in a tank of tropical fish, where "the world outside ceased to exist" (11), symbolizing an escape into an imagined, psychological space. At the same time, the ferocity of nature reflects Jay's inner turmoil: "The southeaster moved rapidly over Devil's Peak, down the barren mountain slopes, and battered the city below. Papers whipped off the street. Sign boards rattled. Tempers were fired" (3).

The Genuine Half-Moon Kid tells of Jason's search for clues to his past, a search that takes on a concrete nature in the quest for his grandfather's yellow-wood box. This search leads him out of his own physical space, in a white area of Cape Town, into an unknown environment—the black township of Khayelitsha: "White boys had no reason to go to Khayelitsha" (Williams 1992: 45). Getting there requires the help of someone who "belongs" in that other space, a Xhosa boy who has himself crossed over into a formerly white area of Cape Town. Linguistic division is also highlighted in this novel, a division that is mostly ignored in youth literature. Jason and his companions are shown to be totally dependent on Lungile in order to communicate with others in this other space.

The contrast between physical and mental space in this story is made explicit. The search for identity and the need to belong reflects alienation from one's physical surroundings and a mismatch between physical and mental space. Through Jason's memories of his grandfather, Williams voices feelings that would be only too familiar to young readers: "He said that too many people here either had their heads in the sand or were living in some European fantasy; not enough people were living *here*, in this country, this South Africa" (Williams 1992: 121).

In Jason's quest for his grandfather's box, he comes to realize that the space between races persists in people's minds rather than in reality. He finds his grandfather, himself, and his identity as a South African in the yellow-wood box containing his grandfather's diaries and stories.

Williams continues the theme of reclaiming space and identity in *The Secret Song* (1997). This story centers on a young colored boy, Bosman, who goes on a pilgrimage to Koombu to find his origins. In Cape Town he was an orphan who had fallen in with a criminal gang, desperate for a place to belong. Escaping from a life of juvenile crime, he hitches a lift out into the middle of the Karoo—"an unfamiliar landscape" surrounded by the "immense silence of the veld" (Williams 1997: 11). In Koombu, he discovers that he is the son of the leader of the people of the valley, that he was "T!kiri, a first-born son of Ikri! He had an identity, a family history, a home" (140). As Bosman finds his identity, so do the orphan children of Koombu, culminating in their casting a vote in the elections—the outward manifestation of claiming citizenship in their own country. Many of them turn out to be the illegitimate children of the dead landowner and they duly inherit the land to which they belong, as their community itself experiences a process of renewal.

In many of the works, rain and floods are used to reflect character and plot development. The onset of rain often serves as a revitalizing and rejuvenating conclusion, as in the "reviving rain" at the end of *My Father and I* (Williams 1989), or as a sign of change and renewal as in the opening paragraphs of *Into the Valley*, when Walter looks up into a tree: "Through its scarlet flowers I see grey storm clouds gathering. I can smell a freshness in the breeze, as it passes through the valley, chasing the still, hot air from the land, and promising rain" (Williams 1990: 2).

In other instances, the rain is a force of nature against which the protagonists have to pitch their strength. For example, in Bransby's *A Mountaintop Experience*, Kat finds herself in the middle of a sudden and terrifying storm: "Almost instantly she was drenched. The violence of it was shocking, breathtaking. . . . She felt she was going to die, plucked off the side of the mountain and crushed like an insect by fingers of lightning" (64).

Lesley Beake (1989) uses rain in a similar way in *A Cageful of Butterflies*. The story builds up with images of heat and drought, and then the rains come—Mponyane, the deaf child at the center of the story, is washed away, but not before he saves the child with him. The familiar feeling of cleansing and renewal experienced after a storm is made explicit: "We sat where we could look out over the valley, at peace below us, green, green after the rain" (Beake 1989: 102).

In other cases, the rain becomes a flood, washing away buildings, lives, and attitudes, and the flood becomes a test of endurance on the road to a new sense of self. Toward the end of *Into the Valley*, Ravi comments: "The flood has washed away many things. It is an old story, told in many cultures" (Williams 1990: 152). The floods open the way to a new order and a brighter future, signifying upheaval and renewal. Peter Slingsby's *Flood Sunday* (1992) tells the true story of a devastating flood, and the power of nature to wash away prejudice and hatred. Ralph, the chief character, and his former enemy, Nico, are both forced to confront the barriers of class and race, when the flood levels parts of the town, leveling their relationship at the same time.

In all of these works, and many others not examined here, the physical space in which the characters find themselves is fundamental to their image of self in relation to the environment and to others. The physical space in which they move is symbolic both of a common heritage and of the division still existing in society. Very often, but not exclusively so, the natural landscape is used to symbolize a shared identity and a sense of belonging, whereas the urban environment represents alienation, division, and deprivation of ownership. By using the physical environment and examining the child's and young person's relationship to it, the authors are constructing the child in a new space. The texts explore the changing nature of the child's relationship with the external environment, and, in certain cases, illustrate how young people are reclaiming that space as their own, empowering themselves with a secure identity in a new world.

The differences between characters are foregrounded in almost all of these works, whether or not they are eventually resolved. Characters are portrayed in a process of redefining themselves in relation to the land they live in and renegotiating their relationships with the people they live with. There is a clear progression from alienation and division to belonging and a growing sense of unity. From separate but adjacent spaces, there is a clear move toward shared and overlapping space. The theme of the search for identity has become somewhat clichéd in youth literatures from other countries, but remains central in South African youth literature, as writers seek to come to terms with the portrayal of characters in a changing and contradictory society.

BIBLIOGRAPHY

Beake, L. 1989. *A Cageful of Butterflies.* Oxford: Heinemann.
Bransby, L. 1989. *Down Street.* Cape Town: Tafelberg.
Bransby, L. 1990. *Homeward Bound.* Cape Town: Tafelberg.
Bransby, L. 1992. *A Mountaintop Experience.* Cape Town: Tafelberg.
Bransby, L. 1995a. *The Boy Who Counted to a Million.* Cape Town: Human & Rousseau.
Bransby, L. 1995b. *Outside the Walls.* Johannesburg: Heinemann.
Bregin, E. 1992. *The Boy from the Other Side.* Cape Town: Maskew Miller Longman.
Case, D. 1991. *92 Queen's Road.* Cape Town: Maskew Miller Longman.
Davidow, S. 1996. *All Anna's Children.* Cape Town: Tafelberg.
Hofmeyr, D. 1990. *A Red Kite in a Pale Sky.* Cape Town: Tafelberg.
Robson, J. 1995. *Dark Waters.* Cape Town: Tafelberg.
Slingsby, P. 1992. *Flood Sunday.* Cape Town: Tafelberg.
Slingsby, P. 1996. *The Joining.* Cape Town: Tafelberg.
Williams, M. 1989. *My Father and I.* Cape Town: Tafelberg.
Williams, M. 1990. *Into the Valley.* Cape Town: Tafelberg.
Williams, M. 1992. *The Genuine Half-Moon Kid.* Cape Town: Tafelberg.
Williams, M. 1997. *The Secret Song.* Cape Town: Tafelberg.
Williams, M. 1998. *Crocodile Burning.* Oxford: Oxford University Press.

CHAPTER 4

Exploring Otherness: Changes in the Child-Animal Metamorphosis Motif

Maria Lassén-Seger

THE MYTH OF THE ANIMAL-CHILD

When studying the motif of metamorphosis in late-twentieth-century English-language children's literature, one soon notices that most stories feature an animal transformation of the child protagonist. Initially, I interpreted these stories as dealing with a subject that touches on a deep human anxiety about transgressing the border between different species, but recently I have come to recognize that animal metamorphosis in children's fiction is surprisingly seldom concerned with the nature and interests of animals. Instead, at the center of these narratives, we tend to find human characters, human needs, and interests made more visible in the process of reflecting humanity in the otherness of the animal.

The marginalized position of the animal lends itself easily to a comparison with the position of the child in Western society. The great number of animal characters in children's literature is generally considered as evidence of a special connection between children and animals. Such an assumption presupposes that there is a connection between this phenomenon and some universal state of childhood innocence and animism. However, children's literature criticism in the 1980s and 1990s, especially with the publication of Jacqueline Rose's highly polemic and influential study, *The Case of Peter Pan: or, the Impossibility of Children's Fiction*, in 1984 has shown increasing awareness of the plasticity of the image of childhood as a social, cultural, and historical construction. Thus, to me, it seems more probable to assume, along with Perry Nodelman (1996), that because children's literature is created mostly by adults for children, the great number of animal characters in children's fiction is primarily a reflection of an adult preoccupation with regarding children and animals as interchangeable.

Regardless of how one might feel about this matter, the myth of the animal-child is still comfortably lodged within Western thinking today. However, associating the child uncritically with animals and nature is not unproblematic. This point of view reflects the sentimental Romantic notion of an innocently natural child uncorrupted by adulthood, as well as the stereotypical image of the child as an uncivilized savage (Jenks 1996). Marina Warner argues that adults today endorse a cult of the child that projects all their hopes, dreams, and fears onto the image of the child, forgetting that "childhood doesn't occupy some sealed Eden or Neverland set apart from the grown-up world: our children can't be better than we are" (Warner 1994: 60). Defining children in opposition to adults and marginalizing and othering them in terms of animality and closeness to nature will inevitably reduce them to mere vessels for the aspirations and nightmares of the adult world.

Attitudes toward both children and animals have, of course, changed extensively over the years. Not surprisingly, this change is reflected in the stories I have chosen to explore, and in this chapter I attempt to sketch an overview of some of the major changes that have occurred in the use of the motif of child-animal metamorphosis.

THE BEASTLY CHILD: CHILD-ANIMAL METAMORPHOSIS AS PUNISHMENT

Because adult hopes for the future so often are pinned on the child, we should not be surprised that many of these stories fill didactic purposes. Traditional children's stories typically employ the motif of metamorphosis as a punishment that enhances the child character's moral development. A. L. O. E.'s *My Neighbour's Shoes: or, Feelings for Others* ([1861] 1904) is a case in point of a cautionary tale in which a cruel and selfish boy is reformed by being transformed successively into those he has mistreated. Carlo Collodi's *The Adventures of Pinocchio: Tale of a Puppet* ([1883] 1986), a late-nineteenth-century toy story under the influence of Darwinian and Cartesian ideas, also depicts the wooden doll's moral and intellectual development as a "metamorphosis from one species to another" (Kuznets 1994: 141). Collodi's novel and its motif of metamorphosis are firmly lodged within the Judeo-Christian tradition that regards humankind as intellectually and morally superior to animalkind. It is, after all, Pinocchio's first and foremost wish to acquire human form, and his temporary transformation into a donkey is depicted as a frightening and regressive metamorphosis contrasted with the more noble and progressive change into a human boy.

Although the traditional motif of punishment through metamorphosis by no means disappeared completely when we entered the twentieth century,[1] the motif of human-animal transformation gradually took on profoundly new and different meanings. Marina Warner (1994) claims that whereas the classic myth of animal metamorphosis used to be regarded as a fall from grace, it has now become an appealing fantasy. Warner's theory is based on a study of video games, but her ideas are also applicable to many contemporary children's books, such as K. A. Applegate's widely popular formulae fiction series, *Animorphs* (1996–2001, as cited in Lassén-Seger 2002), in which the child characters acquire animal shapes in order to be physically empowered to fight their enemy. Still, alongside the modern attractive fantasy of animal transformation, traditional ideas of the dangerous and frightening nature of transgressing the border between the species live on in contemporary stories.

ADVENTURES INTO ADULTHOOD: NEW SUBVERSIVE FUNCTIONS

Reflecting the changing attitudes toward the human-animal dichotomy, the function of child-animal metamorphosis in stories for children underwent a profound change during the early and mid-twentieth century. Not until then do we encounter stories that involve a deeper psychological exploration of what it means to really become an animal in terms of putting a human soul of a child into an animal body. Edith Nesbit's "The Cathood of Maurice" ([1912] 1988), T. H. White's *The Sword in the Stone* ([1938] 1971), and Paul Gallico's *Jennie* (1950)[2] are groundbreaking narratives in this respect (Blount 1974).

The idea of depicting a human self within an animal body, however, is not new. As children's literature gradually grew more child centered, "animal biographies" that encouraged child readers to imagine themselves in the position of animal heroes flourished around the turn of the nineteenth century (Avery and Kinnell 1995), perhaps the most influential and long-lived novel of this kind being Anna Sewell's *Black Beauty* ([1877] 1965). However, the stories featuring children actually undergoing a fantastic bodily change from human into animal are often concerned with more subversive issues than the implied child reader simply empathizing with an animal hero. At the core of these early-twentieth-century texts, the metamorphosis functions as a narrative vehicle highlighting human, rather than animal, issues, such as the power imbalance between children and adults, as well as the mysteries of adulthood.

Whereas animal metamorphosis in Nesbit's ([1912] 1988) short story reveals to the boy Maurice, who exchanges his body with his cat, that neither is better off when it comes to being bullied by the adults in charge, it allows the Wart in T. H. White's ([1938] 1971) novel to peep into adult life, because the animal characters that the Wart encounters during his metamorphic adventures are shrewd caricatures of adults. Nesbit and White appear to have set the scene for the new kind of metamorphosis story: abandoning didacticism in favor of employing animal transformation as a means of subverting the ways of adult life. The result is stories that are less didactic and perhaps more child centered, but also less optimistic about what growing up will mean for its child characters. The child's time in animal form is now described as either an adventure out of childhood into adulthood, or is used as a means of highlighting or subverting adult authority and power over the child.

In a similar manner, a cat transformation (this time caused by a traffic accident) is the vehicle that allows the boy protagonist, Peter, in Gallico's *Jennie* (1950) to undergo an adventure out of childhood into adulthood. As a cat, Peter is literally thrown out into the streets to fend for himself, and the novel's main motif is his love story with the feline stray Jennie. Whereas Margaret Blount (1974) finds a moral lesson in the accounts of Peter's cat-hood, Ann Swinfen (1984) maintains that the book is primarily about Peter growing up. In my opinion, both readings are made impossible because of the, admittedly unsatisfactory, ending. The novel closes when Peter lays down his life in a fight for Jennie, but he dies only to wake up as a boy again discovering that his cat adventure was only a dream. Peter's fantasy of "growing up" is thus stunted by his abrupt return to boyhood; his "adult" experiences of love and death are dismissed as a dream that he must forget in order to be able to return to the innocence of childhood.

Due to the circular ending of Gallico's novel, the child-animal metamorphosis expresses a twofold function of subverting, as well as confirming, the status quo of the power imbalance between child and adult. Like Nesbit's and White's narratives, Gallico's novel subverts adult authority over the child only temporarily through metamorphosis. The child character is only allowed to taste the mysteries of adulthood for a short period of time before being returned to childhood. By following such a carnivalesque circular pattern (Bakhtin 1984), these narratives subvert, as well as confirm, the status quo of the power imbalance between child and adult; or, to quote John Stephens (1992: 133), "disguise situates carnival in parentheses." This tradition of circularity and closure in narratives of metamorphosis for children (and in traditional epic children's literature as a whole for that matter) still dominates twentieth-century children's fiction, but, as is discussed below, an increasingly common trend to break this circular plot pattern emerged toward the end of the century.

EXPLORING ADULT AUTHORITY OR ESCAPING ABUSE THROUGH METAMORPHOSIS

Before discussing the rising trend to subvert the traditional circular pattern of the child-animal metamorphosis motif at the fin de siècle, let me first demonstrate that the power imbalance between children and adults is still the key issue explored within late-twentieth-century children's fiction with circular plot patterns.

In Ian McEwan's episodic novel, *The Daydreamer* (1994), the boy protagonist Peter's dreams of otherness are both appealing and frightening uncanny events that allow him to have experiences of his own, unmonitored by the adults in charge. Peter's one and only animal transformation into a cat is comparable with Maurice's in Nesbit's short story referred to above. Both boys are tempted to exchange bodies with their cats in order to escape their disadvantaged positions. Whereas Maurice is about to be punished by his parents, Peter is simply motivated by boredom. However, the outcome of their physical change is profoundly different. Peter's cathood involves no un-settling blurring of the boy's identity with that of his cat. It is a pleasurable experience away from adult restrictions. It is also a means of expressing his implicit desire to never grow up, which is not unlike the boy-mouse trans-formation in Roald Dahl's *The Witches* (1985; originally published in 1983). Peter would prefer to remain a cat, but he cannot because his cat does not want to remain a boy. Maurice, on the other hand, is horrified to see his cat posing as "himself" and is quite happy to return to human form.

Whereas Nesbit's story plays with the traditional myth of animal meta-morphosis, describing childhood and cathood as equally undesirable in terms of their disempowerment, McEwan's tale follows the modern myth of animal metamorphosis, portraying it as an appealing alternative to being a human child raised and governed by adult authority. The plot pattern of metamor-phosis may still be circular, but the return to human shape is notably an unsatisfactory solution for the child character in question. Stories that express such a profound desire on a child character's part to give up his or her hu-manity for the increased freedom of animal life can, in my opinion, be re-garded as the ultimate outcome of the ever-present power imbalance between child and adult that is constantly under negotiation in books for children.

Let me emphasize that there is nothing essentially "new" about employing the motif of metamorphosis to allow a fictional character a temporary em-powering liberation in the shape of an animal. Myths and fairy tales often employ a flight into nature, such as a transformation into an animal or a tree, in order to grant a marginalized or persecuted female heroine agency or refuge (Lassén-Seger 2001, Pratt 1981, Tatar 1992, Warner 1995). Gillian Cross's novel, *Pictures in the Dark* (1998; originally published in 1996), also employs metamorphosis, not so much as an appealing alternative for the fictive child, but as a desperate last resort to stay sane. The novel tells the story of Charlie Willcox, who gradually befriends Peter, a young outsider at school. Peter's odd withdrawn behavior makes him the school's scapegoat and an easy victim of bullying. Because his point of view is never shared by the readers, it is hard to immediately sympathize with Peter, and readers are made painfully aware of how easy it is to adopt the bully's notion of the frighteningly odd and distanced boy. Peter is prone to falling into trancelike states of mind, which people around him tend to find deeply disturbing. Furthermore, his "other-ness" is frequently referred to in terms of animality and wildness. When Char-lie tries to comfort him after a vicious assault by his classmates, Charlie feels "as if he were reassuring a frightened animal" and Peter responds by biting him (Cross 1998: 71). The bite is of crucial importance to Charlie's later understanding of Peter's dilemma, because it gives him a kind of double vision that enables him to look at the world from a different, or animal/wild, point of view. Eventually, Charlie discovers Peter's secret. In order to escape abuse, at home as well as at school, Peter finds his only refuge in shifting his soul into the body of an otter.[3]

In the horrifying closing scenes of the book, Peter barely survives being drowned by his two main adversaries at school. The two girls bring their superstitious accusations against Peter to the limit as they tie him up and throw him into the river in order to perform a traditional trial by order: if he is a witch, he floats; if not, he drowns. The scene is no less unsettling in its vivid expression of the girls' act being, simultaneously, one of astounding ignorance and premeditated calculation. In the course of the assault, Peter leaves his body and takes refuge in animal form. But danger appears in new form when Charlie, unable to stop the girls' assault on Peter, has to save Peter-the-otter from being killed by Peter's own father, who is infuriated by the otter trespassing into his garden and symbolizing a wilderness that lies beyond his control. Sadly, however, the story abandons Peter immediately after Charlie has rescued him, rendering any positive outcome for the abused boy non-credible, despite Cross's attempts to convince her readers. The depth of Peter's injuries seem far too profound to be simply overcome by the two bullies' and his father's sudden return to their senses. The optimistic ending, during which Charlie suddenly ruminates on all the wonderful things you can see if you know how to look for them, feels hopelessly tacked on. What remains, however, is a shattering account of ignorance, brutality, and power abuse that is equally a part of the lives of both children and adults.

The tendency to foreshadow the disintegration of the rigid circular pattern of child-animal metamorphosis noted in McEwan's novel can also be seen in Melvin Burgess's *Tiger, Tiger* (1998; originally published in 1996). The novel is a problematic attempt to depict a young boy's coming of age through animal metamorphosis. Steve is still a child when he encounters Lila, a Spirit Tiger, who has transformed herself into a girl in order to escape being killed by gangsters. Steve's initial reactions to the tiger-girl are suffused with abjection—he finds her both fascinating and frightening. Lila-the-girl cannot speak and Burgess increases the problematic "othering" of the animal-girl by combining the young body of a mute girl with references to untamed, animal desires. At the close of the story, Lila's and Steve's obscure relationship culminates as he follows her into the wilderness, where he changes into a tiger and they mate. In the morning, Steve wakes up remembering nothing:

He had no memories of the previous night, no knowledge of having been a tiger. But he knew that Lila had given him an unimaginable, unaccountable gift, and that he would never be the same again. He had grown up overnight in a way no one had ever done before. She had left inside him forever a streak of tiger in his soul. (Burgess 1998: 140–41)

Steve's rite of passage into manhood has been sealed through his sexual experience with the tigress. In other words, his maturation process is constructed around him accepting, although unconsciously, a sexuality characterized by wild, untamed animality. Instead of feeling alienated by such a construct of masculine sexuality, as Jo Coward (1999) has shown other boy-animal characters to be—for example, in William Rayner's *Stag Boy* (1972) and Gillian Rubinstein's *Foxspell* (1998; originally published in 1994), Burgess's boy protagonist comes of age through accepting that very construct of his becoming a man. From the point of view of feminist criticism, Melvin Burgess's *Tiger, Tiger* thus represents a backlash in the depiction of male maturation in young adult fiction. However, the novel also foreshadows the collapsing of the circular metamorphosis pattern that Burgess is to carry out in full later on in his picture book, *The Birdman* (2000), illustrated by Ruth Brown; and his young adult novel, *Lady: My Life as a Bitch* (2001).

BREAKING THE TRADITIONAL PATTERN: ABANDONING CLOSURE

One of the easiest ways to pin down variations in the functions of the metamorphosis motif is to examine how the stories end. John Stephens (1992) argues that closure in children's literature is of special interest due to the socializing intent of children's literature and that: "[i]ntentionality can only be fully attributed to a text from the perspective of the close" (42). Children's literature has a strong intertextual tradition of closure—or the sense of a "happy ending" as Bettelheim (1978; originally published in 1976), Inglis (1981), Tolkien ([1964] 1975) and other scholars have chosen to call it, because they ascribe its therapeutic, as well as socializing qualities. In other words, the expectations of a closed ending in books for children are usually very high. Furthermore, metamorphosis is always staged within the realm of the fantastic, where, traditionally, a strong literary convention prevails that a fantastic adventure beginning in reality should return to reality at the end (Gilead 1992).

According to Kimberley Reynolds (1994: 44), the "refusal to grow up is no longer a dominant motif in juvenile fiction but has been replaced by writing which is specifically preoccupied with facilitating the maturing process." Stories of child-animal metamorphosis at the end of the twentieth century seem, however, to be the exceptions that confirm the rule. During the 1980s and 1990s, an increasing number of books for children break the carnival pattern, leaving the child character in animal shape. This breach of circularity is, of course, also partly explained by a shift in the ideological attitude toward the human-animal dichotomy. However, in some of these stories, such as Roald

Dahl's *The Witches* (1985; originally published in 1983), metamorphosis clearly also functions as a vehicle for allowing the child to escape from growing up and, consequently, remain a child forever. In other narratives, such as those written by Melvin Burgess, the motif emphasizes adult anxiety about the future of humanity and about the child leaving childhood behind and approaching life as an adult. These stories subvert adult authority over the child thoroughly, but how empowering are they really for the child character?

One novel, Patrice Kindl's *Owl in Love* (1994; originally published in 1993), presents the perhaps even more unusual solution of not forcing the young protagonist to choose between becoming either animal or human, but rather allows her to remain "in between" as an empowering possibility. This book is one of the few—but apparently increasing in number—stories in which a female character undergoes animal metamorphosis.[4]

The novel features a shape-shifting girl coming to terms with growing up.[5] Kindl uses first-person narration, which has been rare within fantasy novels for children and young adults, but has become an increasingly common narrative device in postmodern children's fiction. Moreover, allowing the metamorph to speak in the first person also functions as a means of making metamorphic ironies more explicit and productive (Clarke 1995: 35). The tone of the narrative voice in Kindl's novel is indeed ironical and far from sentimental.

Owl Tycho is consumed with a passionate infatuation—not lacking in self-irony—for her science teacher, whom she stalks at night while in the shape of a bird. Owl is a shape-shifter, descended from a long line of shape-shifters, and her parents are witches. Although her owl existence is mainly restricted to nocturnal activities, her eating habits are always those of an owl. This makes Owl Tycho inherently different from ordinary teenagers. Given her birdlike appetite for rodents, she shows a rather unhealthy (from a human point of view) interest in her classmate's pet hamster. Moreover, if she eats human food she will lose her ability to undergo metamorphosis. Being this indefinable mixture of two species, Owl epitomizes monstrosity (Cohen 1996), and—as a monster eluding and disturbing a clear notion of identity, system, and order—Owl's reaction toward her split self results in a twofold emotional response corresponding to Julia Kristeva's (1982) notion of abjection understood as a feeling of disgust, repulsion, and degradation mixed with pleasure and desire. The complications surrounding the body of the teenage girl are thus staged on many levels in the novel: first, in the dual nature of Owl's anorectic girl/animal body; and, second, in the repeated emphasis on food as both pleasurable and repulsive. The abjection that Owl feels toward her own body is physical evidence of her inner turmoil: who or what is she?

Unlike many other protagonists in young adult fiction, Owl does not feel alienated or in need of rebelling against her parents, who, in her opinion, are "more fond than wise" (Kindl 1994: 16). Still, she feels the urge to cut the cord between herself and her parents in order to take charge of her own life.

Ultimately, Owl has to come to terms with being an outsider, neither human nor animal, but both. In the process, she survives her infatuation for her teacher, learns the give and take of true friendship, and finds a soul mate in a boy shape-shifter who has given in to madness because he cannot come to terms with his true nature. Eventually, both Owl and the boy have to accept their own dual natures. The young protagonists of *Owl in Love* seem thus to undergo an empowering development, because they manage to reveal and accept their dual identities in the face of an uncomprehending adult world. Kindl's novel is, in this respect, a refreshing, tongue-in-cheek fantasy of animal metamorphosis that resists rigid categorization into different species.

CONCLUSION

Exploring late-twentieth-century English-language children's fiction featuring child-animal metamorphoses, one can observe a marked change from the traditional didactic stories in which the child protagonist is punished, chastened, or forced into submission through a change into animal shape. Regardless of whether the animal transformation has been instigated by free will or by force, by the desire to grow up and be true to one's own nature or to withdraw from growing up or abuse, the child character's time in animal shape is usually a time of nocturnal pleasures, dangers, and violence, often alluding to adult mysteries such as love, sex, and death. In some stories, violence seems sanctioned simply because the characters indulge in it while in animal form. Peter Cat in McEwan's *The Daydreamer* (1994) fights the cat next door using unfair, human tricks and Peter in Gallico's *Jennie* (1950) acts like a trained soldier when he gives up his life in a fight for his feline love Jennie. The *Animorphs* series by K. A. Applegate (1996–2001) is an even more obvious example, because the whole point of the children changing into animals is to become a violent force to be taken into account.

The remarkable changes in the function of this ancient literary motif reflect changing attitudes about human-animal relationships as well as about the relationship between the constructions of childhood and adulthood, often depicted as a difference in power. The stories I have explored in this chapter repeatedly emphasize the power imbalance between children and adults through animal metamorphosis. This power imbalance is most often only temporarily subverted as the children partake in animal adventures that eventually bring them back to their own shape again, reinstating closure. However, as I have also noted, toward the close of the previous century, an increasing number of books break the traditional pattern and present animal form, or remaining in between categories, as both appealing and empowering alternatives.

Animal metamorphosis is most often used in contemporary children's fiction to grant the child characters some form of agency to move beyond the boundaries and restrictions of what the adults in power have meted out as the realm of childhood. At the end of the narrative, the children must either return to the innocence of childhood once their adventures into "otherness" are over, or abandon life as a human being and an adult altogether. Consequently, these stories indirectly reflect a deep adult anxiety about the depiction of fictive children growing up, leaving childhood behind, and becoming adults. What it is to really become an animal is usually of secondary importance.

NOTES

1. In *The Voyage of the Dawntreader* ([1952] 1989), for instance, C. S. Lewis uses metamorphosis as a vehicle for reforming one of his child protagonists. Eustace's transformation into a dragon is a punishment fitting the crime in the sense that his beastly behavior literally turns him into a beast. Not until he repents and improves his manners is he deemed worthy of returning to his human shape again (Lassén-Seger, 2000).

2. The American edition is titled *The Abandoned.*

3. I am indebted to my colleague Jenniliisa Salminen for bringing to by knowledge the association between Peter's last name, Luttrell, and the Latin name for otter, *Lutra lutra.*

4. Jo Coward (1999) has noted that contemporary authors of young adult fiction mainly use animal metamorphosis to depict teenage boys' rites of passage into manhood metaphorically. To this I would like to add that according to the material I have collected it seems as if boy/animal transformations by far outnumber girl/animal transformations whatever the age of the protagonist.

5. Kindl's young adult novels often elaborate on the motif of young girls coming of age. Her novels offer metaphorical descriptions in which she subverts traditional plot patterns. In *The Woman in the Wall* (1998; originally published in 1997), for instance, a shy girl escapes into invisibility and becomes a prisoner of her own home. Anna, who cannot dare face the world outside, builds herself a home behind the walls of her own home. There she becomes an invisible "angel of the house" serving and caring for the rest of her family. Playing with the real and the imaginary, as well as with the house metaphor, Kindl makes the coming of age of her girl character tangibly liberating as Anna steps out of her isolation, resumes visibility and makes herself a "home" within her own body.

BIBLIOGRAPHY

A. L. O. E. [Tucker, Charlotte Maria]. [1861] 1904. *My Neighbour's Shoes: or, Feelings for Others.* Stockholm: Norstedt.

Avery, Gillian, and Margaret Kinnell. 1995. "Morality and Levity 1780–1820." In *Children's Literature an Illustrated History*, ed. Peter Hunt, 46–76. Oxford: Oxford University Press.

Bakhtin, Mikhail. [1968] 1984. *Rabelais and His World*, trans. Helene Iswolsky. Bloomington: Indiana University Press.

Bettelheim, Bruno. 1978. *The Uses of Enchantment: The Meaning and Importance of Fairy Tales.* London: Penguin.

Blount, Margaret. 1974. *Animal Land: The Creatures of Children's Fiction*. New York: William Morrow.

Burgess, Melvin. 1998. *Tiger, Tiger*. London: Penguin.

Burgess, Melvin. 2001. *Lady: My Life as a Bitch*. London: Andersen Press.

Burgess, Melvin, and Ruth Brown. 2000. *The Birdman*. London: Andersen Press.

Clarke, Bruce. 1995. *Allegories of Writing: The Subject of Metamorphosis*. Albany: State University of New York Press.

Cohen, Jeffrey J., ed. 1996. *Monster Theory: Reading Culture*. Minneapolis: University of Minnesota Press.

Collodi, Carlo. [1883] 1986. *The Adventures of Pinocchio: Story of a Puppet*, trans. Nicholas J. Perella. Reprint, Berkeley: University of California Press.

Coward, Jo. 1999. "Masculinity and Animal Metamorphosis in Children's Literature." In *Something to Crow About: New Perspectives in Literature for Young People*, ed. Susan Clancy with David Gilbey, 135–45. Wagga Wagga, NSW, Australia: Centre for Information Studies.

Cross, Gillian. 1998. *Pictures in the Dark*. London: Penguin.

Dahl, Roald. 1985. *The Witches*. London: Penguin.

Gallico, Paul. 1950. *Jennie*. London: Michael Joseph.

Gilead, Sarah. 1992. "Magic Abjured: Closure in Children's Fantasy Fiction." In *Literature for Children: Contemporary Criticism*, ed. Peter Hunt, 80–109. London: Routledge.

Inglis, Fred. 1981. *The Promise of Happiness: Value and Meaning in Children's Fiction*. Cambridge: Cambridge University Press.

Jenks, Chris. 1996. *Childhood*. London: Routledge, 1996.

Kindl, Patrice. 1994. *Owl in Love*. New York: Penguin.

Kindl, Patrice. 1997. *The Woman in the Wall*. New York: Penguin.

Kristeva, Julia. 1982. *Powers of Horror: An Essay on Abjection*, trans. Leon S. Roudiez. New York: Columbia University Press.

Kuznets, Lois Rostow. 1994. *When Toys Come Alive: Narratives of Animation, Metamorphosis, and Development*. New Haven: Yale University Press.

Lassén-Seger, Maria. 2000. "The Fictive Child in Disguise: Disempowering Transformations of the Child Character." In *Text, Culture and National Identity in Children's Literature: International Seminar on Children's Literature*, ed. Jean Webb, 186–96. Helsinki: Nordinfo.

Lassén-Seger, Maria. 2001. "Barnbokens trädflickor—fantasilek eller fåfänga flyktförsök," (Tree-girls in children's literature: Imaginary play or vain attempts at escape) *Horisont*, 2: 22–29.

Lassén-Seger, Maria. 2002. "Child-Power? Adventures into the Animal Kingdom—The Animorphs Series." In *Children's Literature as Communication: The ChiLPA Project*, ed. Roger D. Sell, 159–76. Amsterdam: Benjamins.

Lewis, C. S. [1952] 1989. *The Voyage of the Dawntreader*. Reprint, London: Collins.

McEwan, Ian. 1994. *The Daydreamer*. London: Jonathan Cape.

Nesbit, Edith. [1912] 1988. "The Cathood of Maurice." In *The Magic World*, 7–24. London: Penguin.

Nodelman, Perry. 1996. *The Pleasures of Children's Literature*. 2nd ed. New York: Longman.

Pratt, Annis. 1981. *Archetypal Patterns in Women's Fiction*. Brighton: Bloomington: Indiana University Press.

Rayner, William. 1972. *Stag Boy.* London: Collins.

Reynolds, Kimberley. 1994. *Children's Literature in the 1890s and the 1990s.* Plymouth: Northcote House in association with the British Council.

Rose, Jacqueline. 1984. *The Case of Peter Pan: or, the Impossibility of Children's Fiction.* London: Macmillan.

Rubinstein, Gillian. 1998. *Foxspell.* London: Orion.

Sewell, Anna. [1877] 1965. *Black Beauty.* Reprint, London: Bancroft & Co.

Stephens, John. 1992. *Language and Ideology in Children's Fiction.* London: Longman.

Swinfen, Ann. 1984. *In Defence of Fantasy: A Study of the Genre in English and American Literature since 1945.* London: Routledge.

Tatar, Maria. 1992. *Off with Their Heads! Fairy Tales and the Culture of Childhood.* Princeton, N.J.: Princeton University Press.

Tolkien, J.R.R. [1964] 1975. *Tree and Leaf.* London: Allen & Unwin.

Warner, Marina. 1994. *Six Myths of Our Time: Little Angels, Little Monsters, Beautiful Beasts, and More.* New York: Vintage.

Warner, Marina. 1995. *From the Beast to the Blonde: On Fairy Tales and Their Tellers.* London: Vintage.

White, T. H. [1938] 1971. *The Sword in the Stone.* London: Collins.

CHAPTER 5

A Happy Blend of Universality and Novelty: *Julie of the Wolves* and *A Ring of Endless Light* as Stories Crossing the Animal-Human Boundary

Darja Mazi-Leskovar

Books in which animals play a prominent role appeal to readers cross-culturally. They are read by people of all ages, and some even address a double audience: adults and children. In children's and young adults' literature, animal heroes have always been a prevalent characteristic. Animals have appeared in realistic fiction and in fantasy: in fantasy their portrayal knows no restrictions as far as anthropomorphism is concerned, whereas in realistic fiction there seems to be an expectation of true-to-life representation. The attempt to present the animal in its "animal nature," however, remains a speculation because "we do not and cannot know what it feels like to be an animal" (Townsend 1990: 94). True, the natural environment, the habitat of the animal hero, adds, to a certain degree, to the verisimilitude of the presentation, but any portrayal inevitably includes "that perilous imaginative leap into the animal mind" (ibid.) that reveals, above all, the person and the time in which the leap occurred. This is one of the invaluable sources of change and renewal in animal story writing.

Children's literature as a whole (and art in general), and not only books featuring animals, does not exist in isolation, and its significance cannot be properly appreciated unless it is read in the broader cultural context. Hence, what is revealed in the fictional "animal mind" also depends on the author's suppositions with regard to the reader's expectations about the world—about nature and a particular species, about the society and the child, or about the adult who enters into a relationship with the animal. It is thus a complex perspective that conditions the choice of "animal" themes and their elaboration within the framework of a certain genre. Changes in the view of the world, accordingly, induce novelty in the efforts of writers to make the untamed nature with its animal life meaningful to human existence in a particular historic moment or period and in a specific place or area. Sometimes new features in the portrayals of animal heroes appear, and new relationships between humans and animals are established. In some instances new aspects of old themes, pertinent to animal-human fictional relations, reflect changes that have directly or indirectly influenced the living conditions of certain species and of their ecosystems.

Two American young adult novels—*Julie of the Wolves*, by Jean Craighead George (1972), and *A Ring of Endless Light*, by Madeleine L'Engle (1980)—rank highly among books published in the last century that offer a happy blend of an old theme and new motives that reveal change and renewal in children's literature. Both novels explore various methods of animal-human communication and the consequences related to the crossing of animal-human boundaries in the fictional world that bear the characteristics of the twentieth-century setting.

In *Julie of the Wolves*, winner of the 1973 Newbery Medal, the author has produced a young adult novel defined as an adventure romance (Lomax 1983: 207) and a wilderness survival quest story (Hourihan 1997: 120). However, the story is also a tale of crossing and recrossing the animal-human boundary. The book is divided into three sections, each of which contains a crossing of borders between the animal kingdom and human society. In the opening section, "Amaroq, the Wolf," the eponymous heroine, who is referred to by her Eskimo name, Miyax, manages to enter into the mysterious world of the wolves. Lost on the Alaskan tundra with no food and few supplies, the 13-year-old girl knows that she needs to break the wolves' code in order to survive. She is not afraid of these powerful representatives of the animal kingdom. Her father, Kapugen, once told her that wolves had saved him when he was starving in the wild, but he did not explain to her how he had communicated with them. Miyax thus carefully observes the pack and gradually comes to understand the wolves' ways and language. At first, she tries to "discern which of their sounds and movements" express "goodwill and friendship" (Craighead George 1972: 7). Next, she names the animals that stand out from the group. Amaroq is the leader, Silver is his companion and the pups' mother, Kapu is the leader of the pups, and Jello is a cowardly wolf living on the edge of the pack. Miyax then tries to decipher the wolves' code. After practicing the postures and sounds to convey helplessness and friendship, she approaches Amaroq. Staying on all fours and imitating movements expressing goodwill, she convinces him. She is sprayed and accepted almost as one of the pack. Still, her learning of the wolf code has only started, and it is later, when the puppies also understand her, that she shouts in triumph: "I'm talking wolf! I'm talking wolf" (22). Finally, the protagonist realizes that she can even dominate Jello and is allowed to walk on two feet. She can thus remain fully herself—a human—even though she is accepted in the wolf society. For her, Miyax of the Eskimos is dead, and she considers herself "Julie of the Wolves," traveling southward to her San Francisco pen friend.

The second section is a long flashback recounting Miyax's life before her journey, explaining how she acquired the ability to break the wolf code. As a little girl, she was acquainted with Eskimo folklore and rituals. In addition, her father taught her about the importance of respecting all living beings in the environment. He imitated the wolves by performing traditional dances and storytelling, and Miyax learned to admire the animals for their strength and their brotherly love toward humans. She believed that anyone approaching them in the right way would be accepted and helped. They would know with one sniff "if you were male or female, adult or child, if you were hunting or not hunting—even if you were happy or sad" (Craighead George 1972: 27). The girl completely trusted her father and admired his ability to approach birds and smaller animals by imitating their language. The Eskimo belief that humans are not superior to animals became inherent in her view of life, and the fact that communication between the two worlds is possible formed her personal experience.

In the third part of the novel, Miyax continues alone on her way toward her destination, San Francisco, and does not depend directly on crossing the human-animal borders, yet her rapport with the wolves does not cease. When she is in trouble, her animal friends rescue her. She, on the contrary, can do nothing when tourist hunters in a plane shoot and kill Amaroq. Terrified, she decides to live exclusively according to the traditional ways of her ancestors, which give animals and the environment due respect. However, when confronted with the death of a bird she had rescued, named, and domesticated, she understands that life in the wilderness, even if supported by communication with animals, is not possible any more. She heads back to her father's new home, ready to compromise with his Westernized lifestyle. Her quest for change, which had evolved into a search for ways to communicate with the wolves, ended as a quest for survival for herself, the wolves, and the Eskimos. She finds her place in life. She will not leave her native land, and will have to accommodate to modern ways.

The power of survival based on the accommodation that has enabled the heroine to enter the animal kingdom has taught her the wisdom of life. She survives "because of her sensitivity and empathy, traditionally 'feminine' attributes" (Hourihan 1997: 221). The choice of a female protagonist is thus a sign of novelty as the heroes in wilderness and animal stories are, as a rule, boys, and, accordingly, the attributes that are associated with masculinity are the ones that are presented as life saving. Still, Miyax is not just full of intuition and sensitivity; she is also endowed with flashes of surprising rationalization, attributed to her father's teaching. For example, when she notices that a certain way of acting does not bring the expected results, she is able to take an opposite standpoint. The single-parent education obviously has not mutilated her feminine nature even though she has had no positive female model. The women in the story she has to live with are totally dissatisfied with their social status, and show no understanding for her dreams related to education and knowing the world.

Only when feeling that her existence is endangered does she decide to find her own place in life. She embarks on a journey during which she confronts herself with the crossing of the animal-human borders and with her own double nature. As is not unusual for a postmodern literary hero, she is split between her two selves, symbolized by her two names: Miyax and Julie. Miyax is her Eskimo part, the one she refuses when hoping to find a fairer status in the south, in the prosperous American society. As Julie, she can see herself continuing her schooling and enjoying the same luxuries as her San Francisco pen friend. However, her self-image increasingly depends more on her understanding of the relation between wilderness and civilization.

The name Miyax stands for whatever is related to the Inuit lore, and her English name merely connects her with the civilization that she has to meet as a citizen of the United States of America. As a student, acquainted with the knowledge of her people, she only wonders how it is possible that Americans look for the answers to the problems that Eskimos have solved long ago. Later, when her survival depends to a certain degree on the application of Eskimo survival skills in the harsh environment, she reconsiders her Eskimo roots and starts seeing herself as an Eskimo, saved by the wolves. While crossing the animal-human borderline, she has also been growing in wisdom: her understanding of her people and of the wilderness increases. The protagonist discovers the wilderness as a place of supreme beauty, in spite of its scarce human friendliness. Civilization, on the other hand, reveals itself as a brutal destructive force, represented by one of the twentieth-century pollution symbols: oil drums. However, it is mainly because of the wolves that Miyax's fondness of the wilderness grows.

The great representatives of the nature are not anthropomorphized, even though they are attributed distinctive identities. Amaroq resembles Kapugen, the hunter. The noble black leader possesses the qualities that Eskimos traditionally identify as signs of wealth: fearlessness, intelligence, and love. Amaroq's intelligence is evident with respect to Miyax, because he realizes that the girl cannot change her human ways. At the other end of the social ladder is Jello, a coward who demonstrates that not all wolves are friendly toward humans. The pack is organized similarly to Eskimo society and the wolves' behavior is described, as "similar to that of humans in significant ways" (Hourihan 1997: 220–23). They are affectionate and friendly toward each other, family life is important, and decision making is the father's privilege. Each member has to fulfill precisely defined duties, and transgressions are not tolerated. The puppies, on the other hand, have to play in order to become able to live in a pack and are carefully protected by their elders; and Miyax discovers that cubs resemble Eskimo children: they compete in games, gain self-confidence, and establish a hierarchy of their own.

By living with the wolves, Miyax learns to live in harmony with the environment and with herself. She experiences "a sense of profound well-being" (Hourihan 1997: 222) and comes to appreciate Eskimo culture for recognizing the unity of the universe and the interdependence of all living beings. Her journey through the wilderness and her experience of life on both sides of the animal-human boundary brings her the maturity of recognizing the signs of the times. At the end of the story, she is able to accept these signs as reality to be considered when making decisions.

Coping with reality is also essential in *A Ring of Endless Light* (L'Engle 1980), a story in which crossing the boundaries between humankind and nature is encouraged by scientific research. Adam, a 19-year-old marine biologist who is working toward his veterinary and doctoral degrees, is researching dolphin language and the possibility of human-dolphin communication. He has a summer job at the Marine Biology Station, where he works with Dr. Jeb, an established researcher of the communication code of dolphins.

Adam has been working on the premise that intuition could play a decisive role in breaking the mystery; thus, he is eager to involve 16-year-old Vicky in his project, even though her special interest is literature. She writes poems and stories; however, nature has an important place in her life and it acts as a bridge to her inner self and the outer world. By contemplating plants, small animals, and the beauty of the sky, she approaches the mysteries of life.

Fascinated by the dolphins, Vicky is willing to join the experiment with Basil, a dolphin from a nearby bay. Adam calls him by imitating the blowing balloon sounds and strange whistles, similar to the ones made by the dolphins. Basil responds, and when Vicky has overcome her fear of meeting a mammal, she starts responding to Basil's exuberant friendliness. She discovers that Basil reacts in a doglike way to her petting, and his body movements seem to say, "go on stroking me" (L'Engle 1980: 105). The speed with which Vicky and Basil befriend each other confirms Adam's hunch that dolphins can detect a person's feelings and convey their knowledge to a human. When Basil's mate presents their baby to Vicky, the protagonist names the female Norberta and the baby Njord. The teenager plays with them, makes them perform different tricks, and even gets information on questions no human has been able to answer. Vicky's advances with the dolphins go far beyond Adam's plans, even though he expects her to be capable of the "archaic understanding" (239), as he calls the comprehension of life in the deepest, mythic sense. However, when Vicky displays her ability to communicate nonverbally with Adam, the young researcher gets upset and forbids her "intrusion" into his mind. He becomes afraid of trusting her.

When a baby dolphin born in the pen dies, Adam reveals to the girl that Dr. Jeb sympathizes strongly with the female dolphin because he has lost his wife and only child in a car accident. The animals and the man mutually console each other. The rapport between them is so close that when the researcher lies seriously injured in hospital, the dolphins stop eating. Meanwhile, Vicky is also deeply hurt because her grandfather's health has deteriorated due to terminal illness. She seems to see death everywhere and when a little girl, ill with leukemia, dies on her lap, she breaks down. Unknowingly, by using the ways of communication she has learned from the dolphins, she calls Adam for help. The young man responds, only to find her numbed. Vicky does not recover until he takes her to meet the dolphins. It is this "therapeutic" encounter with the dolphin pod that gives her the strength to face life again. The animals have dispersed her depression and have awakened her from the darkness to the light of the realities of life.

A Ring of Endless Light is as much a narrative of death and dying and of maturation as it is a story of crossing animal-human boundaries. The fictional researchers of human-dolphin communication emphasize the insufficiency of science alone in the search for clues to the enigma about the possibility of communication between a man and a dolphin. The twentieth-century rediscovery of the holistic approach—in the sense of teamwork and interdisciplinary collaboration among experts in various scientific fields—thus is echoed in the novel. The traditional theme of animal-human communication is approached according to the holistic views of research that makes use of the discoveries of twentieth-century neurobiology, neuropsychiatry, and neuropsychology. Even though it was confirmed that in the human brain neither of the hemispheres is completely passive and that they mutually support each other's processes, it is still believed that a particular discipline or activity makes a pronounced use of one of the two cerebral hemispheres. Ways of thinking and conclusion-making are therefore to a certain extent different in such opposing activities as scientific research and the writing of poetry, which brings advantages to multidisciplinary collaboration (Russel 1979). Therefore, it is no wonder that what Adam learns about the dolphins through his research is obvious to Vicky through intuition.

During their conversations about dolphins, Vicky naturally poses questions and expresses suppositions that scientists have been able to formulate only after studying various sources, making long observations, and conducting experiments. Thus, when Adam mentions that whales and others of their kind, like dolphins and porpoises, are the only land creatures that returned to the sea, Vicky thinks of the mermaids of folklore and art. She is afraid of sounding unscientific, but is reassured with the explanation that "some people think mermaids came from porpoises and their singing sounds like dolphins chirruping" (L'Engle 1980: 97). Dr. Jeb is recording such "gabblings" and "underwater whistling" to see if these sounds "are part of a real language with a complex vocabulary" (100). However, dolphins use another type of language to communicate with him. They lower their supersonic sounds to within human range when they want to convey a message to him, "which shows consideration and intelligence" (109). Adam tries to imitate such sounds when he calls the animals living in their natural habitat, but Vicky communicates differently.

Her special manner of establishing contact confirms Adam's thesis that communication between humans and dolphins is possible through nonverbal ways of the language of knowing, "knowing without having to speak . . . maybe even across time and space" (175). The intuitive flashes of knowing might reveal what is unseen when there is conscious control. Adam explains to Vicky that "All the great scientists, like Newton, like Einstein, repeat the same thing—that discoveries don't come when you're consciously looking for them. They come when for some reason you've let go conscious control. They come in a sudden flash" (L'Engle 1980: 167). Such thinking should be related to the unhindered imagination of childhood and is supposed to fade out with the imposition of the Cartesian approach to the world. The novel describes this quality as the willingness to go along with the unexpected or with whatever cannot be controlled. It is thus presented as being enhanced by artistic creativity.

The role of science in *A Ring of Endless Light* has a lot in common with the role it plays in science fiction books, speculating "about something that hasn't happened yet, but might be possible some day" (Sleator 1996: 207). Adam and his boss believe that the parallels between the animal and human worlds should enable a sort of communication. Their thesis is made plausible due to a few motifs that are manipulated within the text. For example, reference to the size of a dolphin's brain will induce readers to speculate about the mammal's intelligence, despite scientific proof that the size of the brain is not a decisive element in defining intelligence. In addition, the fact that dolphins do not have vocal cords is presented as opening a possibility for new ways of communication: through vibration or through the language of knowing. The former is presented as being parallel to the communication experienced by deaf people "who can feel vibrations" and in this way "hear music" (L'Engle 1980: 175). The suggested ways of communication are considerably stretched "beyond the limits of reality" (Sleator 1996: 209). Moreover, the concept of nonlinear thinking, presumably applied to animals, is also discussed by Adam and Vicky. Adam also claims that "scientists need the poets, mystics, people who can escape our logical, linear thinking" (179). The fictional credibility of dolphin-man communication is furthermore strengthened with the drawing of parallels with precognition and teleportation, the two parapsychological phenomena that received considerable attention from the twentieth-century general lay public.

The text of the novel also reveals some similarity to science fantasy books. In dealing with the mysteries of dolphin-human communication, it conveys a "transcendental view of nature and a powerful spiritual approach to life" (Khorana 1997: 2). The mammals seem to have a double nature: on the one hand they are presented as friendly communal creatures, fond of playing and showing off their abilities to men; on the other hand, allusions to their "strangeness" are repeated. These hints or insinuations reach their climax in the final scene, where the duality of the dolphin's nature is put into the limelight. During the therapeutic session the sea mammals display a majestic coordination of various tricks that leads to Vicky's healing .

The protagonist is cured by the entire school of dolphins, even though she does not enter the dolphin society. In fact, Vicky spends only short periods of time with the dolphins, and the societal life of the sea animals is not described in as much detail as the wolf society in *Julie of the Wolves*. Nevertheless, the dolphin family structure is represented as displaying some fixed characteristics: roles in a family are clearly defined. For instance, the mother is the one to supervise the baby dolphin, and it is with her that the baby appears first to the "outside world"—to the human friends. Even though the dolphin world remains full of mysteries to the protagonist, the dolphins succeed in curing her. By crossing the animal-human boundary, Vicky regains her vitality and re-enters life.

However, despite the happy ending of the story, the conclusion is somewhat equivocal, as it is not only the protagonist who is cured, but also Adam, who has liberated himself of his fear of showing Vicky his love. It is not certain to what extent Vicky will be immune to the blows she will have to encounter in the future. The ending is open to speculation, similar to the conclusion in *Julie of the Wolves*, in which the reader does not know how Miyax will manage to adjust to a completely new lifestyle. However, the growth and development of Julie and Vicky leaves the reader with a belief that they are ready for life. At the same time, these books exhibit also a trust in nonadult readers to be able to read the implicit messages of the text. This double confidence reflects the respect that this audience has won in an age that proclaims various types of rights and freedoms. The two novels thus offer a set of specific features, from the application of the nonauthoritative point of view to the elaboration of themes and motifs reflecting twentieth-century ways of thinking and feeling about the child and the animal world.

Change and renewal have indeed taken place in young adult novels featuring animal-human characters. Among the motifs related to the time of the publication of these two books, those evoking ecological problems are particularly stressed. Both novels convey a strong ecological message. In *A Ring of Endless Light*, a newspaper item stating "a thousand porpoises beaten to death with clubs" (L'Engle 1980: 27) provokes a lively discussion about the protection of animals. The incident and its consequences are presented from various angles that reveal a kind of dialogic attitude between the author and her characters and readers. Multiple points of view are expressed through different opinions voiced in the story. For instance, Adam explains that fishermen depend entirely on fish; hence, their need for survival comes first. However, the fervent advocates of animal rights hardly accept the idea, and the discussions evoke parallels with the meetings of animal rights associations.

The issue of killing animals is also dealt with in *Julie of the Wolves*, in which white men kill wolves for enjoyment. Once the animals are dead they are not interested in them any more. Such transgression of the borders set between the animal world and humanity is strongly condemned and is contrasted with the crossing performed by the young protagonists who are sensitive to the laws and customs of the natural habitat.

Miyax and Vicky, who cross and recross animal-human borders, have much in common, even though they belong to different ethnic and social groups. The two protagonists have both retained their capacity for wonder and are open to the beauties and mysteries of nature. The reasons for their entering the animal kingdom are different; however, the steps they take to establish a relationship between the two worlds are similar. They are aware that over-coming the fear of the animals is a precondition to showing their gestures of goodwill. Naming the individuals is another act with which they express their involvement in the new environment, because it is an essay to establish par-allels between their society and animal social structure. Once a relation of mutual trust is established, there are no serious hindrances for the develop-ment of communication, because the protagonists pay attention to the animal code. The relationship is further facilitated when both parties accept each other's individuality, admitting that there are traits that cannot be shared.

The protagonists' way of penetrating the world of animals reflects, on the one hand, the contemporary animal-friendly attitude of the lay public to fauna, and, on the other hand, echoes the findings recently discovered or confirmed by scientific research about wolves and dolphins. "The depiction of the wolf pack is based upon careful and detailed zoological observation of the behavior of actual wolves in their natural habitat and highlights the in-accuracies of the traditional image of the wolf in folk tales and popular lit-erature" (Hourihan 1997: 221). The term "traditional" used in the citation evidently applies to the picture conveyed by Western folk tradition, in which the animals were presented as the enemies of man. The contemporary inter-disciplinary research of wolves in their ecosystem (e.g., in Northern America by the International Wolf Center in Minnesota [www.wolf.org]) has con-firmed most of the Eskimo beliefs about arctic wolves, even if the experts admit that "man is only just beginning to reach a simple knowledge of the wolf and does not know how to come to terms with it" (http://users.ap.net/chenae/wolfhome.html). Among the researchers who contribute to this In-ternet site is Debra McCann, who claims that "with its uncanny perceptions and a social structure that closely resembles our own, wolves challenge us to be wise" (ibid.). Not to be ignorant means also to admit that there are "many documented cases of wolves nurturing lost human children" (Hourihan 1997: 221). Therefore, the image of the wolves in *Julie of the Wolves* is realistic.

The same is true, to a certain extent, with the depiction of the dolphins in *A Ring of Endless Light*. In special maritime medical institutions, dolphins have helped patients and handicapped people with various impairments to regain their health (Carwadine and Hoyt 1998: 27). Particular attention has been paid to the study of the dolphin's senses: taste, smell, and hearing. On an Internet site presenting the issues related to the protection of this animal (http//librarythinkquest.org//7963/captivity.html), the capacity of echolocation receives special attention. Reports on the social structure, ranging habits, and even the character of the animal all confirm the observations from the book. For instance, Vicky remarks on several occasions that the dolphins are funny, and on the Internet site, researchers claim that these creatures "seem to have been blessed with a well developed sense of humor."

The fictional world, however, has gone beyond that of reality. Although no negative consequences of the breaking of the wolf code are indicated in *Julie of the Wolves*, there is a hint of the possible negative consequences of applying nonverbal ways of communication in *A Ring of Endless Light*. The "telepathic" communication transposed onto the human-human level is envisaged as both positive and negative: it can either save lives or it can be misused to invade privacy, limiting freedom, independence, and integrity. If the fictional crossing of the human-animal boundary may have such an impact on interhuman communication, and consequently on society, the book implicitly conveys a message similar to the one explicitly expressed in *Julie of the Wolves:* there is no real gap between humanity and the animal kingdom. Human society and the world of animals seem to be two entities of one and the same reality, heavily dependent on humans. The verse from *Julie of the Wolves* "the hour of the wolf and the Eskimo is over" (Craighead George 1972: 170) indicates parallels between the future of the endangered animal species and the Eskimo culture. Neither can resist the impact of Western civilization unscrupulously exploiting the environment, lacking respect for the weak, and promoting a lifestyle in which acquisition of money and enjoyment at all cost seems to have acquired value status. The issues related to responsibility for one's own life, society, the environment, and life in general are therefore brought into the limelight. Old problems in a new context are raised anew. Will intuition and reason solve the great mysteries of the nature and life? Is the (de)mystification of the functioning of the universe needed or desired? Open questions that neither of the two novels tries to answer are related to universal and timeless themes of growing up and maturation, of bridging gaps between ideals and reality, of accepting life and death, and of establishing communication not just between humans and animals but also among people and peoples. All issues touch the core of human nature, encouraging readers to critically face their world and time. The question about boundaries among living beings has been raised from time immemorial, and the crossing of borders between the animal world and human society is a traditional challenge to authors writing animal stories. The answers given in literature are varied and manyfold, as are the genres in which the issue is addressed. Since the twentieth century, research in the field of zoology and ecology has made unpredictable advances and the topic of animal-human communication gained in appeal. The reading public was ready for novelty. Among the authors who have responded to the expectations of this audience were Madeleine L'Engle and Jean Craighead George. Their contribution to the renewal of children's literature has been an enrichment to the literary production featuring animal and human protagonists.

BIBLIOGRAPHY

Carwardine, Mark, and Erich Hoyt. 1998. *La grande famille des cetaces: Baleines, dauphins et marsouins* (translation of *Whales, Dolphins, and Porpoises*). Konemann: Weldon Owen.

Craighead George, Jean. 1972. *Julie of the Wolves.* New York: Harper.

Hourihan, Margaret. 1997. *Deconstructing a Hero.* New York: Routledge.

Khorana, Meena G. 1997. "To the Reader." *Bookbird* 35/4: 2–3.

L'Engle, Madeleine. 1980. *A Ring of Endless Light.* New York: Crosswicks.

Lomax, Earl Dean. 1983. *After "The Outsiders": The Literary Characteristics of Contemporary American Young Adult Fiction, 1968–1979.* Columbia, Mo.: University Microfilms International.

Russel, Peter. 1987. *Knjiga o mozganih.* Ljubljana: Drzavna zalozba Slovenije; originally published as *The Brain Book: Know Your Own Mind and How to Use It* (London: Routledge and Kegan Paul, 1979).

Sleator, William. 1996. "What Is It About Science Fiction?" In *Only Connect*, ed. Sheila Egoff, 206–12. Toronto: Oxford University Press.

Townsend, John Rowe. 1990. *Written for Children.* London: Bodley Head.

CHAPTER 6

Me, Myself, and Him—The Changing Face of Female Cross-Dressing in Contemporary Children's Literature

Victoria Flanagan

Despite a perception that the associations of cross-dressing with sexuality, homosexuality, and immorality make it an unsuitable topic for younger readers, children's narratives that contain cross-dressing references abound. Not surprisingly, the cross-dressing that typically occurs in children's literature is dissociated from the adult arenas of transvestism and transsexualism. It is constructed as a harmless act of childish experimentation and imagination, and its transgression of social mores is recognized, in most instances, through the implicit suggestion that cross-dressing behavior is somewhat mischievous and naughty—although this rarely translates as a direct condemnation of transvestism as wrong or immoral. Cross-dressing is reconstructed in children's literature as nonsexual and temporary, distinctions that sever connections with the adult world of transgender and effectively absolve its inclusion in children's narratives from controversy. However, the recent proliferation of young adult children's literature that has demonstrated an unprecedented willingness to embrace adult concepts previously considered off-limits to younger readers is responsible for sowing significant seeds of change in the depiction of cross-dressing in children's narratives.

Until recently, the construction of cross-dressing in children's literature has conformed to a basic paradigmatic structure that ensured its distinction from the adult realm of transgender and created a unique strategy for gender criticism. Cross-dressing in children's literature is generally female to male, a temporary act, and definitively nonsexual. The cross-dresser is usually a young girl living in a patriarchal society who discovers liberation and empowerment by disguising herself as a male. Although such a representation constitutes an effective method of critiquing the socially constructed nature of gender categorization, it is somewhat difficult to ignore the fact that this strategy is based on artifice and deception—its success dependent on the negation of trans-genderism as a cultural reality. This phenomenon, however, is slowly begin-ning to change, and the great chasm of difference between the children's literary world of cross-dressing and its adult counterpart is quietly being bridged by a small minority of children's authors.

The renewal of cross-dressing as a relevant theme for texts directed at "young adult" readers is evident in its changing construction. The presenta-tion of cross-dressing in my chosen examples of young adult fiction (discussed below) is closely related to contemporary "adult" transgender concepts, embracing the subjective complexity that these notions encompass. The tra-ditional dichotomy between children's literature (playful, harmless, experi-mental) and adult (sexual, deviate, abnormal, psychological) cross-dressing is re-addressed to a certain extent in these texts. The result is a portrayal of cross-dressing that refuses to disengage itself from reality and involves itself in the previously deemed adults-only world of transgender.

In order to discuss the significant shift that is currently occurring in the representation of cross-dressing in literature produced for children, it is first necessary to examine the manner in which cross-dressing has been presented in the past. One of the most important aspects of this portrayal is its feminine subject, an element that has carried through to its evolving presentation in contemporary texts. Children's authors have used female-to-male cross-dressing in the past for a range of purposes that share much thematic commonality, despite the fact that the texts in which it occurs differ greatly from one another in terms of cultural context, historical positionality, and literary genre. Direct associations and parallels can be made between chil-dren's *sword and sorcery* fantasy, historical Chinese legend, Russian folklore, and seventeenth-century French fairy tales, indicative of a cross-dressing par-adigm that is able to transcend genre-related limitations of meaning.

Female-to-male cross-dressing in children's literature has traditionally per-formed a symbolic, as well as narrative, function. Texts that contain female-to-male cross-dressing usually conform to a basic structure that involves a young girl living in a patriarchal context, who escapes (or is forced to flee) her limited female existence by disguising herself as a man. Dressed as a man, she gains access to a world formerly denied to her and amply demonstrates her ability to perform masculine tasks and feats more successfully than her biologically male peers.

Children's texts generally use female-to-male cross-dressing to interrogate traditional gender values and stereotypes. These texts depict biological fe-males who disguise themselves as males and perform not only as ably as their biologically male peers, but more so—receiving accolades from all whom they encounter for their superior abilities in the masculine arena. The biologically female protagonists of these texts are clearly capable of being "better" men than their male counterparts. This provokes a re-evaluation of traditional masculinity and femininity based on the cross-dressers' own nonconformity to such categorizations.

The re-evaluation of the concept of gender evident in the majority of children's female-to-male cross-dressing narratives manifests itself in the phenomenon of the cross-dressing heroine's apparent ability to change her gender at a certain textual point, moving in and out of gender roles as an actor changes characters for different performances. This act of gender transformation seeks "to reveal the construction of the sexes and deconstruct the established conceptions of them" (Westin 1999: 92). Female cross-dressing narratives in children's literature question socially assumed understanding in relation to gender by playfully exposing the redundancies of two, polarized, gendered identities. They gently ridicule the limitations that such a system imposes on supposedly autonomous individuals.

Although the critical function of female-to-male cross-dressing in children's literature can be usefully discussed in the context of the work of gender theorists such as Judith Butler (1999), who specifically analyzes gender in relation to the destabilizing powers of the transgendered subject, such works do not delve directly into the actual day-to-day experience of the transgendered person. The trauma, mental anguish, and social stigmatization, which commonly play a primary role in the experience of adult transvestites and transsexuals, are not phenomena usually dealt with in children's literature; nor is the issue of homosexuality widely perceived as acceptable subject matter in children's texts. Children's texts that contain any form of cross-dressing have, up until the present time, carefully de-sexualized each representation, removing the most distinctive element of, and any association with, adult transvestism and transsexualism.

Two children's texts that substantively challenge this presentation of cross-dressing and offer a renewed perspective on issues relating to the act of transvestism are *Touch Me* (Moloney 2000) and *Johnny, My Friend* (Pohl 1991; originally published in 1985). Both depict female-to-male cross-dressing in a manner that attempts to re-dress the traditional disjunction between the presentation of female-to-male cross-dressing in children's literature and contemporary adult transvestite/transsexual reality. Peter Pohl's *Johnny, My Friend* is a Swedish coming-of-age mystery novel that offers a particularly unusual portrayal of female cross-dressing. Narrated by Chris, who begins the story when he is 11 years old, it is about his short-lived friendship with Johnny, a mysterious and peculiar boy who suddenly enters his life and becomes his best friend. At the close of the novel, a tragedy unfolds, and Johnny's murdered body is discovered. Only after his death does Chris discover that Johnny is actually a girl—a trapeze artist from a traveling circus who, it is suggested, is killed because of her cross-dressing transgressions. *Touch Me*, by James Moloney, is an Australian work of young adult fiction that revolves around the relationship between Xavier, a conventional teenage boy, and a rather unusual girl named Nuala. Nuala is a charismatic and vivacious young woman who is regarded as strange and enigmatic by her peers because of her unusual presentation—she dresses as a man. *Johnny, My Friend* and *Touch Me* uniquely address contemporary issues relating to transvestism and transsexualism.

Johnny, My Friend, which broaches the taboolike subject of transgender (it is unclear whether Johnny is displaying transvestite or transsexual tendencies), offers a portrayal of cross-dressing that deals with the alienation, psychological anguish, and social intolerance that are inseparable from contemporary transsexualism but are not usually acknowledged in children's fiction. Johnny's death is indicative of the social consequences that may flow from the subversion of established gender codes. The novel imbues the act of cross-dressing with a gravity that is lacking in most portrayals of female cross-dressing in children's literature—in which the heroine's transvestism is typically forgiven because of the admirable deeds she has performed while in disguise, which elevate her beyond reproach. The depiction of cross-dressing in *Touch Me* also indicates a departure from the conventional portrayal of female transvestism in children's texts. This is particularly the case in relation to the issue of cross-dressing sexuality. When Xavier finds himself attracted to Nuala's unconventionality, his blossoming romance is not welcomed by his male friends, who seem unable to comprehend Nuala's disdain for "normal" feminine conventions. Her visual oddity is construed as an abnormality to these boys, and explained in terms of abnormal and "othered" sexuality: they believe that Nuala is a lesbian. Of course, this does not offer an explanation for Xavier's relationship with her. His friendship with Nuala is rationalized in similarly illogical terms: because Xavier is spending time with a girl of questionable sexual orientation who dresses as a boy, his friends interpret this behavior as an indication of his own homosexuality. *Touch Me* is not an exploration of homosexuality, however, but rather a voyage into the problematic and nuanced arena of transgender sexuality—which encompasses elements of both homosexuality and heterosexuality.

The issue of sexuality is integral to *Touch Me*. Sex plays a primary role in Nuala's cross-dressing, differentiating it from the more common representations of female-to-male cross-dressing. It is born out of an incident that occurred prior to the commencement of the narrative, when Nuala first became aware of her emerging sexuality and began a holiday romance with a fellow male student. The relationship later soured because of the disturbing actions of the boy, who attempted to construe Nuala as a sexual plaything to his friends and classmates. He did this by creating digitally enhanced pornographic pictures of her and displaying them at school, as well as spreading rumors about Nuala's promiscuity. The public humiliation that Nuala suffered as a result of this behavior led to her decision never to be similarly mistreated by (or fall victim to) a male again. She angrily responds by ridding herself of any outward signifiers of femininity or female sexuality—cutting her long hair and disguising her hips in loose male clothing. Dressed as a male, she feels safe from masculinity and the traditional sexual threat it poses to femininity.

The construction of cross-dressing as an escape is also evident in *Johnny, My Friend*. Johnny's motivation for disguising himself (I refer to Johnny with the masculine pronoun because this is the pronoun used throughout the text) is never made explicit, although it is suggested that it is the result of a repressive and unforgiving environment. The decision to disguise himself as a male can be interpreted as an attempt to completely dissociate him from his other existence (as a female trapeze artist, forced to perform in a ballerinalike ensemble). It also constitutes a camouflage least likely to betray his female biology. Johnny's ability to carry off this masquerade almost flawlessly also points toward a natural affinity with the masculine persona he adopts. The question of whether "Johnny" is simply the most effective hiding device available to an unhappy and daring young girl or a deliberately constructed image of the male she would rather be is left open. The possibilities offered by Johnny's cross-dressing are cruelly closed by his death. This ending ultimately warns of the hostility that accompanies gender subversion in a realistic context.

The destabilizing and subversive power of the cross-dresser, evident from the murderous reaction to Johnny's transgender behavior in *Johnny, My Friend*, is displayed very differently in *Touch Me*. Nuala's ability to unsettle those around her is constructed in subtler, yet no less confrontational terms. Nuala's cross-dressing and the conflicting sexual messages it sends to her peers are further complicated by her own attitude toward it.

Although dressed convincingly as a man, she does not actually pretend to be male. Her cross-dressing pleasure is born out of the very gender confusion her projected persona creates. She identifies as female when interacting with people, yet seeks to appear male to those outside her acquaintance. The visual dilemma Nuala presents to others is further problematic by the fact that her masculine clothing accompanies a face that is dramatically enhanced with cosmetics. She wears dark lipstick that makes "a cherry-colored slash across her face" and her eyebrows are plucked into "thin, coal-black lines that curved over gaudy eye shadow and teased-out lashes" (Moloney 2000: 26). In short, Nuala is an embodiment of male drag. As argued by Vern and Bonnie Bullough (1993: 246), drag is a "confusion of costume whereby the illusion of assuming the opposite sex is not intended to convince the viewer of authenticity but to suggest ambiguity." The notion of drag as gender confusion is also supported by Esther Newton (cited in Butler 1999: 174), who writes:

At its most complex, [drag] is a double inversion that says, "appearance is an illusion." Drag says "my 'outside' appearance is feminine, but my essence 'inside' is masculine." At the same time it symbolizes the opposite inversion; "my appearance 'outside' is masculine but my essence 'inside' myself is feminine."

This function of drag is not lost on Nuala. She is acutely aware of the effects of her gender bending: "She smiled contemptuously. 'They can't work out whether I'm a cross-dressing female or a boy with serious cosmetic dysfunction' " (Moloney 2000: 28). Nuala is quick to learn that her cross-dressing has powerful potential. She treats it as a game, relishing the perplexity that she constantly encounters from people unable to read her scrambled gender messages. She particularly enjoys male reactions, conscious of the fact that she is the more powerful individual as long as she remains "unknowable" and inexplicable.

Gender is constructed in both *Johnny, My Friend* and *Touch Me* as something transformable and subject to individual manipulation. Johnny and Nuala successfully subvert conventional gender constructions, although the path of subversion for these characters is not as easy or simple as it is for cross-dressing heroines in more traditional female-to-male children's cross-dressing texts. Johnny and Nuala's gender subversion is less extraordinary, and although they present convincingly as males in some circumstances, their biological femininity is not always hidden from view. In Johnny's case, this is evident when characters such as Chris, and Chris's parents, first meet him and perceive some element of his physical presentation as feminine. After interacting with him, however, his masculine behavior soon convinces them that their initial impression was incorrect. Despite these instances in which his female sex is indirectly recognized, Johnny is able to maintain a successful masculine persona throughout the novel. Chris thinks of him as strange and mysterious, but never as female. To Chris, Johnny's masculine gender performance is completely authentic.

Nuala's cross-dressing, in contrast, is successful only to those people not in her immediate circle of friends. From afar she presents as a male, but on closer inspection she is recognizable as female, due to her feminine name, voice, and the fact that she does not hide her biology in the context of her school life and social interactions. This said, Nuala's attempts to subvert traditional gender conventions are perhaps more significant than Johnny's. In presenting herself as a girl in drag, Nuala confuses and undermines the assumptions regarding gender that inform even the most basic levels of human interaction. As Freud argues, "When you meet a human being, the first distinction you make is 'male or female?' and you are accustomed to make the distinction with unhesitating certainty" (Freud [1933] 1964: 113). Nuala presents simultaneously as male and female, causing a disturbance wherever she goes. She is a testament to the artificiality of traditional gender constructs, constantly demonstrating the ease with which such constructs can be challenged and rendered meaningless—all that is needed is the requisite clothing and a knowledge of gendered behaviors. Nonetheless, this success comes at a price. Nuala is perpetually misunderstood because of her gender rebellion, and alienated even from those people who attempt to see past the barriers she has erected around herself. The presentation of gender in these texts is complex and multifaceted. Each clearly reveals the artificiality of traditional gender divisions through the portrayal of characters who successfully achieve a gendered persona at odds with their biological sex.

The treatment of cross-dressing in *Johnny, My Friend* and *Touch Me* is radical and progressive, sympathetically introducing the concept of gender transgression to younger audiences. Johnny and Nuala's transgendered status, however, is not depicted as symptomatic of a contemporary relaxation of limited gender roles in a modern context. Gender is revealed as an artificial social construct in each text, yet its traditional significance in a wider cultural context is maintained. The repercussions of transgender behavior are serious and far-reaching, as is evident through the hostile reactions that each character encounters. Gender is presented as a restrictive concept with the potential to be challenged, but such a challenge is carefully depicted as fraught with difficulty and the possibility of negative social impact.

The willingness of *Touch Me* and *Johnny, My Friend* to explore the concept of cross-dressing in a realistic fashion is indicative of a newly emerging desire to present complex social issues to children in a manner that is informative and relevant. In dealing with the issue of transgender, *Touch Me* and *Johnny, My Friend* are both pioneering texts. They tread sensitively around the issue of cross-dressing, choosing to use a biological female (rather than the more commonly occurring male subject) as the cross-dresser. The issue of sexuality, pertaining particularly to the relationship between transgender and homosexuality, is also raised in each text. Perhaps most significantly, the cross-dressing featured in *Touch Me* and *Johnny, My Friend* is not presented as ongoing at the close of each text. The final pages of *Touch Me* see Nuala accepting the present of a dress from Xavier, signifying that she is finally ready to re-embrace conventional femininity. Johnny's death similarly closes the door on his cross-dressing in *Johnny, My Friend*. The construction of cross-dressing as temporal is a key feature of more traditional female-to-male children's cross-dressing narratives, and the retaining of this strategy in texts that have otherwise strived to explore the adult-oriented subject of transgender realistically symbolizes a hesitance to fully embrace, or endorse, cross-dressing as it exists in an adult context.

The attempt made in each of these novels to engage with the adult transgender arena does not, however, exactly validate transgendered behavior as a viable gender existence. Although cross-dressing is used to reveal the artificiality of traditional gender constructs, and is portrayed as a means through which such constructs can be successfully subverted, the overriding message is overtly negative—serving as a warning against transgendered behavior. This position is made clear by the conclusion of each text, in which the cross-dressing of the protagonist dramatically ceases. Despite this, however, it is still possible to perceive these contemporary children's texts as offering a renewed and progressive representation of cross-dressing—one that sympathetically introduces younger readers to the complex notion of transgender and also to the negative social attitudes it typically attracts.

The caution with which *Touch Me* and *Johnny, My Friend* approach the subject of cross-dressing is easily appreciated. In choosing to depict transvestite and transsexual behavior realistically, these texts immediately place themselves in an unknown and uncertain realm of children's literary realism. Although issues such as divorce, youth suicide, sex, teenage pregnancy, and even homosexuality are increasingly featured in children's literature, transvestism and transsexualism are subjects that are largely left untouched. This is, I would suggest, the result of a popular sentiment of uncertainty that surrounds the issue of transgender—a residual notion that transvestism is sexually devious and immoral, and a tendency to discount transsexualism as implausible.

The ambiguity of social attitudes toward transgender (i.e., in an adult context) is magnified in a children's context, as the ability to direct an impressionable reader becomes increasingly problematic because a general consensus has yet to be reached on the manner of direction. In this respect, *Touch Me* and *Johnny, My Friend* perform admirably. Both novels present the complex, and often controversial, adult-oriented concept of transgender to younger readers in a manner that is sensitive and compassionate. While the construction of cross-dressing within these books does not wholly accord with the adult transgender experience, each text voices a powerful message about the values of tolerance and acceptance in the face of behavior considered to be socially subversive.

BIBLIOGRAPHY

Bullough, V., and B. Bullough. 1993. *Cross-Dressing, Sex and Gender*. Philadelphia: University of Pennsylvania Press.

Butler, J. 1999. *Gender Trouble—Feminism and the Subversion of Identity*. New York: Routledge.

Freud, S. [1933] 1964. "Femininity." In *New Introductory Lectures on Psycho-Analysis*. Vol. 22, *The Standard Edition of the Complete Psychological Works of Sigmund Freud*, ed. James Strachey. Reprint, London: The Hogarth Press and The Institute for Psycho-Analysis.

Moloney, J. 2000. *Touch Me*. Queensland: University of Queensland Press.

Pohl, P. 1991. *Johnny, My Friend*, trans. Laurie Thompson. England: Turton and Chambers.

Westin, B. 1999. "The Androgynous Female—(or Orlando Inverted) Examples from Gripe, Stark, Wahl, Pohl." In *Gender in Children's Literature*, ed. L. Pastemak, 91–95. Stockholm: Baltic Centre for Writers and Translators.

CHAPTER 7

Voyeurism and Power: Change and Renewal of the Eroticized Figure in Australian Books for Teenagers

Margot Hillel

In many children's books of the nineteenth and early twentieth centuries, the child character was eroticized. This eroticizing appeared in a number of ways; the most frequent depicted the child as subordinate in a relationship in which the wielding of power became an erotic experience for the dominant figure. Among such books are Rudyard Kipling's *Stalky and Co.* ([1899] 1962); Frederick Farrar's *Eric or Little by Little* (1907); and, in Australia, Ethel Turner's *St Tom and the Dragon* (1918), with its brutal father chaining his daughter to the table and stripping and beating her until she bleeds, and *Seven Little Australians* (1894) in which Captain Woolcott's whip frequently is heard swishing over the buttocks of hapless Pip. Pip's father clearly subscribed to the "link between flogging and learning . . . [the view] that whipping boys would result in masculine valor and civilized behavior" (Favret 1998: 26). Furthermore, as James Kincaid (1993: 263) argues, such beatings were frequently conducted with "hypocritical righteous fervor." In many of these books, the erotic interaction between the characters seems to be depicted as a substitute for "legitimate" sex. The child figure in such encounters is eroticized through the power exercised over her or him by the stronger character and becomes a fetishized object for that character. A number of these figures are further eroticized by the voyeuristic gaze of other characters in the book and, through them, of the reader. The voyeuristic gaze sometimes operates apart from the violence in, for example, books like James Barrie's *Peter Pan or the Boy Who Would Not Grow Up* (1928). In such books, the erotic voyeurism operates on a number of levels in much the same way as Laura Mulvey (as cited in Perry 1999) has described the viewing of films: there is the level of the artist (or author) who produces the image, the level of the viewer (or reader), and the level of the characters within the narrative.

This chapter demonstrates the ways in which—perhaps surprisingly, given changed societal attitudes toward the sexuality of teenagers and its representation in books—these constructions of the erotic child were renewed in the latter part of the twentieth century. Although it might perhaps be expected that a more open acknowledgment of the sexuality of teenagers in their recent reading matter would preclude eroticism, there is, however, persistence in the trope of the eroticized child. Although the eroticization of the child in nineteenth- and early-twentieth-century texts was, as Jan Kociumbas (1997) has argued, frequently linked with innocence, in the later twentieth century this has often been culturally succeeded by the eroticization of the teen figure linked with pubescent sexuality.

Some of this eroticization still involves gazing on a young person's body. In instances where the eroticism is configured in this way, the protagonist, as in many earlier books, becomes a voyeur, and the author makes the reader complicit in that voyeurism. Margaret Olin (cited in Perry 1999: 27) describes gaze as being a "literary term for what could also be called 'looking' or 'watching'. . . . While most discourse about the gaze concerns pleasure and knowledge, however, it generally places both of these in the service of issues of power, manipulation and desire." Furthermore, as Perry (1999: 27) goes on to point out, "modern theories of the gaze . . . have helped to give an important critical edge to our concept of looking, encouraging us to see the social and gender relations involved." These theories can be applied to a study of children's literature in the same way as they can to studies of film or fine art. In this way, these theories allow us to see how certain forms of eroticizing child and teenage figures in their literature are repeatedly renewed.

A number of contemporary books, for example, contain an (either temporarily or permanently) impotent male character as voyeur, through whose eyes the action and gaze are directed and who, in turn, is the object of the gaze of the adult author. Such characters can be seen as the descendants of, for example, the Tom of Turner's *St Tom and the Dragon*, an 18-year-old boy whose own sexuality would, no doubt, have been repressed by early-twentieth-century attitudes toward teenage sexuality. This form of eroticizing highlights gender differences, especially in recent books, in which it is the male characters who are most frequently the voyeuristic observers—the ones who do the gazing—whereas it is the female characters who are usually the objects of the male gaze.

One book that contains an impotent male voyeur is Jocelyn Harewood's *Voices in the Wash-house* (1990). Peregrine (Perry), who is 17, has a bed made up for him in the laundry after he breaks his leg in a car accident. His parents are divorced and his mother, Maddy, has a new boyfriend who is a policeman. Perry is one of four children and feels very left out when he is confined to his bed. His friend brings Perry back into contact with the whole household by rigging up a set of microphones and a small cassette player so that Perry doesn't miss out on what is going on in the house. "Mono['s] . . . covered three areas: the lounge, the kitchen and Mum's bedroom" (Harewood 1990: 15) The whole idea is somewhat prurient, because Perry is able to listen to other people's conversations, including some on quite intimate subjects—for example, the discussion between Perry's mother and his 16-year-old sister, Ashley, on the latter's first attempt at sex (Harewood 1990: 17–18), and later Ashley's description of this conversation to her friends (Perry can also over-hear telephone conversations) (Harewood 1990). Perry's mother's telephone conversations with the various men in her life also provide him with a great deal of prurient amusement (Harewood 1990). Even Perry's description of his sister eroticizes her: "All my mates lust after Ashley and I must admit she's a pretty neat shape—if you're into long legs, big boobs, long blonde hair and an aristocratic way of walking" (Harewood 1990: 16). There is recognition in the book of teenagers' sexuality that is mixed up with this curious kind of eroticizing of Perry's sisters and his mother, especially in her relationship with Barry, the policeman: "Maddy, . . . come here, close to me." [Maddy replies] "I love to drift into your body space." [Barry] "I feel so calm with you, yet breathlessly excited as well." [Maddy] "I'm pretty scared of any . . . Barry . . . Barry, could you hold me, forever . . . do you think?'" (Harewood 1990: 146). Perry is thus the means by which we, as readers, become part of this intimate moment between his mother and her boyfriend. Perry is eroticized implicitly by the voyeurism and prurience of the teenage reader whose gaze is directed through Perry. He himself is the object of the gaze of the author as she directs all the action through him.

Prurience and eroticizing are also part of Gary Crew's *Angel's Gate* (1993) as Kimmy, the younger child of a doctor in an isolated town, watches the world around him, especially his older sister, Julia. She is very much a sexualized figure, flaunting her body in seductive nightdresses and bright red dresses. The dress she buys to go to the local dance was not, as Kim expected it to be, "pink and pretty and with puffy sleeves," but as he describes it in careful detail, a "very, very short . . . bright red, shiny, dress which was skin tight across her stomach and cut low, revealing the beginnings of her breasts" (Crew 1993: 81). Mulvey (1989: 19) describes this type of behavior as women who are in their "traditional exhibitionist role" where they are "simultaneously looked at and displayed, with their appearance coded for strong visual and erotic impact so that they can be said to connote *to-be-looked-at-ness.*"

Julia and her brother often share a bed, despite their father's disapproval. In addition, Kim watches Julia and her boyfriend Bobby together, at which time she becomes eroticized for both Kim and Bobby, a point made by Heather Scutter (1999) in her examination of the book. In *Angel's Gate*, the first description of Julia suggests voyeurism; her younger brother Kimmy, the narrator, is 10 and she is 15. He watches her all the time and we see her filtered through his gaze. On this occasion, he is in bed and she is standing framed in the window of his bedroom, backlit, as it were, by the light from the cars outside. The description given is not that of a 10-year-old boy; there is a slippage between the adult narrator looking back and the 10-year-old persona he is trying to recreate. "She was staring into the yard, concentrating. She looked very beautiful; the moonlight on her face, her dark hair out and spilling down her back, her white nightdress falling in straight folds like marble" (Crew 1993: 1). The gaze here is directed through the eyes of the author, who, in another instance of renewal, is like the Victorian photographer gazing on the eroticized child subjects of his work—an adult gazing on the adolescent body of his character.

Kim is prepubescent and is therefore an impotent voyeur whose sexual longings seem directed toward this eroticizing of his sister. Kim himself is both feminized and infantilized. He is prone to excessive fears at night—fears that allow him the opportunity to sleep in his sister's bed—"Julia threw the sheet back, 'Here,' she said, 'get in with me.' I crawled in beside her and the sheet fell gently over me" (Crew 1993: 33). There is complicity by the author here in eroticizing the relationship between the children (and Julia, at 15, is still a child, albeit a willful one). There is a sense in which the two are wrapped, literally and metaphorically, in the sheet in a way that keeps out the outside world and its disapproval of this physical, if not consummated, relationship between the two. Despite the nonconsummation, there is a strong undertone of incest in these encounters, prevented only by Kim's lack of sexual maturity. Kim is, somewhat contradictorily, both infantilized and sexualized in his dependence on his sister.

Kim, whose name is androgynous, enjoys the "artistic" things of life, whereas the only thing that Julia really likes studying at school is mathematics. The attempted reversal of stereotypes and disturbance of heterosexual notions of masculinity is not convincing, however, because of the emphasis on Julia as female, an emphasis that writes much of her being on her body—in a way that rehearses the earlier defining of Anne in *St Tom and the Dragon* (Turner, 1918), whose public persona is constructed for her by adults in the way that they dress her. Kim's friend Keithy, who comes to stay one night, describes Julia as "the best looking girl I've ever seen" (Crew 1993: 108). This is after Kim, as narrator, has told us of Julia's arrival into his room: "Keithy's eyes were round as saucers. Julia in a nightdress, her hair spilling over her shoulders, was a sight to see" (Crew 1993: 107–8). The clichés used here—"round as saucers," and "sight to see"—are a sort of junior romance-novel language, but are intended to convey the strength of the sexual emotion of these two prepubescent boys, who—even though they are impotent voyeurs—can make Julia into a powerful, erotic object. The reader is also meant to respond to her formidable and manipulative sexual attraction. Even she sees herself as an erotic object, a persona she uses quite consciously to manipulate many of the males around her, especially Kim and her boyfriend Bobby. Keithy becomes the means of a form of betrayal of Julia, as well as a further eroticizing of her.

He asks Kim if he can see Julia's room, as a payback for Kim's own betrayal of the story Keithy has told him about the capture of one of the feral children. For Keithy, even Julia's personal belongings are erotic as he sees them as an extension of her. There is something sexual in the way he prowls around her bed, touching, fingering, sniffing and stroking her things. It's an experience Keithy "truly" appreciates (Crew 1993: 146–47). The teenage female is eroticized for the benefit of males—the characters in the book—and for the culture that both supports and encourages such eroticizing.

Julia, however, is not the only eroticized child in the book. Both of the feral children, Leena and Micky, who are brought to Kim's house—Kim's father is a doctor and his mother nurse—are eroticized to some extent, most particularly Micky. He becomes the object of the gaze of many of the characters in the book. He is configured as both "primitive" and "other." This form of gazing, as Perry Nodelman (1992) points out, constructs a form of power relationship in which the dominance of the gazer is emphasized. It also echoes the kind of gazing that occurs in nineteenth-century books, in which there is a kind of racial eroticism as white men gaze on the bodies of the "primitive savage" (an example of this is the 1896 *The Secret of the Australia Desert* by Ernest Favenc). The first time the reader—and Kim and his family—see Micky, he is captured in the headlights of the doctor's car as the family drives home from a dance to which Julia and other "civilized" people have been:

The thing stood and turned to face us. It wore trousers, or what remained of trousers. As we sat staring, it raised one hand to protect its eyes from the glare of the headlights. The other hand hung at its side, gripping the limp body of a hare. Then, without any sign of urgency or fear, it stepped out of the light and vanished into the darkness of the forest. We had disturbed its feeding. (Crew 1993: 87)

The use of the pronoun it, rather than the more personal him, blurs the child's gender, dehumanizes him, and emphasizes his otherness to the family. Micky becomes the primitive savage, to be both feared and desired. Micky renews a kind of Tarzan image, as well as emphasizing a fascination with the feral child, and construction of the "other" (Scutter 1999, Wallace 1994). Micky refuses to wear clothes, except for a pair of Kimmy's shorts, and for most of the time, he refuses to speak. He is an object of fascination to the household, especially Kim, who spends a lot of time looking at him, as he has done previously with Micky's sister, Leena. As Claire Pajaczkowska (1999: 236) has stated, "psychoanalytic theory has pointed out that the pleasure of the gaze is closely connected to unconscious fantasies of control and power." As Kim has been powerless with Julia, it may be that he is gaining a feeling of power with this gazing. Just as Kim has been feminized to some extent, so too is Micky. There are, in this book, a number of interlinked dualisms that combine to eroticize the children, especially Micky. As with Julia, in Micky, wildness equates with femaleness, wild equates with primitive, and wild also equates with erotic. Micky is a wild, primitive, feminized, and eroticized boy.

Micky's lack of speech also emphasizes his "otherness" and makes it impossible for him to communicate his own needs. As a result, Kim's family has ultimate power over him; they can decide the direction of the rest of his life and change him body and mind. There is a conflating of Puritan and Romantic notions of childhood here, notions that are frequently rehearsed in books for young people throughout the twentieth century. On the one hand, Micky is fascinating because he is free and natural; on the other hand he is seen as too wild and must be tamed and civilized. The latter notion prevails and he is sent away to learn to speak properly and acquire at least some of the approved attributes of civilization. He will presumably be transformed from the erotic exotic to the less exciting, but more socially acceptable, child.

John Marsden's *Dear Miffy* (1997) is a book that, although openly recognizing teenage sexuality, nonetheless renews the image of the eroticized figure. Indeed, it actually contains two eroticized teenagers. The entire relationship of Tony and Miffy is based on the body (or more accurately two bodies). As in a number of his other books, Marsden uses the narrative form of letters in *Dear Miffy*, this time from one character only. Because the narration uses the epistolary form, the story is told in the present tense, the function of which is "to convey an illusion of immediacy and instantaneity" (Stephens 1999: 63). Tony is writing from an institution to his (ex)girlfriend Miffy. During the course of this correspondence, we discover that Tony is a very violent character who has beaten up Miffy's mother and has tried to commit suicide and has ended up with both his legs cut off after throwing himself under a train. Tony uses the language of women's romance novels in his descriptions of Miffy: "Miff, I want to see your breasts again. You had the most beautiful breasts I've ever seen. It was like God made them out of sand, golden sand that was lying in the sun a thousand years. They were so warm and alive and firm" (Marsden 1997: 32). The reader is thus positioned as "a voyeur who is accessing secret, personal and sensitive material" (Gorme 1998: ii). Marsden, although acknowledging the teenagers as sexually active beings, still eroticizes the female character, who is the object of the gaze of both the writer and of Tony. Discourses of sexuality and eroticization intersect. It is significant that the audience intended for the book is not an exclusively male one, and indeed is predominantly female. Teenage females are thus also being asked to join in the voyeurism. What is difficult to establish is whether they are being asked to identify as the object of the gaze or the gazer. In other words, as Mulvey points out in discussing the female audience's role in watching action movies with a male hero, is the female spectator (reader) being expected to take on a masculine "point of view"? (Mulvey 1989: 30). It seems as if the female reader is oscillating between accepting Tony's viewpoint on things and enjoying being in the position of Miffy. Thus, the reader becomes the one doing the gazing and the one enjoying being gazed at.

Because of his incarceration and his physical injury, Miffy is no longer accessible to Tony and she thus becomes an erotic fixation for him. The reader becomes both an onlooker of, and participant in, Tony's erotic dreams about Miffy. The warning given in capital letters on the back cover emphasizes this voyeuristic aspect of the book: CONTENTS MAY OFFEND SOME READERS. The other text on the back cover—a quotation from the book—further emphasizes this aspect: "Dreamed about you again. Like I do most nights. Sometimes it's nightmares, sometimes it's good dreams, sometimes I have to change the sheets." In a sense, Marsden is also eroticizing his teenage readers in this way, as he asks them to join in Tony's dreams, to understand how he is feeling and to place themselves in his position of frustrated eroticism. Tony feels his whole life revolves around sex, and that now he'll "probably never have sex with anyone again" there is "no fucking life anyway" (Marsden 1997: 90). Such a view means that he is determined, if he ever manages to leave the facility, to make sure his second suicide attempt is successful.

The language of popular fiction becomes interspersed on some occasions with what Marsden regards as the realistic language of teenagers: "When I was with you the sun and the moon and the stars were in the fucking room, and heaven was in your mouth and your breasts and between your legs" (Marsden 1997: 77). The language used is also supposed to help build the characterization and differentiate for the reader the classes of Tony and Miffy. On occasion, however, the determinedly working-class language of Tony is inconsistent, as in the last quoted passage in which the expletive is gratuitous and seems to be included only to remind readers of Tony's working-class status and his usual paucity of language. In the context of the statement, too, the word has an almost comic overtone, an overtone that is presumably unintended by the author. Such a speech is also designed to signify again the idea of Miffy as an erotic object and to emphasize the construction of her whole being as written on her body. One journalist has even described such scenes as "soft porn" (Bolt 1999: 20). The popular romance aspect is emphasized in a number of the erotic episodes. Marsden is attempting to write as he imagines a teenage boy would express his erotic feelings and yearnings for his girlfriend, but the effect is contrived; the authorial adult voice making that attempt comes through too clearly.

Tony uses violence as a means of gaining power, a construction Marsden previously used with his characters Steve and Tracey in *Letters from the Inside* (1992). Violence gives Tony power over others, especially women. Marsden is thus eroticizing Tony by giving him the power of male sadistic violence, allowing him to indulge in what Kincaid (1993: 338) describes as "sadistic revelry." The most striking examples are when he stabs his father's new girlfriend whom Tony blames for the breakup of his parents' marriage and when he assaults Miffy's mother. The former incident is another form of eroticized violence that is depicted as almost justifiable because she is the dangerous "other woman," dressed in a way that clearly signifies her as such: "this tall chick with red hair and kind of leopard skin pants . . . and me dad and this chick are all lovey-dovey holding hands and shit" (Marsden 1997: 9–10). This incident follows Tony overhearing a discussion between his uncle and aunt in which they make it clear that they don't really want to have him and in which the image of the "bad mother," a recurrent feature in Marsden's books, appears. His aunt says that any woman who walks out on her family is worse than a man who does the same thing: "I still think it's a woman's job, I don't care what anyone says, and what happened to Owen [Tony's baby brother, who died after his mother left the family] is all her fault as far as I'm concerned" (Marsden 1997: 8–9). There is also a strong suggestion that Tony's violence is a symptom of his abandonment; he is therefore also constructed as a vulnerable child lacking the guidance of a "good mother." When he is at his lowest point in the hospital, he writes to Miffy about how much he hates his mother, but that, nonetheless, he might try to find her, because he still believes that "she'll be able to fix everything up for me somehow" (Marsden 1997: 98).

The scene in which Tony attacks Miffy's mother is a signifier of class. Although Marsden makes gestures toward a kind of egalitarianism in violence—Mandy's middle-class brother Steve is a violent psychotic in *Letters from the Inside* (1992) and Marina's upper middle-class father damages her face in the acid incident in *So Much to Tell You* (1987)—it is more often his working-class characters who are violent. Violence seems to be part of a larger power struggle. In much of *Dear Miffy*, Miffy is described as a rebel, one not averse to using a bit of violence to get her own way. Ultimately, however, as Tony recognizes, she is "not that tough" (Marsden 1997: 74). Tony, too, is unable to change his spots. He tries to make himself more middle class so that he is less conspicuous and more approved of when he mixes with Miffy's family, but ultimately doesn't change; the violent reaction to Miffy's mother seems automatic as he uses violence as a way of trying to control the situation and gain some ascendancy: "I didn't know what to do or where to go, I was just running around in circles grabbing for me clothes and trying to find stuff and shaking like crazy. I didn't mean to hit her Miff, it was just the way she was screaming, I couldn't stand it, then what she said, she shouldn't have said that, about me being filth and all, she didn't have the right" (Marsden 1997: 84).

This is the oft-repeated justification of male violence—that somehow the victim brought it on herself—and recalls Kincaid's (1993) previously referred-to description of beating in Victorian books displaying "hypocritical righteous fervor." This justification is also similar to that given by Marina in *So Much to Tell You* to excuse the violent actions of her father against her mother—actions that disfigure Marina herself: "He would never have wanted to hurt me, not the way he did. . . . There were a few times when he belted me . . . but only when he was really angry and half the time I'd provoked it by being rude or something" (Marsden 1987: 73). Despite the violence of the scene in

Dear Miffy, there are elements of French farce in it too, although one can assume that that is not how Marsden intended it. Tony runs down the stairs after the assault, wearing only half his clothes and struggling to dress himself properly. Miffy stands naked, staring at her mother who is lying on the floor with blood pouring from her nose. In this scene, there is, to use Barbara Creed's phrase, a kind of "masochistic looking" on the part of the reader (1993: 154). *Dear Miffy* is therefore a book containing two kinds of eroticism: Miffy is the object of the erotic gaze of the author, Tony, and the reader; and Tony is eroticized by having the power of male sadistic violence. This latter construction renews that of earlier books such as those of Ethel Turner mentioned earlier, in which violence is used as a means of gaining power and in which the violence is a signifier of "manliness." In Turner's *The Little Larrikin* (1896), for example, Lol, the youngest of a family in which both parents are dead, is frequently the victim of corporal punishment (cuffings) from his eldest brother. Lol likes these "cuffings" because they make him feel "manly" (11); furthermore, he is eroticized by the way in which the older boy gains physical power over him.

Rather different is *Loving Athena*, by Joanne Horniman (1997), which tells the story of 18-year-old Keats and his journey of first love, during which he finds out the secrets of his own past and learns more about the many people he lives with on a commune called Elysian Farm. Keats's new awareness of his own sexuality makes him see things in an erotic way, although he is not, during the course of the book, sexually active. He writes poetry, some of which eroticizes the everyday. One poem, entitled "Plate Tectonics," includes the following (Horniman 1997: 81):

> These soft, slow rubbings,
> this drawing apart
> and together
> and apart
> causes intense geological activity
> at the boundaries.
>
> . . . strange rumblings
> upheavals
> eruptions
> hot liquid issuing from cracks and fissures
> the soft slurp of subsidence
> over and over again.
> The earth is very old
> very alive
> and very sexy.

Athena, the girl of the title and the object of Keats's interest, too, is eroticized by Keats, and through him for the reader. She is described as "wearing a black ruffled skirt, so short it barely covered her knickers: her legs went up and up" (Horniman 1997: 24). On another occasion, when he is lying on the grass with Athena, Keats wants to lick Athena's belly button: "He imagined his tongue going into that soft, smooth hollow. In and out, until she called for him to stop" (Horniman 1997: 66). Much is made of the fact that Keats has "seven mothers"; his birth mother committed suicide when he was a baby. When his mother died, all the other women on the commune took turns feeding him: "He had grown up surrounded by women. All those little girls, those sort-of sisters. All those milky breasts that had nurtured him. Fourteen of them. Keats's early memories teemed with breasts" (Horniman 1997: 31). The author is thus eroticizing female sexuality, both adolescent and adult, through the gaze of the teenage male protagonist.

In addition, the cover of the book emphasizes an erotic reading of Athena using an image that owes something to advertising. Athena's face is the central image, but much of it is concealed by a mask made of feathers, the wings of a magpie, and frangipani. Her face is framed with the blossoms of the bird of paradise plant. These blossoms can be seen to symbolize both the unfettered sexuality of the Garden of Eden and a vagina. Lurking in the undergrowth around the edges of the pictures are various phallic symbols, including pistons with tubes attached. The framing of Athena's face also serves to emphasize her lips and eyes, the two features most frequently eroticized. There is a quite deliberate enticing of a voyeuristic gaze from the reader in this design.

The eroticizing of the teenage figure thus appears in a number of ways: through gazing at the child's body, through eroticized violence, and through the construction of the child as adult. All of these rehearse earlier constructions. Peter Hollindale (1997: 92) claims quite rightly, that neither "death nor sex is any longer a taboo subject in children's books: in these ways recent work has reconstructed fictive childhood, freeing it from a protective voluntary censorship which is out of line with children's knowledge and awareness." However, the trope of the eroticized child figure who is, after all, constructed in these books by adults, has long been a part of children's literature—even in the time of "voluntary censorship"—and remains surprisingly persistent, even after the development of a more open attitude toward sexuality in books for young people. The earlier eroticized figure of the innocent child has, however, been frequently supplanted in contemporary literature by the eroticizing of the teenage figure linked with pubescent sexuality. In the context of the theme of change and renewal, therefore, this can perhaps be summed up as *plus ça change, plus c'est la meme chose* (the more things change, the more they stay the same).

BIBLIOGRAPHY

Barrie, James. 1928. *Peter Pan or the Boy Who Would Not Grow Up.* London: Hodder & Stoughton.

Bolt, Andrew. 1999. "Are You Sure You Want Your Kids Influenced by the World of John Marsden?" *Herald-Sun* (6 September): 20.

Creed, Barbara. 1993. *The Monstrous-Feminine: Film, Feminism, Psychoanalysis.* London: Routledge.

Crew, Gary. 1993. *Angel's Gate.* Melbourne: Mammoth.

Farrar, Frederick. 1907. *Eric or Little by Little.* London: Adam and Charles Black.

Favenc, Ernest. 1896. *The Secret of the Australian Desert.* London: Blackie.

Favret, Mary. 1998. "Flogging: The Anti-Slavery Movement Writes Pornography." In *Romanticism and Gender,* ed. Anne Janowitz, 19–42. Cambridge: D. S. Brewer.

Gorme, Adrienne. 1998. "A Keyhole View of Life: John Marsden's Institutional Novels." Master's thesis, School of Arts and Sciences, Australian Catholic University, Sydney.

Harewood, Jocelyn. 1990. *Voices in the Wash-house.* Sydney: Pan.

Holland, Patricia. 1992. *What Is a Child? Popular Images of Childhood.* London: Virago.

Hollindale, Peter. 1997. *Signs of Childness in Children's Books.* Stroud, Gloucestershire, UK: Thimble Press.

Horniman, Joanne. 1997. *Loving Athena.* Adelaide, Australia: Omnibus Books.

Kincaid, James. 1993. *Child-Loving: The Erotic Child and Victorian Culture.* New York: Routledge.

Kipling, Rudyard. [1899] 1962. *Stalky and Co.* Reprint, London: Macmillan.

Kociumbas, Jan. 1997. *Australian Childhood: A History.* Sydney: Allen and Unwin.

Marsden, John. 1987. *So Much to Tell You.* Sydney: Walter McVitty.

Marsden, John. 1992. *Letters from the Inside.* Sydney: Pan Macmillan.

Marsden, John. 1997. *Dear Miffy.* Sydney: Pan Macmillan.

Mulvey, Laura. 1989. *Visual and Other Pleasures.* Basingstoke, Hampshire, UK: Macmillan.

Nodelman, Perry. 1992. "The Other: Orientalism, Colonialism, and Children's Literature." *Children's Literature Association Quarterly* 17 (1): 29–35.

Pajaczkowska, Claire. 1999. "Psychoanalysis, Gender and Art." In *Gender and Art,* ed. Gill Perry, 229–39. New Haven, Conn.: Yale University Press.

Perry, Gill, ed. 1999. *Gender and Art.* New Haven, Conn.: Yale University Press.

Scutter, Heather. 1999. *Displaced Fictions.* Melbourne: Melbourne University Press.

Stephens, John. 1999. "Analysing Texts for Children: Linguistics and Stylistics." In *Understanding Children's Literature,* ed. Peter Hunt, 56–68. London: Routledge.

Turner, Ethel. 1894. *Seven Little Australians.* London: Ward Lock.

Turner, Ethel. 1896. *The Little Larrikin.* London: Ward Lock.

Turner, Ethel. 1918. *St Tom and the Dragon.* London: Ward Lock.

Wallace, Jo-Anne. 1994. "De-scribing *The Water-Babies:* The Child and Post-Colonial Theory." In *De-Scribing Empire: Post-Colonialism and Textuality,* ed. Chris Tiffin and Alan Lawson, 171–83. London: Routledge.

CHAPTER 8

Fostering Controlled Dissent: Democratic Values and Children's Literature

Eva-Maria Metcalf

Readers of Karin Gündisch's novel *Im Land der Schokolade und Bananen. Zwei Kinder kommen in ein fremdes Land* (*In the land of chocolate and bananas*; 1987) follow eight-year-old Uwe, a recent immigrant from Romania, as he adjusts to a new life during his first weeks in Germany. He has his first concrete lesson in democracy in school when his classmates, who are unhappy with a physical education teacher who comes late repeatedly, get together and write a petition, demanding that the teacher be on time from now on. They hand it to the teacher, and to Uwe's great surprise the teacher does not reject it or get angry (as his Romanian teacher surely would have); instead the teacher apologizes, explains the cause for his repeated tardiness to the class, and promises to improve. This episode from Gündisch's novel models an ideal situation of conflict solution and child-adult interaction following democratic principles of mutual respect and orderly conduct that may not be representative of most teacher-student interactions in German schools, but that is representative of a fundamental shift in attitudes toward children that has affected both the lives of children and their fictional representation.

During the past decades, democratic structures and procedures have left their mark on public institutions such as the military, church, corporate life, and school and have intruded into the private sphere of the family as well, contributing to the demise of traditional bourgeois family patterns. Children's literature—especially in Germany and Scandinavia, which is the focus of this chapter—has reflected this development and, by modeling it, has given it some degree of legitimacy.

In an article published in *The New Republic* in May 2001, under the title "Why Literature? The Premature Obituary of the Book," the Peruvian author Mario Vargas Llosa claims that a high level of literacy is essential for the health of a democracy. In defense of literature, he calls it "one of the most primary and necessary undertakings of the mind, an irreplaceable activity for the formation of citizens in a modern democratic society" (32). The act of reading itself, according to Vargas Llosa, will help readers to develop a permanent spiritual mobility—a necessary attribute of independent thinkers—by being challenged by unfamiliar fictional worlds and ideas. Vargas Llosa bases his argument on the premise that the reading experience should be a challenge to the imagination; thereby he excludes all literature that is formulaic in character and confirms reader expectations. When he claims that escapes into fantasy have a subversive effect because they will increase the reader's dissatisfaction with the status quo, he likely does not consider the instrumentalized escape into dream worlds that advertisement provides. He could, however, be speaking of children's classics, as Alison Lurie does, who has made similar claims. She too sees in good literature an agent for gaining a more critical perspective on life and an antidote against the discourse of the market place. Basing her arguments on selected classics, she writes in *Don't Tell the Grown-Ups: Why Kids Love the Books They Do* (1990) that "The great subversive works of children's literature suggest that there are other views of human life besides those of the shopping mall and the corporation" (xi). How subversive are "good" children's books today? Are they still, as Lurie asserts, an antidote against the discourse of the marketplace?

In the following chapter, I discuss how since the 1970s high-quality children's literature, written for the dominant and culture-defining class, does not just implicitly contribute to the formation of a democratic mindset by challenging the imagination and cognitive powers of the readers through the narrative mode, but often explicitly propagates more democratic child-adult interactions that mirror developments in the social and legal status of children in the Western world. In addition, I point out how challenging children's literature can also be regarded as a training ground for success in the corporate world.

German author Peter Härtling has given us a recipe for a "good" children's book in his *Erzählbuch Geschichten, Gedichte, Texte, Proben* (*Book about narration: Stories, poems, texts, samples;* 1992), which could serve as a guideline for all quality children's literature during the past decades. He urges writers to tell stories that provoke readers and make them think and perhaps act, and he advises them to write in such a gripping manner that readers will want to go beyond the open end of a story. He asks them to help children understand the world and help them doubt, question, and if necessary challenge it. With regard to the narrative stance, Härtling adds that adults in children's books should not be presented as authorities, but as equals and as human beings that readers can relate to and identify with. This recipe for writing good children's fiction is based on a concept of childhood quite different from the nineteenth-century bourgeois ideal. Communicating with readers today presupposes a narrator-reader/adult-child interaction that is based on the democratic concepts of equality, self-determination, and codetermination.

Granting children human and civil rights is clearly a twentieth-century phenomenon. Ellen Key's designation of the twentieth century as the century of the child is fully justified from the point of view of children's rights. Granting children more rights is a gradual process that has its roots in early modern times. It parallels the development of the concept of childhood, which in turn is intimately connected with the development of reading and child literacy, as John Morgenstern (2001) cogently and convincingly argues in his article, "The Rise of Children's Literature Reconsidered." Awareness of the special needs of the child and concern for the child's well-being and favorable development can be traced as far back as Locke, but it was Rousseau's positive re-evaluation of childhood that eventually led to a more empathetic attitude toward children. The educational climate in the nineteenth century remained overall authoritarian and disciplinarian, but educational reformers such as Pestalozzi and Fröbel began popularizing child-oriented approaches to pedagogy.

When Ellen Key (1849–1926) and Maria Montessori (1870–1952) led campaigns against what they called the torturelike conditions of disciplinarian education at the beginning of the twentieth century, they found many followers who felt as they did: that children should be allowed to develop freely in an environment adapted to their specific needs and desires. Both deemed corporal punishment a disgrace for humanity, because it contradicted the notion of human dignity that should be applied to children as well as adults. In *Mischievous Meg* (1960), Astrid Lindgren, who remembers corporal punishment from her own school days, uses Mischievous Meg's father in her novel by the same name as a mouthpiece to condemn it in no uncertain terms. Now, both Sweden and Germany have a law against striking children, but approximately 30% of Germans still condone the practice according to a brochure published jointly by the German Ministry for the Family, Women, and Youth and the German television station ZDF (Schick and Kwasniok 2000: 10).

The acceptance of corporal punishment is most likely higher in Mississippi, where "paddling" is still accepted in many public schools. In other words, change occurs slowly and unevenly, but the general trend of a more empathic attitude toward children, as Lloyd deMause (1974) has argued in his psychohistory of childhood, still persists in the way children are represented in fiction and treated in everyday life.

Often authors are at the forefront of new movements, both responding to and shaping new ideas, as was the case with Astrid Lindgren and Tove Jansson in the 1940s, 1950s, and 1960s. Both were effective spokespersons for the child-oriented education that was championed by Ellen Key and Maria Montessori by modeling it in their fiction. However, initially at least, there had to be an accepting audience as well, because their books would not have been published and sold without a predisposition on the part of publishers and parents toward the new mode of adult-child interaction they contained. Not only did adult mediators have to approve of the many escapades of the main characters in *Pippi Longstocking, Emil in the Soup Tureen,* or *Karlsson-on-the-Roof* (and their sequels) that go unpunished; they also had to sympathize with these characters' mothers, who were unusually empathetic to the needs and desires of their children and whose educational practices were exceedingly liberal for their time. For example, in *Pippi Longstocking* (Lindgren 1950), Mrs. Settergren tolerates and even defends Pippi's behavior when most mothers in town feel the need to tame the wildness of Pippi's childish exuberance and would never send their offspring to the South Seas with Pippi. In general, Lindgren's mothers or mother figures allow their children to find their own way, protest, make mistakes, and develop into strong independently minded individuals in any setting, from small town to robber's forest.

Tove Jansson launches sharp criticism against disciplinarian education of children in her short story "The Invisible Child," in *Tales from Momminvalley* (Jansson 1963), about a young girl who became invisible because she was shamed into behaving, was treated coldly, and lacked love. The invisible child has been a popular metaphor to describe not only abuse and neglect on the part of the parents, but their unwillingness to see and accept the child as a human being who possesses both strengths and weaknesses. Maria Gripe's novels about Elvis (*Elvis and His Secret*, 1976a [originally published in 1972], and *Elvis and His Friends*, 1976b [originally published in 1973]) and Tormod Haugen's early novels (such as *The Night Birds*, 1982 [originally published in 1975], and *Keeping Secrets*, 1994 [originally published in 1976]) provide variations on that theme. Scandinavian psychological children's novels, in particular, propagate children's rights to be loved and cared for—very often illustrated by negative examples—and demand, in compelling and sensitive ways, greater understanding for a child's individuality and dignity.

The conception of the child was reconfigured again when calls for greater empathy toward the child converged with socialist ideas of emancipation and empowerment. The socialist perspective opened the path for a critique of the bourgeois conception of childhood and radically changed the projection of adult dreams and desires onto children from naive innocents to responsible individuals. The ultimate aim of socialist plays, parables, stories, and fairy tales directed at children was the creation of a new human being in the spirit of an egalitarian democracy, often enough transported by means of rather crude didacticism. By laying bare the mechanisms of power and politics in society, this kind of literature invited child readers into the public sphere and asked them to become openly critical of the status quo within the given confines of the socialist ideology.

Neither the socialist children's literature that was published by a fairly small socialist press nor the radical experiments in democratized schooling had a significant effect on society at large at the time. Around the turn of the century, a number of experimental children's republics had emerged in the United

States and in Central Europe in the form of schools and summer camps where children were to experience democracy concretely and either participate in or shoulder the decision-making process themselves. One of the earliest such experiments, in which children ran the institution, was William Ruben George's Junior Republic from 1890 (in Freeville, New York). In *King Matt, the First* (1923), Janusz Korczak fictionalizes a children's reign—without glorifying the outcome of such an experiment—doubtlessly incorporating his experiences while directing an orphanage in Kraków. Alexander Sutherland Neill's children's republic-school at Summerhill, founded in 1921, was perhaps the most influential and definitely the most long-lived of these experiments. His publications had an enduring influence on the antiauthoritarian movement that swept the Western world in the 1970s.

Children's rights campaigns that followed in the wake of women's and minority rights movements, were embedded in the socialist tradition. In the 1970s, avant-garde authors and author collectives rediscovered proletarian children's literature and the child conception that formed its basis. Democratic values, such as peaceful coexistence and conviviality, had been championed in children's literature in various forms since World War II in books such as Erich Kästner's *Konferenz der Tiere* (1949), but assumed greater prominence within their new ideological setting in the 1970s. The spirit of egalitarianism and cooperation applied to publishing cooperatives as well as the messages in the books they published. At the radical fringe were books such as *Die Geschichte von der Verjagung und Ausstopfung des Königs* (Röhrbein 1971), published in Berlin, which, as the title reveals, deals with the dethroning of a king, the representative of traditional patriarchal power and traditional values. A radical break with tradition applies to the creation and production of this book as well. It features a complex and layered narrative structure and a Brechtian alienation technique to shock readers into awareness. The introduction reveals the cooperative effort behind the creation of the book, giving the semblance of a book that emerged out of the fantasies of children at play assisted by an assortment of adult writers, photographers, editors, and publishers.

The rather slim production of the leftist book cooperatives was admittedly the radical fringe. However, more moderate children's authors from that period (Peter Härtling, Paul Maar, Christine Nöstlinger, Ursula Wölfel) used modernist narrative techniques to make readers active and critical readers. Empowerment of the reader is reflected in the transparency of the creative process and an emphasis on reader participation. These authors also wrote stories that contained heavy-handed social criticism, but they were less concerned with the message than with the literary quality of their works.

Christine Nöstlinger's novel, *Wir pfeifen auf den Gurkenkönig (The cucumber king;* 1972), which was awarded the German youth book prize (Jugendbuchpreis) in 1973, is representative of the period. It too is a throw-out-the-king story that exposes the happy bourgeois family ideal as a myth. Nöstlinger, who remains one of the leading German language authors of that generation, takes a stab at the authoritarian structure of the Hogelmann household, which is mirrored in the dictatorial rule of the Cucumber King over his Kumi-Ori people in Hogelman's cellar. The Hogelman children follow the example of the Kumi-Ori people who have emancipated themselves and thrown out their oppressor. By revealing and refusing their father's dictatorial family regime, they open the road to an uneasy, fledgling family democracy.

Most avant-garde books from the 1970s follow the general pattern of villainizing authoritarian parents or teachers against whom children unite, grab power, and make the world a better place. In the 1980s, the tone becomes less militant and the teleological certainty of the early years gives way to subdued hope, disillusionment, or cynicism, but the democratic tenor remains the same. The decreasing militancy of the demands for children's rights parallels the institutionalization of children's rights on national and international governmental levels in the intervening years.

The Geneva Declaration of the Rights of the Child (1924) and the United Nations Declaration of the Rights of the Child (1959) ensured children the right to special protection, education, and social security. These were general guidelines based on a traditional, bourgeois concept of childhood, appealing to the responsibility of caretakers, but giving children themselves no say. The United Nations Convention on the Rights of the Child from 1989, however, differed from the two previous documents by changing the underlying conception and the status of the child. The document that was adopted by the General Assembly of the United Nations on November 20, 1989, and ratified by 191 countries (all except Somalia and the United States) viewed children as citizens and human beings in their own right. While protecting their dignity, the Convention on the Rights of the Child gives children a voice. According to the convention, children, as well as adults, must be heard in the case of a conflict. (Naturally, as is the case in any legal document, these rights are open to interpretation by representatives of governments and institutions, and the enforcement is yet another matter.) To make sure that these laws take effect, a provision of the convention states that all signatory countries are obliged to make the convention's principles widely known to children and adults alike.

Searching the Internet for *"Kinderrechte"* (children's rights), one finds thousands of sites. In Germany alone, 90 organizations from government institutions to nongovernment organizations to private citizens assist in spreading the word. Most sites provide informative and entertaining ways to remind children and their parents of children's equal rights status, their right to privacy, and their right to information and self-expression.

The episode from Karin Gündisch's novel *Im Land der Schokolade und Bananen. Zwei Kinder kommen in ein fremdes Land* (1987), to which I referred at the beginning of this chapter, is hence very much in line with the legal status and public discourse about the child. In the idealized conflict resolution in today's German public school setting portrayed by Gündisch, children assume the rights and duties of citizens and their voices are heard. Gündisch is no exception in this respect. The same model of conflict resolution is applied to all child-adult interactions, including the family setting, in most novels by Christine Nöstlinger. She has passed through a range of moods from optimistic idealism to resigning pragmatism in her writing career from 1970 to 2001, reacting to social and cultural developments in Austria, Europe, and the world, but her portrayal of desirable adult-child interactions has remained stable. Its underlying paradigm has been one in which children constantly question and undermine adult authority watching out for their own interests; however, they never take power themselves, as had been true in the radical social and fictional experiments.

From Hugo in Nöstlinger's *Hugo, das Kind in den besten Jahren* (1983), who calls for the unionization of children as a means of their empowerment, a straight line leads to Bonsai in Nöstlinger's novel *Bonsai* (1997). In this latter novel by Christine Nöstlinger, conflict resolution by way of less formal negotiation takes place within the minifamily consisting of a divorced mother and teenage son. Their negotiations are not always peaceful and are laced with emotion, displaying the uneasy fusion of the disparate discourses of the public and private sphere in the democratized family. The public sphere's social-contract model (based on autonomous, self-interested individuals) and the private sphere's community model (based on affective bonds and interdependence) are as often at odds, as are Berti Bartolotti and Mr. Thomas in Nöstlinger's novel *Konrad oder Das Kind aus der Konservenbüchse* (1975), which concludes with a telling image.

Seven-year-old Konrad stands between the extremes of creative anarchy and nonconformism, represented by his foster mother, and orderliness and adherence to norms, characterized by his foster father. Konrad, who models the situation of his readers, will have to chart his course between these extremes. In order to defend his rights and interests, he will first have to know what they are and how to defend them. This is difficult enough for Bonsai and not an easy task for seven-year-old Konrad, who will have to internalize controlled dissent, a constant give-and-take between subversion and affirmation that is characteristic of Western democracies.

Controlled dissent presupposes what Henry Giroux has termed *emancipatory authority;* that is, an authority that continuously works at its own destruction. Emancipatory authority thus institutionalizes subversion, and the question remains how subversive the many models of emancipatory authority that we find in the novels of Gündisch, Nöstlinger, and many well-established authors actually are. Do these stories help readers gain a more critical perspective on life and, hence, foster a democratic mindset, or do they merely prepare them well for the challenges that lie ahead in family life, education, and the work place?

In the corporate world an instrumentalized form of controlled dissent is encouraged and practiced. Were either Konrad or Bonsai to join today's workforce of McKinsey and Co, they would be well prepared for it. According to company policy they would be expected to "think independently, to assert your own point of view . . . is taking" (Hoenig 2001: 66).

This leads me to my final question: What does children's literature foster—learned controlled dissent, benefiting democratic institutions and the corporate world, such as permanent spiritual mobility and a critical mindset or, as Vargas Llosa also demands, a vibrant imagination to resist manipulation? I see the former, but I hope for the latter.

BIBLIOGRAPHY

Archard, David. 1993. *Children: Rights and Childhood.* London, New York: Routledge.
deMause, Lloyd. 1974. "The Evolution of Childhood." In *The History of Childhood,* ed. Lloyd deMause. New York: The Psychohistory Press.
Ewers, Hans-Heino. 1999a. *Kinderliteratur und gesellschaftliche Modernisierung. Entwicklungslinien der Kinderliteratur in Westdeutschland.* Available at: http//www.goethe.de/os/hon/kiju/ewemod.htm. Accessed April 2004.
Ewers, Hans-Heino. 1999b. *Die Kinderliteratur der Gegenwart als Spiegel veränderter kindlicher Lebenswelten.* Available at: http//www.goethe.de/os/hon/kiju/ewekin.htm. Accessed April 2004.
Giroux, Henry A. 1999. "Schooling as a Form of Cultural Politics: Toward a Pedagogy of and for Difference." In *Critical Pedagogy, the State, and Cultural Struggle,* ed. Henry A. Giroux and Peter McLaren, 138–39. Albany: State University of New York Press.
Gripe, Maria. 1976a. *Elvis and His Secret.* Translated by Sheila La Farge. New York: Delacorte Press/Seymour Lawrence.
Gripe, Maria. 1976b. *Elvis and His Friends.* Translated by Sheila La Farge. New York: Delacorte Press/Seymour Lawrence.
Gündisch, Karin. 1987. *Im Land der Schokolade und Bananen. Zwei Kinder kommen in ein fremdes Land (In the land of chocolate and bananas).* Weinheim und Basel: Beltz & Gelberg.
Härtling, Peter. 1992. *Erzählbuch. Geschichten, Gedichte, Texte, Proben.* Weinheim und Basel: Beltz & Gelberg.
Haugen, Tormod. 1982. *The Night Birds.* New York: Delacorte Press/Seymour Lawrence.
Haugen, Tormod. 1994. *Keeping Secrets.* New York: Harper Collins.
Hoenig, Christopher. 2001. "All for One and One for All: Mc Kinsey Co Evolves from a Network to a Living Community." *Continental Magazine* March: 66.
Jansson, Tove. 1963. *Tales from Moominvalley.* New York: Farrar, Straus & Giroux.
Kästner, Erich. 1949. *The Animals' Conference.* New York: D. McKay.
Korczak, Janusz. 1923. *King Matt the First.* New York: Farrar, Straus & Giroux.
Koren, Marian. 2001. "Human Rights of Children: An Emerging Story." *The Lion and the Unicorn* 25 (2): 242–59.
Lindgren, Astrid. 1950. *Pippi Longstocking.* Translated by Florence Lamborn. New York: Viking.
Lindgren, Astrid. 1960. *Mischievous Meg.* Translated by Gerry Bothmer. New York. Viking.

Lindgren, Astrid. 1970. *Emil in the Soup Tureen.* Translated by Lilian Follett. Chicago: Follett.

Lindgren, Astrid. 1971. *Karlsson-on-the-Roof.* Translated by Marianne Turner. New York: Viking.

Lurie, Alison. 1990. *Don't Tell the Grown-Ups: Why Kids Love the Books They Do.* New York: Avon Books.

Morgenstern, John. 2001. "The Rise of Children's Literature Reconsidered." *The Children's Literature Quarterly* 26 (2): 64–73.

Nöstlinger, Christine. 1972. *Wir pfeifen auf den Gurkenkönig (The cucumber king).* Weinheim und Basel: Beltz & Gelberg.

Nöstlinger, Christine. 1975. *Konrad oder Das Kind aus der Konservenbüchse.* Hamburg: Oetinger.

Nöstlinger, Christine. 1983. *Hugo, das Kind in den besten Jahren.* Weinheim und Basel: Beltz & Gelberg.

Nöstlinger, Christine. 1997. *Bonsai.* Weinheim und Basel: Beltz & Gelberg.

Röhrbein, Karin. 1971. *Die Geschichte von der Verjagung und Ausstopfung des Königs.* Berlin: Basis Verlag.

Schick, Benno, and Andrea Kwasniok. 2000. *Die Rechte der Kinder von logo einfach erklärt. Herausgegeben vom Bundesministerium für Familie, Senioren, Frauen und Jugend.* 3rd ed. Stuttgart: PV Projektverlag.

Vargas Llosa, Mario. 2001. "Why Literature? The Premature Obituary of the Book." *The New Republic* (14 May): 31–36.

Zipes, Jack. 1977. "Down with Heidi, Down with Struwwelpeter, Three Cheers for the Revolution: Towards a New Socialist Children's Literature in West Germany." *Children's Literature* 5: 162–79.

CHAPTER 9

Childhood as the Sign of Change: Hans Christian Andersen's Retellings of the Concept of Childhood in the Light of Romanticism, Modernism, and Children's Own Cultures

Helene Høyrup

This chapter explores historic concepts of childhood as they appear in Hans Christian Andersen's work, which could be said to embody Danish Golden Age children's literature.[1] Studying Andersen's view of childhood is like reading a story of cultural perspectives at war with themselves. Overriding Western clusters of ideas concerning childhood are represented and often deconstructed in his work, revealing an ongoing questioning of how childhood relates to adulthood. Andersen's fluctuations are interesting to study in terms of the history of evaluations that underlie our critical language for children's literature, inasmuch as a paradigm is changed and laid open for serious discussion. By analyzing the author's destabilizing discourse of childhood, we can picture significant links between Romanticism and Modernism in childhood definitions. More importantly, we can trace how post-Romantic "childhood" tends to be configured as a pattern of empathic identification and alterity, enabling adults to question and change their positions in culture and, in turn, perhaps renegotiate their views of lived childhood.

In the beginning of Andersen's novel *Kun en Spillemand* (*Only a Fiddler;* 1837), the narrator presents a special, culturally codified vision of how children and adults tend to perceive the same thing differently:

Den Ældre vilde her kun see en smuk, lille Have I rig Flor, med mange sjeldne Blomster, Viinranker opad væggene, et Poppeltræ og længer henne to Akasier; men vi maae

see den, som den Indtrædende saae den, vi maae med ham aande den stærke Blom-
sterduft, føle de varme Solstraaler, beskue den rige Pragt.

[An old person would here only see a beautiful little garden in bloom, with many rare
flowers. . . . But we must see it as the person entering the garden saw it. We must
breathe the strong smell of the flowers with him, feel the warm rays of the sun, see
the splendor.] (17)

Schooled as we are in generational dividing lines, any post-Romantic reader
would automatically make the deduction that the person entering the garden
is a child. On one level, the boy in the garden is related to the Romantic
pedigree of children as *"seers blest"* or incarnations of ideals that adults may
have long lost, but which in the Romantic and Victorian cults of childhood
were ardently recuperated through various kinds of retrospection. Along this
line of thought, Andersen's discourse could be said to be a part of attempts
by Lewis Carroll's generation to freeze time and hark back to childhood as a
vital state questioning civilized adulthood. The quoted schism between adult
and childlike perception finds parallels in many of Andersen tales, notably
"Little Ida's Flowers," "Grief," and "The Daisy." The adults are Hobbesian
or Arnoldian citizen-intellectuals who classify and hierarchize reality according to cultural principles that work against the richness of the moment, and
make the colors of the day fade. The children, on the other hand, are receptive
to life in its horizontal splendor. They make use of the senses in a way that,
paradoxically, points forward in time to the free language of Modernism. Take,
for instance, in the field of Danish literary history, the famous slaughtering
scene in Johannes V. Jensen's *The Fall of the King* ([1900–1901] 1992) where
the world is a feast for the senses: the scenes come alive in colors, lines, and
smells. In the quotation from *Only A Fiddler* (Andersen 1837) above, the narrator sides with the reader, who is not a child but an implied adult reader, and
invites him or her to apply a *double vision* in order to learn to see from an
angle that works as an alternative to the one spurring the usual trite descriptions and socially inhibited viewpoints, labeled as "old." On the whole, the
phrase in *Only a Fiddler* harks back to a latent child self as an emblem of
cultural alterity. The later Modernist deconstruction of metaphysics and hierarchies of age and culture is only embedded. What is envisioned is an in-
vitation, but in some Andersen tales (e.g., "The Shadow"), the inclination to
perceive from new, unsanctioned positions has been accepted by the narrator.
This is also the case in Baudelaire's *Les Fleurs du Mal* (1857): the chief narrator
in this tale discovers intensity, although not beauty, in realms unexpected.

It has often been argued that Andersen's genius is related to his being a
"medium" or a prism of autobiographical yet cultural tensions. His pen was
an instrument of continuous positioning and interpretation—in necessity
close to breathing—as is amply illustrated by his prolific writings and extensive
diaries. Many of the tales can, indeed, be read as synergies of metafiction and
autobiography, with an abundance of "rises" through the tower of language

with subsequent "lapses" from the steep linguistic arches (Brostrøm and Lund 1991). His well-known perspectivism and metonymical ambivalence in terms of biographical and fictional levels foreground the conflation of culture and subjectivity and aesthetics and life, in his work as a whole. Critics from Søren Kierkegaard to Peer E. Sørensen to Jack Zipes have emphasized how Andersen never came to rest on the permanent outlook on life prescribed by the *Bildungsroman*, and Andersen's adulthood was never a stable plateau. By examining his configurations and symbolism of childhood, I hope to demonstrate his active inscription of classical Danish children's literature in the wider cultural paradigms of Romanticism and Modernism, thereby testifying to his frequently noted "childishness" as an adult projection paradoxically changing the paradigm of children's literature. From the gap between self and other, mind and matter, and from nineteenth-century historiography, the child perspective emerged.

NOTIONS OF CHILDHOOD

The Romantic rhetoric of childhood is considerably more complex than the Rousseauistic view of childhood as an Edenic state outshining adulthood. Admittedly, this is in itself a popular, romantically biased misreading of Rousseau, who did not renounce the influence of experience. Rather, he subsumed it to the new concepts of organic individualism. First, the Romantic idea of childhood is related to notions of change, growth, and continuity that were also on the agenda in contemporary novels and autobiographies. Robert Folkenflik (1993: 8) has outlined part of the background of the Romantic autobiographical boom as a superstructure imposed on eighteenth-century empiricism:

Our enquiry into the earliest use of the term "Romantic autobiography" suggests several reasons why the major tradition of autobiography began with (or slightly before) the advent of Romanticism in the eighteenth century. First, such writings, building upon eighteenth-century empiricism and individualism, were encouraged by Romantic subjectivity and its expressive poetics. Second, the Romantic search for origins and its child cult led writers to narrate their own lives from the beginning, and to find more significance in their early years. Third, the breakdown of the prestige of genres encouraged the multiplicity of forms of writing.

Ultimately, secularization was the background of the hermeneutical turn that triggered both autobiography and the Romantic "double vision" of childhood, which, in turn, paved the way for children's literature as a distinct form of writing. However, the Romantic notion of childhood was never a totally uniform complex of ideas. In Andersen's collection of tales (e.g., "The Girl Who Stepped on Bread" or "The Red Shoes") can be discerned remnants of a much older, Augustinian view of childhood as a fallen state that needs strict disciplining.

Andersen, Oehlenschläger, and Thorvaldsen (the Danish national poet and sculptor) belonged to a generation that was socially mobile and therefore had the chance to choreograph their own lives in astonishing, historic contours. At first sight, Andersen may indeed seem to adhere uncritically to the Wordsworthian phrase that the child is the father of the man. This view would accentuate essence, continuity, and expression in its emphasis on an unbroken, yet revolutionized line of growth from child to adult. However, in *Levnedsbogen* (Andersen [1832] 1962) from 1832, which was mainly composed for himself and the Collin family, and whose form is less fairy tale–like than *The True Story of My Life* (1847), there is a description of how, already as a child, he stages the concept of childishness as a *construction* that questions the Romantic concept of the child as naive and spontaneous:

Justitsraad Falbes Have stødte op til mine Forældres og tæt ved laae den gamle St Knuds Kirke; naar nu om Aftenen Klokerne ringede, sad jeg I underlige Drømme og saae på Møllehjulet og sang da mine Improvisationer. Ofte lyttede de Fremmede i Falbes Have . . . jeg mælrkede ofte mine Tilhørere bag Plankeværket og det smigrede mig.—Saaledes blev jeg bekjendt og man begyndte at sende Bud efter mig for at høre, som man kaldte mig, "den lille fynske Nattergal."

[Chancellor Falbe's garden bordered on my parents' garden, and close to this was the old church of Saint Canute. At night when the bells were tolling, I would sit in strange dreams looking at the mill wheel, singing my improvisations. Often the strangers in Falbe's garden would be listening. . . . I often felt my listeners behind the fence and I was flattered.—In this way I became known and they began to send for me to listen to what they called "the little nightingale from Funen."] (*Levnedsbogen* [1832] 1962: 28)

In the Danish Andersen scholar Klaus P. Mortensen's reading, the juxtaposition of naïveté and the concomitant consciousness of childish improvisations as a tool to fascinate his audience becomes a key to understanding Andersen's mental makeup. In his bracketed self-quotation—a linguistic parallel to his position behind the fence—the protagonist only acts as a naive and childish hero. The narrator's reflection indicates that he has made the turn from the naive to the sentimental, as described by Schiller. Selfhood and childhood engage in an ultimately unstable semiotics.

According to Alan Richardson (1992: 124), many nineteenth-century autobiographies and *Bildungsroman* are marked by a "tension between a developmental faith in the self's continuity and a haunting sense of childhood as distinctly and irrevocably other." Compared with the experiential model of the *Bildungsroman*, childhood in Andersen's tales appears to be more like a *position* that is used to find radically new ways of relating to or signifying a difference from the mainstream. There is a substantial quality of signification in the high-Romantic, Wordsworthian notion of the child, insofar as it is a teleological beginning of immense importance. However, although it clearly demonstrates interest in the innate essence of childhood in tales such as "The Snow Queen," childhood attains additional, even contrasting, layers of meaning in other tales. The tension between viewing childhood as continuity and alterity is certainly present in the difference in terms of the views of childhood in, for instance, "The Snow Queen" and "The Emperor's New Clothes," which, interestingly, was first conceived and written *without* a child perspective relativizer. Here, and in tales such as "Grief," the childhood perspective is employed as a narrative (or heuristic) position enabling its author to question adult reality. Childhood becomes an emblematic platform comparable to the function of animated objects in other tales, such as "The Steadfast Tin Soldier" or "The Shepherdess and the Chimney Sweep," which tend to lead to Modernist abstraction in their dissolution of permanent outlooks at the upper narrative level. From the author's vehement dislike of August Saabye's proposed statue depicting him with a child audience not on his lap, but in close proximity, we know that it was not the Biedermeyer, idyllic content of childhood that intrigued Andersen, but instead its melodramatic and even avantgarde or outsider bearings. The child as a mask or essentially empty sign, as we recognize it in Modernist art from Kandinsky and Paul Klee to the Danish Cobra painters or Isak Dinesen's fascination with the native Africans, who, by analogy, helped Dinesen to escape culturally trammeled ways of seeing.

Andersen's artistic use of the child resembles Baudelaire's admiration for children's "great capacity for abstraction" and for seeing everything "in a state of newness," which he (like Andersen) saw as a contrast to "the impotent imagination of the blasé public" (Baudelaire 1964: 198). According to Jonathan Fineberg, Baudelaire considered children to be receptive to the correspondences between the world and higher truths. In his pioneering study of the relations between Modernist art and children's own drawings, Fineberg (1997: 3) traced the nineteenth century's "virtually universal resistance . . . to the uniform style of the beautiful" as a cultural strain from John Ruskin to Oscar Wilde. The childish eye was seen as innocent of convention, and a certain clairvoyance was ascribed to the child. This, in Andersen's case, is clear in, for instance, the little mermaid's capacity to perceive correspondences and in the mediating role of the child audience in the same tale as well as in "The Emperor's New Clothes," or in little Gerda's sensibility in "The Snow Queen."

However, as is always the case in Andersen's work, the child as an accomplished seer is only one among several choreographies. In some tales, the child is rendered just as conventionalized as the adults, notably in "Children's Prattle," or "The Professor and the Flea," in which everybody—including the little princess, the child audience, and the reader—is deceived by the socially cunning professor-artist, who can also be read as an emblem of authorial selfhood:

Den lille Prindsesse, hendes Fader og Moder, hele Folket med stod og ventede. De vente endnu, og tror Du det ikke, saa reis til de Vildes land, der taler hvert Barn om

Loppen og Professoren, troer at de komme igjen, naar Kanonen er kølet af, men de komme ikke. (Haugaard 1979)

[The little princess, her father and her mother, and all their people stood and waited. They are waiting still and if you don't believe me you can travel to the land of the savages. Every child there will tell you the story of the flea and the professor. They are expecting him back as soon as the "cannon" has cooled off. But he will never return.] (Haugaard 1979: 1025)

In "Grief," the position of childhood as other is marked. The little girl is placed as an ideal outsider in a totally redundant, commercialist universe. Her eyes and the capacity to see are foregrounded, but transcendence is blocked, as a theory of Modernity might put it. Paralleling Klaus P. Mortensen's (1989) reading of Andersen's autobiography as mental theater, there are parallels of agency and staging, subjectivity and reification in the verbal imagery:

Men udenfor Garvergaarden, tæt op til Laagen der, stod en lille pjaltet Unge, saa yndigt skabt, med det deiligste krøllede Haar og Øine saa blaae og klare, at det var en Lyst; hun sagde ikke et Ord, hun græd heller ikke, men saae saa langt hun kunde, hver Gang Laagen aabnedes. Hun eiede ikke en Knap, vidste hun, og blev derfor sørgmodig staaende udenfor, stod der til de Alle havde seet af, og Alle vare gaaede bort; da satte hun sig ned, holdt de smaa brune Hælnder for Øinene og brast i Graad; hun alene havde ikke set Moppens Grav. (Sørensen 1993: 80–81)

[Outside the gate of the tannery yard stood a little girl. Although she was dressed in rags she was lovely; she had the most beautiful curly hair, and eyes so clear and blue that it was a pleasure to look at them. She didn't utter a word nor did she cry; but every time the gate opened she peeked in. She didn't own a button and therefore she stood dejected outside the gate all afternoon, until the last of the children had left. Then she burst out crying and, hiding her eyes in her little sunburned hands, she sat down upon the ground. She alone, of all the children in the street, had not seen the little lap dog's grave! Now that's grief, a sorrow as sharp as a grownup's can be!] (Haugaard 1979: 415)

The fictional construction of the girl mirrors the adult double vision and the view of childhood as alterity, but the girl is simultaneously "frozen" as an adult emotional construction. She is turned into an aesthetic tableau by the adult narrator, who is shut out from the intensity of the real experience. While sitting there as a human in her own right with feelings as full spectered as are the adult's, she is simultaneously a counter image and an emotional projection. The coexistence of alternative figures of childhood testifies to Andersen's rather modern experiments with positioning himself in adult culture. Now, however, let us take a closer look at how he created the "childist" text (to use Peter Hunt's [1991] phrase), and thereby, paradoxically, came to pave the way for avant-garde notions and children's literature in its modern form.

THE CHILDIST TEXT

From a reader's perspective, it is a stroke of genius how Andersen's narrative techniques reflect qualities in children's own play cultures, such as subversion, intensity, receptivity to alternative readings, nonlinearity, decategorization of reality modes, and the priority of feeling over specialized intellect, just to mention a few of the most important. Andersen's tales tend to be dual address narratives implying both child and adult readers. Whereas the adult reader can enjoy the pleasure of constructing a master reading, the child may move on following his or her own paths of reading. Interestingly, the childlike features are the ones that point forward to Modernist and even Postmodern epistemologies.

In Jack Zipes's (1990) interpretation, Andersen's patterns of imagination mediate between his own and children's situations of being structurally dominated. A key to his successful writings for children lies in the strategies of subversion—a marked element in popular children's literature, in which carnivalistic elements of grotesque realism have been preserved from folkloric traditions. The priority of luck, chance, and instant satisfaction in "The Tinderbox," which was severely criticized for its amoral plot in contemporary reviews, might serve as an example (Zipes 1990).

In many of the nonironic tales, childhood becomes a metaphor for reaching a unified vision, a state of subjective totality that is intense because it is framed by the horizon of the moment. Childhood is often antagonistic to established culture. "The Old Oak Tree's Last Dream," for instance, discusses vitality in the light of age. The mayfly's mode of living in one intense, expanded moment is contrasted to the old oak tree's history and durability in a manner that is comparable to the staged contrast between childlike and adult perception in the initial quotation from *Only a Fiddler* (Andersen 1837). Only in its final, lifting, and artlike dream, which is acted out on a cold winter's night, can the old oak tree, allied to Peter Brooks's (1976) understanding of the melodrama as the scene of lost presence, recover the intensity of the mayflylike child. Moreover, Andersen's tendency to establish personal mythologies mirrors vital elements in children's cultures (i.e., role plays in which existential positions are acted out in fictional codes). Through a series of conflations of dualisms, such as child/adult, space/time, and alienation/subjectivity, he creates momentary unities of vision reminiscent of both children's play cultures and the high-Modernist, personally enjoined visions of a Marc Chagall. Andersen's mingling of religion with personal destiny; his translations of nature to personal past in the tales in which the Aladdin myth is questioned; or his analogies of space and time in "The Little Mermaid" or "The Tinderbox" that render autobiographical past, present, and future with spatial signifiers are pointers to an artistic strategy. In the optimistic tales, the attempt to establish a personal mythology is successful. The old oak tree finally experiences its unity of vision, elevating its life to a sphere of meaningful intensity, but notably in contrast to harsh, wintry reality. In the more pessimistic ones, such as "The Pine Tree" or "Auntie Toothache," the unifying vision succumbs to materialism, and the result tends to be either hilarious emancipation or dark nihilism as a reflection of the Modernist exclusivity of vision. Aren't the much-debated endings of the mermaid's and the ugly duckling's stories images of empty transcendence? In both, the idealist, uplifting movements are deconstructed to states of dependency.

Further links between Andersen, children's culture, and Modernism are found in his questioning of mimetic codes. It is a well-known topos in children's literature to anthropomorphize things or animals, to subsume the non-human within to the human realm as a reflection of what Piaget (1958) might term the primitive imaginative centeredness of the child at a certain age. As we know, Andersen twists and subverts this childlike convention to make the deepest human reification central to the plots of his stories. Staging the social world as an object world is more akin to Benjamin's descriptions of the modern loss of aura than to Lafontaine's fables.

Antimimetic techniques of abstraction also feature the freezing of life into a still life. The lyrical, portraitlike quality of "The Happy Family" or "The Dung Beetle" stops epic time and discloses the agents' alienation in a radioscopy that bridges the Modernist focus on shedding layers of meaning (i.e., the "scheletoning" phase in Danish lyrical Modernism of the 1960s) and the philosophic simplicity of some children's literature. Søren Kierkegaard (1838) was deeply critical of the absence of epics and principled structure in Andersen's novels, but damming the flow of time is a prevalent technique in Symbolism, Imagism, or Expressionism. Moreover, turning a dream world into an object world is a familiar feature both in fantasy for children and Modernist art. "Little Ida's Flowers" bridges between reality modes, which was a general trend in Victorian Golden Age children's literature. In the adult arena, this would later on be termed Surrealism.

In conclusion, the reflections of children's culture in Andersen's work can be seen as an expression of the nineteenth-century double vision, whereby the adult self ascribes meaning to childhood, which in turn serves to revitalize adult culture. In "The Snow Queen" (1844) and "The Little Mermaid" (1837), the protagonists go through circular plots and return to states echoing the epithets of Romantic childhood. Additionally, the childish style for Andersen became a way of integrating his personal past, the loss of which to Bildung and sanctioned notions of adulthood so many stories dramatize as an ambivalent amputation. The "primitivist" strain dealing with the mental discomfort of modernization was reinforced in high Modernism, in which it became a pronounced hermeneutic tendency to connect childhood with radical novelty of visions. Andersen's autobiographical images of himself as a gifted child are really not so far from Joan Miró's celebration of childhood: "The older I get and the more I master the medium, the more I return to my earliest experiences. I think that at the end of my life I will recover all the force of my childhood" (Miró, as cited in Fineberg 1997: 138).

ANDERSEN, MODERNISM, AND THE CHILD

From contemporary eye witnesses' and artists' statements, we know that several Modernist artists—for instance Paul Klee, Picasso, and Kandinsky—were intrigued by children's drawings and their styles. Apollinaire reported that Picasso worked like "a newborn child who orders the universe for his personal use" (Apollinaire, as cited in Fineberg 1997: 122). One episode reports Picasso studying a child's work, using it, so to speak, as an eye-opener:

He looks at them as though he had never before seen a drawing. His eyes never leave them. He is totally absorbed by what he is looking at, and indifferent to everything else around him. The entire force of his attention is concentrated here. The greediness of his curiosity and his power of concentration are perhaps the key to his genius. (Fineberg 1997: 122)

Andersen's so-called lack of an exemplary, culturally balanced, idealist perspective from a Hegelian view implies a movement away from the Romantic notion of the artist as a cultural medium—and toward a more experimental, avant-garde role, whose exclusivity is both celebrated and mourned in the tales. It is as if the metaphors will only hold momentarily, but the figure of the child enables Andersen to deconstruct mainstream culture and to "order his universe for his personal use" in a manner comparable to that of Picasso's. The conflation of nature and otherness contained in the adult's perception of the child's perspective enables him to articulate the Modernist tension between sign and thing, where the sign becomes a thing and the thing becomes a sign (i.e., in his rewritings of the fairy tale genre). Walter Benjamin's admiration for children's perception as a capacity of *creative distortion* that places the child as an antidote to the progressivist linearity and streamlined consciousness of the society of commodities seems oddly familiar to Andersen's use of the child as a perspective relativizer. Reflecting on children's art of misunderstanding, Benjamin ([1938] 1987) describes an episode in which, as a child, he himself misunderstood the concept of "Aunt Ellen." Because the word "aunt" was unknown to him, he imagined the concept of "Auntellen" as an independent spiritual creature. It gradually took on a life of its own and grew to something new in his mind. The child's thinking to Benjamin is uncensored, and it can therefore function as a kind of spiritual resistance that is able to create radically new mental patterns that adults have either forgotten or suppressed. Childhood is tied to the forgotten dream side of history. It is potentially noncolonized, and is a cultural vehicle for transporting novelty to the cultural symbolic sphere.

Andersen's artistic methods reveal an openness not unfamiliar to Benjamin's creative distortion. A Biedermeyer drawing by Johan Thomas Lundbye in

Flinch's Copenhagen Almanac from 1843 inspired him to write his ambivalent tale "The Little Match Girl." In his diaries, we can study how his imagination worked. Often the stimulus to a tale would be a concrete occasion that he used metonymically to take off and construct a realigned universe of personal order. Along with the culturally sanctioned Romantic patterns, the stories often simultaneously imply their own deconstruction, or they contain a surplus of meaning pointing anarchistically in different directions, much like a child reading a picture book will tend to notice small details that are overlooked by adult attention to linearity. Modern children's literature nourishes possibilities of displacement and misreading. In Andersen's time, this way of addressing the reader's critical faculties was, on the one hand, considered more questionable, as is testified by his frequent misgivings about the reception of the tales. "I hope they didn't understand the stories," he would write in his diaries after nocturnal reading sessions for the royal family and other powerful members of the Danish cultural elite. On the other hand, generic conventions being less targeted on age at Andersen's time—when a dual audience and cross-writing were common features—there was a possibility of turning writing for children into a highly destabilizing kind of creative discourse.

The Andersen generation's use of the child perspective partook in paving the way for the formal experiments of Modernism. As Rosemary Lloyd (1992) and Juliet Dusinberre (1987) have demonstrated, with regard to French Symbolism and the Virginia Woolf generation, respectively, the canon of childhood reading established by the Lewis Carroll generation and the emancipation and linguistic play in their works, shaped the following generations' reading experiences. Whereas the full critical range of Andersen's tales is accessible only to the adult reader, postmodern, so-called age-ambivalent children's literature tends to question the hierarchy and exclusivity of ages. The reader of, for instance, Philip Pullman's novels or Jostein Gaarder's *Sophie's World* (1994; originally published in Norwegian in 1991)—which was marketed as young adult fiction in the Scandinavian countries, but as an adult novel in the United States—could be said to address "the adult child." Paradoxically, in light of the fact that I have now been arguing that Andersen drew on the child perspective, his tales are also much on par with today's most eminent Scandinavian children's literature because they are exploratory paradigms, reflections on what it means to be placed in modern culture. In Andersen's case, looking back on the child self was really a way of emancipating visions.

According to Mitzi Myers (1999), our critical concepts of period children's literature tend to follow processes of conceptual unification and canon formation, which, as Jacqueline Rose (1984) has also demonstrated, we need to be especially careful to avoid in the field of children's literature criticism. Myers makes the relevant comment that "Romantic ideologies play a much bigger role in children's literary history of the *twentieth* century," and asks whether "*Modernism* in fact fashioned a unified Romantic child, projecting it back onto the past and producing a fallaciously coherent narrative from the illogical and the illegible" (1999: 47). Andersen's work definitely requires the reader to bring complexity of approach to its reading, and we also should try to bring this approach to our studies of children's literature between change and canonization.

NOTE

1. All of the Andersen tales mentioned in this chapter are from *The Complete Fairy Tales and Stories of Hans Andersen* (Haugaard 1979).

BIBLIOGRAPHY

Andersen, Hans Christian. [1832] 1962. *Levnedsbogen*, ed. H. Topsøe-Jensen. Copenhagen: Det Danske Sprog- og Litteraturselskab.

Andersen, Hans Christian. 1837. *Kun en Spillemand (Only a Fiddler)* (Quoted on Det Kongelige Bibliotek' home page: http://www.kb.dk/elib/lit/dan). Accessed 15 July 2002.

Andersen, Hans Christian. 1847. *The True Story of My Life.* Translated by Mary Howitt. London: n.p.

Andersen, Hans Christian. 1981. *81 Eventyr.* Copenhagen: Hans Reitzel.

Baudelaire, Charles. 1857. *Les Fleurs du Mal.* Paris: n.p.

Baudelaire, Charles. 1964. "A Philosophy of Toys." In *The Painter of Modern Life and Other Essays*, ed. Jonathan Mayne. London: Phaidon Press.

Benjamin, Walter. [1938] 1987. *Berliner Kindheit um neunzehnhundert.* Frankfurt am Main: Fassung letzer Hand.

Boas, George. 1966. *The Cult of Childhood.* London: Warburg Institute.

Brooks, Peter. 1976. *The Melodramatic Imagination. Balzac, Henry James, Melodrama and the Mode of Excess.* New Haven, Conn.: Yale University Press.

Brostrøm, Torben, and Jørn Lund. 1991. *Flugten i sproget.* Copenhagen: Gyldendal.

Carpenter, Humphrey. 1985. *Secret Gardens. The Golden Age of Children's Literature.* London: Unwin Hyman.

Dusinberre, Juliet. 1987. *Alice to the Lighthouse. Children's Books and Radical Experiments in Art.* London: Macmillan.

Fineberg, Jonathan. 1997. *The Innocent Eye. Children's Art and the Modern Artist.* Princeton, N.J.: Princeton University Press.

Folkenflik, Robert, ed. 1993. *The Culture of Autobiography: Construction and Self-Representation.* California: Stanford University Press.

Gaarder, Jostein. 1994. *Sophie's World: A Novel about the History of Philosophy.* New York: Farrar, Straus & Giroux.

Haugaard, Erik, ed. 1979. *The Complete Fairy Tales and Stories of Hans Andersen.* London: Victor Gollanz.

Hunt, Peter. 1991. *Criticism and Children's Literature.* Oxford: Blackwell.

Jensen, Johannes V. [1900–1901] 1992. *The Fall of the King.* N.p.: Mermaid Press.

Kierkegaard, Søren. 1838. *Af en endnu Levendes Papirer (Early Polemic Writings: One Still Living).* Accessed on homepage of Det Kongelige Bibliotek's. Accessed 15 July 2002.

Knoepflmacher, U. C. 1977. "Mutations of the Wordsworthian Child of Nature." In *Nature and the Victorian Imagination*, ed. Knoepflmacher and Tennyson, 391–425. Berkeley: University of California Press.

Larsen, Steinar Björk. 1998. "Children's and Young Adults' Literature in the Age of the Millennium: Towards New Concepts?" In *Modernity, Modernism and Children's Literature*, ed. Ulf Boëthius, 95–116. Stockholm: Centrum för Barnkulturforskning.

Lloyd, Rosemary. 1992. *Land of Lost Content*. Oxford: Clarendon Press.

Lurie, Allison. 1990. *Don't Tell the Grown-Ups. Subversive Children's Literature*. London: Bloomsbury.

Mortensen, Klaus P. 1989. *Svanen og skyggen—historienom unge Andersen* (*The Swan and the Shadow: The Story of Young Andersen*). Copenhagen: GAD.

Myers, Mitzi. 1999. "Reading Children and Homeopathic Romanticism: Paradigm Lost, Revisionary Gleam, or Plus ça Change, Plus c'est la Même Chose." In *Literature and the Child. Romantic Continuations, Postmodern Contestations*, ed. James Holt McGavran, 44–84. Iowa City: Iowa University Press.

Piaget, Jean. 1958. *The Growth of Logical Thinking from Childhood to Adolescence*. Translated by A. Parsons and S. Seagrin. New York: Basic.

Richardson, Alan. 1992. "Childhood and Romanticism." In *Teaching Children's Literature. Issues, Pedagogy, Resources*, ed. Glenn Edward Sadler, 121–130. New York: Modern Language Association of America.

Rose, Jacqueline. 1984. *The Case of Peter Pan; or the Impossibility of Children's Fiction*. London: Macmillan.

Shavit, Zohar. 1986. *Poetics of Children's Literature*. Athens: University of Georgia Press.

Sørensen, Peer E. 1973. *H.C. Andersen & herskabet. Studier i borgerligkrisebevidsthed*. Aarhus, Denmark: GMT.

Sørensen, Peer E. (ed.) 1993. *H. C. Andersens Eventyr*. Copenhagen: Dansklælrer-foreningen.

Zipes, Jack. 1983. *Fairy Tales and the Art of Subversion: The Classical Genre for Children and the Process of Civilization*. New York: Heinemann.

Zipes, Jack. 1990. *When Dreams Came True: Classical Fairy Tales and Their Tradition*. New York: Routledge.

CHAPTER 10

Continuity and Change in the Fantasy Tale—with a Focus on Recent Danish Works

Anna Karlskov Skyggebjerg

Fantasy tales have been an extremely popular genre in Danish children's literature over the last two decades. Whereas the seventies were first and foremost a problem-oriented decade, resulting in a predominantly naturalistic (defined as an attempt to imitate reality) sense of aesthetics, the eighties and nineties were decades in which Danish authors of children's literature no longer felt a need to create exclusively recognizable universes. The purpose of this chapter is twofold: first, to show how recent fantasy tales belong to an established genre tradition with canonized works and, second, to show how the same stories challenge and renew the genre tradition.

What is special about fantasy tales as opposed to other genres in which there are references to fantasy figures and fantasy universes is that there is a mixture of recognizable reality and the supernatural in the fantasy tale. This can be seen, for example, when a double world is constructed, in which the hero of the story crosses the boundary between a recognizable and a magical world, or when the hero of the story who inhabits our world is visited by a creature from another world of unfamiliar laws and beings.

THE THEORETICAL UNDERPINNING

Both literary analysts and analysts of children's literature have examined the fantasy tale in depth and have given some pointers regarding the essence of the genre and its possibilities. In my research on the genre, I have relied on Tzvetan Todorov's book *Introduction à la littérature fantastique* (1970), in which he examines the place of the fantasy tale in the divide between the alien and the weird on the one hand, and the wondrous, the supernatural, and the adventure on the other. This duality can, according to Todorov, give rise to doubt or hesitation with regard to the events concerned that is experienced by the hero of the story and/or the reader. The uncertainty for the reader comes from not knowing whether the events in the story should be understood literally or metaphorically.

I further based my research on Rosemary Jackson's psychoanalytic studies of the fantasy genre, which, couched in Jackson's terminology, correspond to my concept of what a fantasy tale is. In Jackson's book, *Fantasy: The Literature of Subversion* ([1981] 1986) the genre is defined as a literature of negation and deals with the spooky, the unknown, the unacknowledged, and the invisible. The consequence of this is that the works do not allow for absolute interpretations and instead indicate dissolution of meaning.

Neither Todorov nor Jackson have shown any interest in the fantasy tale in children's literature, and although it is my opinion that their theories could have relevance for children's literature, some reflection is first needed on those special features that characterize the fantasy tale in children's literature. As for Todorov's (1970) theory, one can claim that the doubt that for Todorov is the hallmark of the genre is often toned down in children's literature. The protagonists in children's literature are often quick to accept the existence of the supernatural, and by using the narrator's voice in support of the main character in the respective work, many works set the scene for a similar unproblematic acceptance of the supernatural by the reader. In the subsequent interpretation, the question of literal or symbolic reference has to be raised and that is why I believe that Todorov's focus on the double orientation of the fantasy tale and the resultant uncertainty in the interpretation of the story has relevance for children's literature.

In Todorov's (1970) system of genres, pure fantasy is bordered on the one side by the uncanny and on the other by the marvelous. The marvelous (or the fairy story) is characterized by a magical world in which there is no problem relating to the supernatural and the interpretation will quite naturally be allegorical. It appears that the fantasy tales of children's literature (or a large number of them), in Todorov's sense, border on the marvelous and, in Todorov's words, belong to a category called the fantastic-marvelous.

Rosemary Jackson's ([1981] 1986) theory also has to be modified for it to have relevance for children's literature. I, however, still find her point that the fantasy tale deals with unspoken or taboo areas relevant. However, the consequent conclusion that works reveal the breakup of meaning or meaninglessness is not valid for children's literature. Fantasy tales in children's literature generally carry several layers of meaning, and there is no question of an absence of meaning or, for that matter, an absence of quite obvious messages.

Göte Klingberg, in *De främmande världarna i barn-och ungdomslitteraturen* (*The Alien Worlds in Literature for Children and Young People*; 1980), has dealt quite specifically with fantasy tales in children's literature. For my work with the genre, it is particularly Klingberg's analysis of motifs that is interesting.

Klingberg shows that fantasy tales in children's literature revolve around the same themes: visitors from the unknown, the fight against evil, and the mythical land, among others. For Klingberg, another essential point is that the genre fundamentally has quality, and that the respective works within the genre discuss universal human problems. According to Klingberg, the works deal especially with realities of consciousness; that is, psychological questions.

In *The Magic Code*, Maria Nikolajeva (1988) talks about a fantasy poetics for children's literature and illustrates this with a series of fantasemes taken from a historical selection of English-speaking works. Fantasemes are found at various levels of the text and are defined as the special structural characteristics that are varied from work to work within the genre. The secondary world, the magic passage, and the messenger are examples of fantasemes. For me, Nikolajeva's analysis of the shaping of the magical world carries special weight. Nikolajeva distinguishes between three different variants of the magical or, in other words, the secondary world: the closed, the open, and the implied construct.

The closed world is the construct in which the action only takes place in a magical—that is—a secondary universe (Nikolajeva 1988). A primary world only exists outside the story as reference for the reader. J.R.R. Tolkien's *The Hobbit: or There and Back Again* ([1937] 1975) is a famous example of this construction. The open construct is found in stories in which there is a normal (primary) world and a magical (secondary) world (Nikolajeva 1988). Lewis Carroll's *Alice's Adventures in Wonderland* ([1865] 1999), J. M. Barrie's *Peter Pan and Wendy* ([1911] 1988), and C. S. Lewis's *The Lion, the Witch and the Wardrobe* ([1950] 1984) are some of the many examples of such a construct. The implied construct is found in works in which a magical agent intervenes in the normal world (Nikolajeva 1988). It is understood that the magical agent belongs to another world. Here I can mention E.T.A. Hoffmann's *Das fremde Kind* (*The Strange Child*; [1817] 1988) as an example.

For Nikolajeva (1988), all three constructs are possible in the fantasy genre, whereas for other researchers, you can only talk about a fantasy or a fantasy tale if two worlds are described in the text itself. Nikolajeva's definition allows for a less exclusive and less rigid concept of genre and it is possible to understand works that are clearly related as being from the same context of genres.

I have chosen to use the concept "fantasy tale" rather than the English term "fantasy." This is partly because the concept of "fantasy tale" points to the connection with Hoffmann and the Germanic tradition, which I think is important, and partly because the word "fantasy" has some inappropriate connotations. In Danish, "fantasy" is used in some contexts about novels that take place in closed mythological universes, and in some contexts it is used pejoratively. The method I used is that of hermeneutic text analysis. As is clear from what I have said above, I have used insights from structuralism and psychoanalysis, but have allowed myself to use the terminology from earlier researchers relatively freely.

MODERN DANISH FANTASY TALES: THE
APPLICATION OF A EUROPEAN TRADITION

The fantasy tale is a genre that can be traced back to the last century. In children's literature, E.T.A. Hoffmann's *Das fremde Kind* (*The Strange Child;* [1817] 1988) and Lewis Carroll's *Alice's Adventures in Wonderland* ([1865] 1999) are two of the earliest and internationally best known examples of fantasy tales. The two works show the beginnings of the genre in partly a Germanic and partly an Anglo-Saxon tradition.

Both *Das fremde Kind* and *Alice's Adventures in Wonderland* have had tremendous significance for Danish fantasy tales as sources of inspiration in structural and thematic areas. In both works, there is a discussion about the relationship between magic and reality, the visible and the invisible; and this discussion is continued and developed in later works within the genre. What defines these works as children's literature is partly the fact that they are written for children and have children as the main characters, but also that they are close to the marvelous in Todorov's sense. The characters marvel at the magic, but they are not seriously beset by doubt, and the reader is forced to share this reaction at first. Reflecting subsequently, the reader (the child, in just the same way as the adult) has to ask himself or herself, however, what the magical elements actually mean, and whether they should be taken literally or metaphorically.

In *Das fremde Kind* (Hoffmann [1817] 1988), childhood is contrasted with adulthood, and a rationalistic view of the child and its upbringing confronts a romantic view of life in the work. The rigidly rationalistic educator is portrayed in the book as a pedantic teacher who is turned into a giant fly, and in this way shows himself to be an incarnation of uncontrollable evil. The destructive magus who emerges out of the teacher is met by the eponymous figure of the tale, the strange child, who represents a positive side of the supernatural. The strange child is a rescuing angel in its embodiment of courage, naturalness, and intuition. We hang our hopes on the unspoiled child, the visitor from a remote and indefinable magical place. Those who can come into contact with the strange child are the main characters in the tale—in other words, other children.

Whereas in *Das fremde Kind* the focus is on the confrontation between various philosophies of life and principles, it is strangeness that is at the center of *Alice's Adventures in Wonderland* (Carroll [1865] 1999). The magic here appears as something that is both demonic and attractive, and the characters that Alice meets in the wondrous world evoke both laughter and horror. Speaking animals and bodiless or physically strange creatures are a part of the theme. Alice's body undergoes various metamorphoses and lives its own life, out of her control. Through Alice's various experiences, such as the physical metamorphoses, the work calls attention to the grotesque and the absurd as elements of the fantasy tale.

Lewis Carroll's book is, moreover, a metapoetic work, reflecting the relationship between language and reality. Alice wonders about language and exploits its onomatopoeic and graphical sides, reciting poems that semantically make no sense. The language is self-generating and creative.

Now I will try to illustrate how two modern Danish children's novels—Louis Jensen's *Skelettet på hjul* (*The Skeleton on Wheels*; 1996) and Knud Holten's *Flamme-Øglens Tåre* (*The Lizard's Tear*; 1999)—are both traditional and innovative within the genre of fantasy tale. The reason I have chosen these two authors is that they deal with the traditions of the genre in very original but very different ways.

LOUIS JENSEN: THE SKELETON ON WHEELS

Until the present moment, Louis Jensen (b. 1943) has written approximately 10 fantasy tales (the number depends somewhat on how one chooses to categorize particular works). The author reveals an affinity with Hoffmann in his use of motifs and his view of the child. The secondary world is understood in *Skelettet på hjul* (*The Skeleton on Wheels*; Jensen 1996) just as it is in *Das fremde Kind* (*The Strange Child*; Hoffmann [1817] 1988), in that the primary, apparently real world is visited by figures with magical powers. The understood construct in *Skelettet på hjul*, however, is not carried through consistently. At the end of the book, the main character enters into the secondary world in the form of a chamber of spirits where one is able to contact the dead.

In *Skelettet på hjul*, the boy, Martin, learns that his parents have killed the dog, Trofast, because he is a nuisance. In this way, right from the beginning of the novel, there is a conflict between the parents and the son. The adults' world and their perception of reality stand in stark contrast to the universe of the child. The adults are rationalistic, insensitive, narrow-minded, and indifferent to both the son and the dog. In contrast, Martin is independent, active, and open to the supernatural.

Martin is visited by an angel of light, which is a variation of the theme of the strange child. In Nikolajeva's (1988) terminology, the angel of light is a variation of the fantaseme called the messenger from the secondary world. The angel asks Martin to cleanse the skeleton of the dog and put the bones on a cart. Martin follows the orders and afterward goes out into the world to search for the dog's soul. Martin and the dead dog undertake a voyage of self-discovery, and Martin learns to find his own position with regard to good and evil. The world Martin travels in resembles the world we recognize. Martin travels by rail and on the motorway, and when he gets a lift in a lorry he hears on the radio that there is an official search out for him. During the journey, however, Martin meets several magical figures, representing both good and evil, who clearly come from another world.

Like Hoffmann, Jensen exhibits great faith in the child. However, in this case, the strange child (the angel of light) is only a contributory element and a catalyst for the actual child's (i.e., Martin's) own will to act. In the beginning, Martin has to bear the lack of understanding and the callousness of the adults on his own, and to a large extent he has to act to free himself from the evil. With Louis Jensen, the main character is not only receptive to magical power; he is also a capable person. In this way, Jensen, like Hoffmann, shows that his view of the child coincides with that of the time. In the 1990s, the view of children was that they are capable, independent beings.

There are further similarities between *Skelettet på hjul* (Jensen 1996) and *Das fremde Kind* (Hoffmann [1817] 1988) in the inclusion of grotesque elements; that is, hyperbolic, gruesome, and tragicomic features. However, in *Das fremde Kind*, the grotesque is tied to the supernatural—for example, the teacher's metamorphosis into the violent monster—whereas the grotesque in *Skelettet på hjul* is part of Martin's daily routine and apparent normality. Martin's parents' ignorant behavior and their sneering laughter when their son confronts them with the dog's death is the most grotesque episode in the book. His parents are watching Laurel and Hardy on TV while Martin tries to establish a dialogue about life and death. Martin's situation is both gripping and extreme; it is incredible that he manages to hold onto his integrity against this background. In summary, one can say that the world we recognize in this fantasy tale is a great deal more problematic than the magical universe.

The basis of Louis Jensen's innovative work on the fantasy tale is largely a sharper focus on known problems—the conflict between the child and the rationalistic world of adults, for example. The gruesome, tragic element in the opening situation is violent, but it merely means that the main character will appear as someone correspondingly strong and independent. The magic serves to strengthen the contrasts between good and evil, and the magical events serve to emphasize the fact that there is a symbolic struggle and spiritual development taking place in Martin's mind. To use Klingberg's (1980) words, one can say that the story is about the realities of consciousness, and with Rosemary Jackson's ([1981] 1986) formulations in mind, one can say that the work actualizes a taboo-ridden area: parents' failings.

Louis Jensen's writing is serious but it is not without humor. Martin's confrontation with his parents has to be seen as tragicomedy. The passion of the situation is juxtaposed partly with the slapstick comedy droning away on the television and partly with the absurd, almost laughable, argumentation of the parents. In the same way that laughter accompanies the sinister in *Alice's Adventures in Wonderland* (Carroll [1865] 1999), the same is true in *Skelettet på hjul*.

In the prominence of the use of language, Jensen also shows some similarities with Carroll. There is a consistent playfulness with words and letters throughout Jensen's works. In *Skelettet på hjul*, the dog, while alive, is called Trofast (faithful), but its skeleton is called Tsafort. The anagram is a code, showing that there is a connection between the dog and the skeleton. However, Tsafort is a word without a soul—that is, without any semantic content—and that is why Tsafort has to become Trofast again before the events gain meaning and the book can finish.

KNUD HOLTEN: THE LIZARD'S TEAR

The other example I would like to put forward is Knud Holten's *Flamme-Øglens Tåre* (*The Lizard's Tear;* 1999). Knud Holten (b. 1945) openly acknowledges his debt to Lewis Carroll. *Flamme-Øglens Tåre* is one part of a series called *Alex på Eventyr (Alex's Adventures)*, clearly a nodding reference to Carroll's *Alice i Eventyrland (Alice in Adventure-Land)*, as it is called in one of the Danish translations. Using Todorov's terminology, *Flamme-Øglens Tåre* verges on the marvelous. There is something " adventurelike" in both of the two parallel worlds, in that there are characters in both worlds with supernatural powers. The first world is the one that resembles more closely the one we experience. Just as in *Alice's Adventures in Wonderland* (Carroll [1865] 1999), the secondary world in *Flamme-Øglens Tåre* is made explicit and, in Nikolajeva's (1988) terminology, the construct is open.

The action centers on the mysterious disappearance of a young girl from an old landed estate. The main protagonist and hero of the book, Alex, finds out that the girl has disappeared into another world where she is held prisoner by a terrifying witch with the symbolic name of Fatalina. Alex's mission is to save the girl and to prevent the witch from practicing black magic. In this secondary world, Alex enlists the help of strange creatures, strange in size and behavior. The story races along and is full of action, but the reader is never in any doubt that Good will triumph, in accordance with the conventions of the genre. The work makes use of a number of stereotypical figures from folk tales in the creation of heroes, villains, friends, and foes. What makes the book innovative is not the depth of the conflict or the psychological complexity, but rather the richness of the language and the metaconsciousness of the creation of two worlds.

An example of the metaconsciousness in the text is when an aging troll is said to have developed its *"magisk-fænomenologiske parallelverden-hypotese"* (hypothesis of a magical-phenomenological parallel world) (Holten 1999: 158). However, this not only evidences consciousness of the nature of a universe, but is also a character's comment on the nature of a genre.

At the beginning of the book, there is the introduction to a play, functioning as a *mise en abîme;* that is, a self-reference containing a particular point with relation to the understanding of the work. The actor, Kalle Vilmersen, and Aunt Clotilde, who is the author and director of the play, discuss to what extent the play can be described as a comedy or a tragedy. The actor makes a case for a comedy and thus for humor as an artistic technique, a point that is also valid for the whole book. Humor is preferable to the seriousness of tragedy, or its taking itself too seriously.

The particular style of the story has parodic and comical elements, which immediately puncture the bombast that occasionally builds up in the description of the magical universe. The narrator uses high-flown language one moment, only to pull the rug out from underneath the meaning the next moment with a modification or a comment. Thus, for example, on page 230:

Og fordi Kugle-Fuglen åbenbart havde tindrende, citrinfarvet blod og gennemskinnelige årer, svøbtes de tre venner i et dæmpet lysskær, som nogle (for eksempel Kalle Vilmersen) ville have beskrevet som "unikt og særdeles delikat"—og andre simpelt hen som "smadderhyggeligt."

[And because the Curd-Bird had sparkling, quartz-coloured blood and translucent veins, the three friends huddled together under the dim ray of light, which some (for example, Kalle Vilmersen) would have described as "unique and délicat"—and others as simply "right snug."]

The high-flown language consists of unusual words such as *"citrin"* (quartz), which has connotations of something refined in that citrin is used as a precious stone. The refined, the unusual, and the high flown contrast with *"smadderhyggeligt"* (right snug), which is made colloquial by the addition of the emphatic "smadder" *(right)*. The whole quotation indicates that language is arbitrary and that the choice of style is largely a personal matter. The use of quotation marks a distance to what is said, and it marks the fact that we have to be skeptical regarding the ability of language to cover a particular content.

There is a similar example in the description of Mille:

hvis hår var så langt og så skinnende gyldenblondt, som det ellers kun ses i unaturliger reklamefilm for shampoo . . . og selv en talentløs digter kunne garanteret skrive alenlange, vidunderlige vers om hendes læbers farve af fylde og smil, hvis han bare ignorerede det lille, hovmodige drag om dem.

[whose hair was so long, so shiny and golden blonde in a way that is normally only seen in artificial commercials for shampoo . . . and even a poet with no talent would manage to write wonderful verses as long as your arm about the colour and fullness of her lips and smile, so long as he just ignored the little arrogant sneer on them.] (Holten 1999: 83)

Here the cliché of all clichés in Western culture is used: the shampoo advertisement. Mille is a cliché herself—that is, a stereotype—and describing her or putting her into words is the task for a talentless poet, the narrator comments self-ironically.

The characters in the book are largely described through their language. A professor imitated by an actor is a parody of academic language, whereas the wood troll Fillitot has his personality expressed through the clichés of folk songs:

Frygt ej længere, skønjomfru . . . jeg svæger . . . at eders grumme kvide snart er omme.

[Fear not, fair maiden . . . I vouchsafe . . . that your great travails soon shall be no more.] (Holten 1999: 293)

Fillitot is romantic and chivalrous, but, as the language shows, he becomes a comic figure by not conforming to the linguistic norms of the girl, his addressee.

In conclusion, one can say that the text is imaginative and burlesque, and what seems to be a simple comedy or a pastiche of a fantasy tale is a detailed reflection on language as a medium. The similarity with Lewis Carroll rests on his predilection for the comic absurdity of existence and a principled de-stabilization of every statement through an unrestricted, imaginative, and self-reflective attitude toward language. As far as actual themes and plotting are concerned, Holten relies much more on folk tales and myths than do his predecessors within the fantasy tale genre.

Louis Jensen and Knud Holten, each in their own way, draw on the legacy left behind by Hoffmann and Carroll, respectively, and represent originality and innovation in the genre. *Skelettet på hjul* (Jensen 1996) and *Flamme-Øglens Tåre* (Holten 1999) do not represent a division between an ethical and an aesthetic interest; rather, as described above, Jensen's focus is largely of a psychological kind, whereas with Holten, it is the language that becomes the content itself of the story. In general, the two examples point to a high degree of awareness of genre in the authors' works. The analysis of Louis Jensen's story can be seen as a general example of how innovation in recent Danish tales of fantasy lies in taking tensions to extremes and in emphasizing the image of the child as someone who is capable and can act with conviction. The analysis of Knud Holten's story reveals a general tendency to pay special attention to language and also to expose clichés through humor.

BIBLIOGRAPHY

Barrie, J. M. [1911] 1988. *Peter Pan and Wendy.* London: Pavilion.

Carroll, Lewis. [1865] 1999. *Alice's Adventures in Wonderland.* Reprint, London: Walker Books.

Hoffmann, E.T.A. [1817] 1988. *Das fremde Kind (The Strange Child).* Reprint, Hanau, Germany: Dausien.

Holten, Knud. 1999. *Flamme-Øglens Tåre (The Lizard's Tear).* Copenhagen: Gyldendal.

Jackson, Rosemary. [1981] 1986. *Fantasy: The Literature of Subversion.* London: Routledge.

Jensen, Louis. 1996. *Skelettet på hjul (The Skeleton on Wheels).* Copenhagen: Gyldendal.

Klingberg, Göte. 1980. *De främmande världarna i barn- och ungdomslitteraturen (The Alien Worlds in Literature for Children and Young People).* Stockholm: Rabén & Sjögren

Lewis, C. S. [1950] 1984. *The Lion, the Witch, and the Wardrobe.* London: Fontana Lions.

Nikolajeva, Maria. 1988. *The Magic Code: The Use of Magical Patterns in Fantasy for Children*. Stockholm: University of Stockholm.
Todorov, Tzvetan. 1970. *Introduction à la littérature fantastique (The fantastic: A Structural approach to a literary genre)*. Paris: Seuil.
Tolkien, J.R.R. [1937] 1975. *The Hobbit: or There and Back Again*. London: Unwin.

CHAPTER 11

Blytons, Noddies, and Denoddification Centers: The Changing Constructions of a Cultural Icon

David Rudd

INTRODUCTION

Certain stories, like fairy tales, are perennials, simply being reworked for different audiences and societies. Within this context, some literary authors have also managed to create evergreen figures, or scenarios: Peter Pan, Alice, Winnie-the-Pooh, Pinocchio, and Peter Rabbit come to mind, living on in numerous different versions. In this chapter, I consider Enid Blyton and her oeuvre, for she also has stood the test of time, although only by going through a number of transformations—partly through her own reconstruction of herself, and partly through critical reactions to her work. There are, in fact, a number of "Blytons" out there, just as there are different versions of her most famous characters—Noddy, the Famous Five, and so on. In addition to showing this process of change and renewal in action, I also point out that it might well be at the expense of some of Blyton's original appeal.

BLYTONS—THE FAMOUS FOUR

First, let's look at Blyton herself, for depending on one's age, she has been seen very differently, although, for many who are professionally involved with children's literature, the enduring image continues to be of someone who epitomizes what children's literature should not be. However, Blyton was not always seen in this negative way, as there have been four discernible constructions of Blyton (for more detailed information, see Rudd 2000), each of which is described below.

The Educationalist (1920s–1930s)

In the 1920s, Blyton was seen as a significant writer, her name appearing in the company of authors such as A. A. Milne. In a special 1923 issue of *Teachers World* on poetry, Blyton's work was published alongside poems by Kipling, de la Mare, and Chesterton (Druce 1992: 31). When an English version of Jan de Brunhoff's *Babar* was produced (Blyton 1941a), it was Blyton who was asked to provide the text (Ray 1982: 13).

She was also, it should be noted, seen predominantly in educational terms. A regular contributor to *Teachers World* for 23 years, her texts on teaching were quite influential, the most substantial being a 3-volume *The Teacher's Treasury* (1926), a 6-volume *Modern Teaching* (1928), a 10-volume *Pictorial Knowledge* (1930), and a 4-volume *Modern Teaching in the Infant School* (1932). Her range was quite extraordinary, writing the equivalent of National Curricula almost single handedly, as well as works on ancient history, religious studies, nature, drama, and a number of class readers.

Golden Days (1930s–1950s)

In the late thirties and early forties, Blyton turned to writing full-length fictional works, including the first "Famous Fives" (1942a), "St. Clare's" (1941b), "Adventure" (1944), "Naughtiest Girl" (1940), and "Mary Mouse" (1942b) books as well as the "Magic Faraway Tree" series (1939), and was gaining an ever-increasing and loyal readership. (Many of these works, it should be noted, grew out of much shorter pieces, often using the same-named characters.) Although reviews of her books were few, they tended to be positive, with one of the "Adventure" series even winning a literary award in America. Moving into the 1950s, there was a shift of interest in her books. Although still a popular writer, the term "hack" started to be linked with Blyton's name, partly as a result of her increasing rate of production (in the early 1950s she was averaging over 50 titles a year, her record being 69 titles in 1955—more than one a week!).

However, with what was seen in Britain as an invasion of American culture (e.g., rock music, horror comics, television, teenage culture, delinquency, and Disney), Blyton was generally regarded as something of a more savory, English alternative—which she capitalized on. She wrote a poem called "American Comics (and Those Who Like Them)," which is very critical, and publicity matter about the character Noddy states that it is "ousting the American creations of Walt Disney from our nurseries and homes" (*Publicity Matter Concerning Enid Blyton Children's Author*: 5). By this time, she was regularly topping polls as the most popular children's writer.

Slow Poison (1960s–1980s)

A more negative tone toward Blyton's work was gathering momentum in the 1950s, with Colin Welch (1958: 21–22) famously calling Noddy an "unnaturally priggish . . . sanctimonious . . . witless, spiritless, snivelling, sneaking doll." Jane Dohm (1955) and David Holbrook (1961) were similarly condemnatory and Edward Blishen (1967: 28), in an educational journal, provocatively asked the question "Are your children addicted to Enid Blyton and what, if anything, do you do about it?" speaking about the need for "denoddyfication centres" for the afflicted. (Ironically, it was Noddy's visual creator, the Dutch artist Harmsen van der Beek, who was most in need of this. He confessed to hallucinating Noddies crawling over his desk after he had been working too hard, trying in vain to match Blyton's output!)

There is also a shift in criticism at this time, from a literary perspective to a more socially concerned one, finding racism, sexism, and elitism in Blyton's work. Thus, we find Lena Jeger (1966) accusing Blyton of writing "more insidiously dangerous" neofascist literature than the British racist groups, and Margery Fisher (1983) describing Blyton's work as "slow poison." However, because this attention only seemed to increase Blyton's sales and popularity and she had a fiercely loyal child readership, many other critics simply began to ignore her. This ploy continues even today; for example, Brian Alderson, although forced to recognize Blyton's centenary year for the Children's Books History Society, still managed to slant it euphemistically so that the discussion was of authors "obscured" by the "Noddy-lady's fame" (Alderson 1997: 7–8).

Sunny Stories Again (1990s)

Despite the official silence of literary critics of the 1970s and 1980s, Blyton continued to top reading polls (although latterly, Dahl often took top spot)—even being featured as a favorite among older, teenage readers (see, e.g., Knowles and Malmkjaer 1995: 38–39). By the 1990s, with increasing numbers of now-adult readers, a new tolerance of her was emerging. Many celebrities confessed to being weaned on her work (e.g., Beryl Bainbridge, Melvyn Bragg, Wendy Cope, Carol Ann Duffy, Ken Follett, and Brian Patten). In addition, amid more recent scares around children—mindless TV consumption, inability to read, video-nasties, crime and violence among the young, ginger-beer giving way to under-age drinking, a perceived decline in moral standards, and abuse of various sorts (physical, sexual, and satanic)—Blyton came to be seen not as slow poison, but rather as a strangely innocuous figure, representing, if anything, a more desirable age of innocence. In addition, given fears over reading standards and moral decline, she was seen as representing a possible answer to such deterioration.

Thus, we have seen how Blyton's reputation has changed substantially over the years—possibly more than any other writer's during their lifetime (many writers' reputations—for example, Kipling's—changed more posthumously). Since her death, Blyton has continued to evolve, entering the public consciousness and folk culture in less formal ways through a number of intertexts.

INTERTEXTUAL BLYTONS IN SEARCH OF THE BLYTON FORMULA

Probably the most famous of these intertexts is *Five Go Mad in Dorset* in the Comic Strip Presents series on British television (Comic Strip 1982), which coined the apocryphal Famous Five line, "lashings of ginger beer," subsequently taken up by others. (A child who wrote Five-style stories for me in class ended one of his offerings with: "Then they all went back home for lashings and lashings.") Other writers have also used Blyton's works, such as Adèle Geras (1990–1992) in her "Egerton Hall" trilogy (Malory Towers), Jacqueline Wilson (1996) in *Double Act* (St. Clare's), and Peter Hunt (1985) in *A Step Off the Path* (Famous Five). The crime writer Denise Danks (1989) has admitted that her detective, "Georgina Powers" was inspired by George from the Famous Five.

Music bands have also referenced Blyton. "Current 93," for example, released an album entitled *Swastikas for Noddy*. Other groups have named their bands "Noddy's Puncture"; and "Die Funf Freunde"; and, most explicitly, "The Enid"—a band that was originally known as "The Famous Five." Their leader, Robert John Godfrey, gives a more subversive playful edge to the Blyton world: "There have never been any fairies at the bottom of my garden apart from myself and the boy next door having fun behind the wood shed. Which one of us was Noddy or Big Ears is my secret" (Godfrey 1996).

In addition, there have been songs and radio programs on how the Famous Five might have matured. There are games on the Internet based on Blyton's works, continuations of her stories, individuals named after Blyton characters, lists of favorite quotations by characters, recipes inspired by her books, soft porn, and much more.

As I discovered from my research, however, the impact of her work went even further, filtering down into the imaginative landscape of children's culture such that her works were being used extensively as springboards for children's games, role-playing activities, personal fantasies, and writing stories (more so with past readers than present ones).

As I shall suggest, there is a huge difference between Blyton with her effortless storytelling ability—updating her stories over the years, reworking her characters, responding to changes in fashion and to new technologies—and the Blyton industry simply trading on what her name signifies. For me, this was epitomized in 1996 at Christmas when the new owners of Blyton's copyright had her name, alone, in huge pink neon hanging over Regent's Street in London. This "floating signifier" seemed to capture the notion that her brand name alone sold merchandise—that her name indeed could signify all and everything—something that seemed rather insulting to her child audience who had sought out *her* books rather than those of others for more than four generations.

Since her death, a number of false Blytons have been appearing. In the

1970s, in France, there were apocryphal "Secret Seven," "Mystery," and "Famous Five," tales produced using Blyton's logo signature on the covers (only inside did they state, "a new adventure of the characters created by Enid Blyton"); and in Germany, again in the 1970s, there were a dozen anonymous sequels to Malory Towers. In the 1990s, when the "Adventure" series was filmed, the scriptwriter proudly proclaimed that "Not one word of Blyton's is in the script" (Brown 1996). Since then, the books have been turned back into "screenplay novelizations," interestingly described in *British National Bibliography* (1998) as "New Zealand" fiction (the film's location). Totally new series have appeared too, such as the "Riddle" series, which rewrites six of Blyton's single novels, running together the characters. There are sequels to the "Naughtiest Girl" stories, written by Anne Digby, and prequels of the Famous Five stories, telling of George and Timmy's pre-Five existence.

As stated above, these reworkings treat Blyton's texts as fairly expendable, trading on her name alone, whereas I have found her readers to be far more discerning. For instance, they noticed that the characters in the reworked Adventurous Four stories, although still set in the 1940s, had inappropriately trendy names (they have been changed from Mary and Jill to Pippa and Zoe); and that the French "Famous Five" stories, subsequently translated back into English, were not nearly as good because they dispensed with much of the period feel (the titles themselves, *The Famous Five and the Z Rays*, *The Famous Five on Television*, are indicative). The German Malory Towers likewise had Darrell Rivers ("Dolly" as she is called in their version) become an adult, marry, and go back to the school as a "housemother"—not even a teacher— thus completely losing her child appeal and feisty edge. One article, by the German academic Gertrud Lehnert (1992), based much of its argument about "The Taming of the Shrew" on these non-Blyton versions, without seeming to realize that they are not Blyton's works. More recent "politically correct" updates of the Famous Five have also blunted George's subversive edge with, for example, all of the Five now washing the dishes. Similarly, the original contrast of George with the more stereotypical Anne has been lost as Anne has herself become more "liberated."

Noddy, however, has suffered more than most (although some say he deserves all he gets!). In the 1980s, Macdonald Purnell produced a version that halved the length of the original texts and simplified the language, making the amazing claim that the original Noddy books "seem very long and have language that [the children] do not experience" (Bates 1987). Ironically, the stereotype of the Blytonesque—not really justified in her lifetime—was increasingly becoming a reality. This 1986 edition didn't sell very well (unsurprisingly) such that a third edition appearing in 1990 reverted to the original format, although it still removed some of the polysyllables (things that Margery Fisher said Blyton could not abide): thus, "unexpectedly" became "just then," "becalmed" became " isn't moving," "surge" was replaced with "come," and so on.

Because it is easier to change a few words of text than it is to alter illustrations, it is of note that Blyton's words have sometimes had to conform to something that an illustrator once misrepresented. At other times, however, illustrations have had to be redone, notably to "degollify" the texts—and, with a hint of homophobia, to put Noddy and Big-Ears in separate sleeping accommodation. [Noddy, a new man before his time, was always seen as effeminate, with his long lashes and domesticated habits, and was supposedly "banned" in parts of Australia for this reason (Knowles 1988)].

All of these revisions appear to have been done without any thought as to how the stories work—or don't. For instance, in the most controversial book of the Noddy series, *Here Comes Noddy Again!* (Blyton 1951), the nodding man goes off with a golly in the original, having been tempted by a bag of six-pences—although he confesses to being worried about meeting goblins. He is subsequently "mugged" by some gollies [as I've argued elsewhere (Rudd 2000), the episode closely reworks one in *Pinocchio* in which that wooden man is also enticed out for monetary gain, sees "two awful black figures" in the dark by whom he is mugged, and then runs off for help]. In the revised version of *Here Comes Noddy Again!*, however, it is goblins that Noddy goes off with and by whom he is attacked. Many child readers I have spoken with, like these nine-year-olds quoted below, have pointed out that the story just doesn't work the same:

Lucy: Yeah, because like, he doesn't know the goblins, but he knew golliwogs.

Patrick: He's silly going off with a goblin cos . . .

Lucy: You can't trust them.

Patrick: Yeah, you can't trust them, never!

Again, such changes have made Noddy more of a "noddy" character and Blyton, the writer, more stereotypically "Blytonesque." What have been removed or revised are often some of the very elements that make Blyton successful—elements that she shares with an older, oral tradition, one that is often less concerned with fashionable notions of being "politically correct." Drawing on nearly 500 children across a variety of cultures and ethnicities, I found that although they had different interpretations and tastes with regard to Blyton's work, the process of reading it was remarkably uniform: she was seen as a very visual writer whose stories unfolded with ease in their heads, like films (which is how she herself described writing them); moreover readers frequently saw themselves as part of the action (and none, need it be said, saw themselves as being marginalized or excluded because of race or gender).

This visually accessible depiction is very much part of the oral style in which stories are frequently set in a fairly vague past with an equally hazy landscape and with characters drawn from stock figures (in Blyton's works, these characters were not just working-class stereotypes but middle-class ones too). She draws on readers' senses, frequently telling them to "Look" or "Listen." Whereas she writes of a message, "Here it is," in the new edition this is simply rendered as "It said." The here and now of the present is thus returned to a more literary, past tense. In addition, Blyton's own intrusions on (and evaluations of) the action, typical of the oral teller, have often been toned down or removed. For example, "I'll pop my head in at the window and hear it for you. Listen!" becomes, "I think it might sound a bit like this" (Blyton [1954] 1990: 60).

Sometimes this oral style involves her in intermingling teller and told and thought and speech, but this is part of the dreamlike feel of her stories in which external reality and more magical, internal thought processes merge. Note, for instance Anne's "thoughtless" shift here from internal to external speech:

"I wish I was like George," she thought. "She wouldn't really mind that toad. I'm silly. I ought to try and like all creatures. Oh my goodness, look at that enormous spider in the corner of the sink! It's sitting there, looking at me out of its eight eyes! Wilfrid, Wilfrid—PLEASE come and get this spider out of the sink for me!" (Blyton 1962: 49)

CONCLUSION

Blyton is "ephemeral," then, not in the sense that her work will quickly date—it always was dated in the manner of many oral folk and fairy tales—but in the sense that it is "for the day," lasting only the duration of the telling. However, if it is tampered with in the way that is currently being done, allowing other writers to retouch her original stories in a variety of different styles as well as write prequels and sequels and, most recently, with the new copyright owners seeking to customize her work for different nationalities, each with its own particularized environment—then I believe that Blyton's work could become ephemeral in a more final sense. Blyton herself will end up becoming increasingly like the Blytonesque stereotype that the critics have always loved to despise. She will then be little more than a brand name, with her works effectively penned by a collective. Change will then no longer lead to renewal but rather to decay.

BIBLIOGRAPHY

Alderson, Brian. 1997. "Putting Blyton in Her Place" [chairman's comments]. *Children's Books History Society Newsletter* 59 (November): 7–8.

Bates, Stephen. 1987. "Golliwogs Lose Their Place in Noddy's Tales." *Daily Telegraph* (2 January).

Blishen, Edward. 1967. "Who's Afraid of Enid Blyton?" *Where* 32: 28–29.

Blyton, Enid, ed. 1926. *The Teacher's Treasury*, 3 vols. London: Newnes.

Blyton, Enid, ed. 1928. *Modern Teaching*, 6 vols. London: Newnes.

Blyton, Enid, ed. 1930. *Pictorial Knowledge*, 10 vols. London: Newnes.
Blyton, Enid, ed. 1932. *Modern Teaching in the Infant School*, 4 vols. London: Newnes.
Blyton, Enid. 1939. *The Enchanted Wood*. London: Newnes.
Blyton, Enid. 1940. *The Naughtiest Girl in the School*. London: Newnes.
Blyton, Enid. 1941a. *The Babar Story Book*. London: Methuen.
Blyton, Enid. 1941b. *The Twins at St. Clare's*. London: Methuen.
Blyton, Enid. 1942a. *Five on a Treasure Island*. London: Hodder & Stoughton.
Blyton, Enid. 1942b. *Mary Mouse and the Dolls' House*. Leicester: Brockhampton Press.
Blyton, Enid. 1944. *The Island of Adventure*. London: Macmillan.
Blyton, Enid. 1951. *Here Comes Noddy Again!* London: Sampson Low.
Blyton, Enid. 1952. *Noddy Goes to School*. London: Sampson Low.
Blyton, Enid. [1954] 1990. *Noddy Gets into Trouble*. London: Sampson Low.
Blyton, Enid. 1962. *Five Have a Mystery to Solve*. London: Hodder & Stoughton.
British National Bibliography. 1998. Boston Spa, British Library, 25 March.
Brown, Maggie. 1996. "Golly—Would Enid Approve?—Lashings of Period Detail or a Radical Updating?" *Daily Telegraph* (1 July).
Comic Strip. 1982. *Five Go Mad in Dorset*. Channel 4, London.
Danks, 1989. *The Pizza House Crash*. London: Futura.
Dohm, Jane. 1955. "Enid Blyton and Others: An American View." *Journal of Education* 87 (August): 358–61.
Druce, Robert. 1992. *This Day Our Daily Fictions: An Enquiry into the Multi-Million Bestseller Status of Enid Blyton and Ian Fleming*. Amsterdam: Rudopi BV.
Fisher, Margery. 1983. "A Reputation Reconsidered." *Growing Point* 22 (2 July): 4119–20.
Godfrey, Robert John. 1996. *Anarchy on 45: Complete Singles Collection*. Mantella Records, London. Compact disc notes.
Holbrook, David. 1961. *English for Maturity*. Cambridge: Cambridge University Press.
Jeger, Lena. 1966. "In Large Print." *The Guardian* (24 May): 18.
Knowles, Murray, and Kirsten Malmkjaer. 1995. *Language and Control in Children's Literature*. London: Routledge.
Knowles, Stewart. 1988. "Noddy's Adventures in the Big Apple." *TV Times* (2–8 April): 8–9, 18.
Lehnert, Gertrud. 1992. "The Taming of the Shrew: Socialization and Education of Young Women in Children's Literature." *Poetics Today* 13(1): 109–22.
Publicity Matter Concerning Enid Blyton Children's Author (for Use either Abroad or at Home). N.d. Unpublished leaflet. Enid Blyton Society Archive, Salisbury, Wiltshire, England.
Ray, Sheila G. 1982. *The Blyton Phenomenon: The Controversy Surrounding the World's Most Successful Children's Author*. London: André Deutsch.
Rudd, David. 2000. *Enid Blyton and the Mystery of Children's Literature*. Basingstoke, UK: Macmillan.
Welch, Colin. 1958. "Dear Little Noddy: A Parent's Lament." *Encounter* 10 (1): 18–23.

CHAPTER 12

Changing Perspectives: Tarzan Recalled and Retold at the Turn of the Millennium

Rolf Romören

INTRODUCTION

In a previous article (Romören 2001–2002), I interpreted Edgar Rice Bur-roughs's novel *Tarzan of the Apes* ([1914] 1990) as a *Bildungsroman* in which the civilizing of Tarzan goes through three stages—the mirror scene; the ac-quisition of literacy; and the encounter with, and subsequent sacrifice of, Jane. I also tried to investigate how these stages or motifs have been treated in later retellings, including the latest Disney film version. Apparently there is more than one Tarzan: there is a "Tarzan of the Books" trying to become a man through the encounter with books and letters; and there is a "Tarzan of the Films," which focuses more on the main character Weissmuller's athletic and sensual body and his romance with Jane.

Retelling means both recalling and interpreting, and in this chapter I pre-sent and discuss some recent Scandinavian contributions that may be said to mark a changing perspective on the Tarzan mythology: they all focus on the authors' childhood reading experiences of Tarzan. Of the four texts presented, two of them—Conny Svensson's *Tarzan i slukaråldern* (*Tarzan in the Book Devouring Age*; 1997) and Bo Green Jensen's *Det forste landskab* (*The First Landscape*; 1999)—are written by middle-aged men of varying academic back-grounds, apparently addressing their own generation, and in prose. The other two are a picture book by Torill Thorstad Hauger, *Tarzan på loftet* (*Tarzan in the Attic*; 1993), and a young adult novel by the HC Andersen Prize Winner, Tormod Haugen, titled *Skriket fra jungelen* (*The Cry from the Jungle*; 1989).

Reconstructing a childhood reading experience, whether it is in fiction or nonfiction, proves to be as risky as children's literature itself: our pictures (of the pictures) of the past are, at the same time, responding to current pictures or constructions and aspirations, for childhood and for reading, as well as for gender. Can these texts be said to reflect a changing perspective on the question of reading and gender? What sort of "socially oriented metanarratives" [John Stephen's term (Stephens and McCallum 1998)] might they convey?

At first, a personal confession: I hardly read Tarzan at all as a young boy. I was raised in a religious home where popular fiction, comic strips, and films were not altogether forbidden, but at least kept out of reach, because spending money on such things was considered a waste. However, I did read some books, especially biographies, on so-called great men and women, and one repeated message from these books was the importance of reading for success in later life. My heroes all grew up in very modest circumstances, they had hard working days, but late at night, in a tiny little room in the attic, from the light of a candle, they finally satisfied their hunger for THE BOOK.

This must have made me sensitive to this particular motif in children's books, and I have tried to find different explanations for its prevalence. One is very obvious: why shouldn't authors and publishers—and critics—use every opportunity to add symbolic value to the act of reading? However, the prevalence of the motif also tells me something about the close link between literacy and modernity. In the case of the biographies of great men and women, it becomes evident: they all play the role as forerunners of human progress, in politics as well as in science.

In my still ongoing project on boys' books, I have been seeking alternative explanations for their great popularity—trying to look beyond the adventure and excitement in the stories themselves. One possible explanation struck me when I came across an advertisement for boys' books in a Danish scout magazine *(Spejderens Magasin)* from the late 1920s. It pictures some happy young scouts on a hike, and the text below reminds the scout boys not to forget to bring a book along in their rucksacks! Thus, physical or real-life adventures in the woods were not enough—you had to experience it in writing as well. The value of literacy is propagated in metanarratives not only in biographies, but in adventure stories as well, and this is where Tarzan comes in.

TARZAN'S HEROIC STRUGGLE WITH THE ALPHABET

This illustration (from the first Norwegian edition of *Tarzan Lord of the Apes*, 1930) bears the subtext: "In the middle of the book he found his old enemy Sabor" [author's translation]. Tarzan acquired literacy on his own, even though he was unfamiliar with human speech. In the original first edition of Burroughs's novel, this scene is orchestrated in this way:

Squatting upon his haunches on the table top in the cabin his father had built—this smooth, brown, naked little body bent over the book which rested in his strong slender hands, and his great shock of long, black hair falling about his well-shaped head and

Midt inne i boken fant han sin gamle fiende Sabor.

Tarzan apenes konge (1930). Published by Windju Simonsens Forlag

bright, intelligent eyes—Tarzan of the apes, little primitive man, presented a picture filled, at once, with pathos and with promise—an allegorical figure of the primordial groping through the black night of ignorance toward the light of learning. (Burroughs [1914] 1990: 67)

As years go by, the civilizing effect of letters becomes more and more underlined:

Tarzan of the Apes lived on in his wild jungle existence with little change for several years, only that he grew stronger and wiser, and learned from his books more and more of the strange worlds that lay somewhere outside his primeval forest. (Burroughs [1914] 1990: 85)

Literacy, in Burroughs's case, evidently means more than a bright future. The entire scene depicted in this illustration makes some very concrete links to the past (see the skeletons in the picture) and points to the fact that heritage is the key to becoming a (hu)man. The most important text Tarzan learns to read is his father's diary (written in French, another great challenge to Tarzan's reading skills).

CONNY SVENSSON: *TARZAN I SLUKARÅLDERN* (*TARZAN IN THE BOOK DEVOURING AGE*), 1997

As I was working with the theme of literacy in boys' books, and in the Tarzan story in particular, I came across a very interesting book in which a Swedish Professor in Comparative Literature, Conny Svensson, reflects upon his childhood reading in a dialogic form. As the author says: "The goal is to understand what once attracted the boy, while scrutinizing the texts historically with the professional literary competence acquired in later years" (Svensson 1997: 202). He modestly calls the result "a mixture of literary criticism and autobiographical essayism that also contributes to the slender history of literary reception in Sweden" (ibid.). Svensson also comments on a large number of books and magazines, many of them not part of canonic children's literature, and the comment on Tarzan is summarized this way:

My acquaintance with Tarzan was made on the screen, in a comic, but first and foremost in Edgar Rice Burroughs's novels. Even in early days books in my eyes were superior to any other medium and thus the written version was the most important. Here I was fascinated by the hero's hard way of learning, how he taught himself to read from the books left him by his deceased parents. I could identify, not so much with the lion-slaying son of the apes, but more with the diligent schoolboy of the wilderness, deprived of his teachers. (Svensson 1997: 205)

What is being described in this excerpt is a boy-reader responding relevantly to "an extraordinary piece of book-reading propaganda" (Svensson 1997: 53 [author's translation])—but what can you expect from a literary critic?

BO GREEN JENSEN: "HANDYRET TARZAN" ("TARZAN THE MALE ANIMAL"), IN *DET FORSTE LANDSKAB* (*THE FIRST LANDSCAPE*), 1999

"For my own part I can wrinkle my nose as much as I want, but I shall never forget my father's entranced reading from *Tarzan and the Golden Lion*" (Green Jensen 1999: 250 [author's translation]). Green Jensen expresses a clearer distance between his past and present reading of Tarzan. However,

Conny Svensson: *Tarzan i slukaråldern*, 1997. Published by Rabin Prisma. Courtesy of Pan Agency
Rabin and Sjvgren/Tiden

like Conny Svensson, his defense is built on a return to the first novel, *Tarzan of the Apes*, and in the original version:

From the beginning, it was a piece of conscious and deliberate escapism, quite in tune with the growing distaste/uneasiness with civilization in the beginning of the last century. In fact *Tarzan of the Apes* is not much of a boy's book, it aims at young men, and it is rather offering an outline of a myth of maleness like the one Ian Flemming created with his Bond-figure half a century later. You read it with the same feeling of melancholy sadness. It's just about becoming too late to take Tarzan seriously, but with Burroughs's original first version in your hands it's well possible to give it a try. (Green Jensen 1999: 250 [author's translation])

Green Jensen's Tarzan is "no swaggering brutal male, but a romantic hero in the last Eden, a man living in harmony with nature, seeking metaphysical

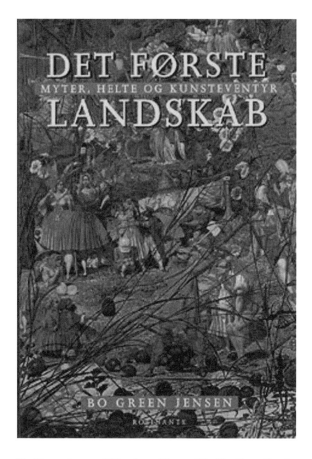

Bo Green Jensen: "Handyret Tarzan," in *Det Forste Landskab*, 1999. Harvey Macaulay illustrator. Published by and
courtesy of Rosinante.

insights in his own way" (Green Jensen 1999: 249 [author's translation]). It's
a paradox, however, that this interpretation has been best taken care of—
according to Green Jensen, and I tend to agree with him—in one of the last
film versions, Hugh Hudson's neo-romantic *Greystoke—The Legend of Tarzan,
Lord of the Apes* from 1984, with the French actor Christophe Lambert playing
Tarzan. Green Jensen is not commenting on the language and literacy theme,
although Hudson's film takes good care of that part, which is more than is
usual in film versions.

   Green Jensen—and Hugh Hudson—seem to interpret Burroughs as if the
conflict between civilization and nature is a question of liberating yourself
from a restricted world of conventions and narrow-mindedness. This, in my
opinion, is to overlook the literary tradition that after all has set its mark on

Burroughs's first novel—the structure of the *Bildungsroman*, describing a civilizing process of a young man. Although Burroughs's project is undermined
by his own irony and doubts, his text seems to suit deconstructionist inter-
preters. Still the "Freedom in the Jungle" theme is definitely there and this
brings us to a third recalling of Tarzan, *Skriket fra jungelen* (*The Cry from the
Jungle*; 1989), a young adult novel written by Tormod Haugen.

TORMOD HAUGEN: *SKRIKET FRA JUNGELEN*
(*THE CRY FROM THE JUNGLE*), 1989

Haugen's novel of 400 pages is very complex and my brief comments will
hardly do it justice. As one can see from the cover, he draws heavily on the
Tarzan mythology: there is the contrast between urban life and the jungle,
and in many ways the author seems to refer to the neo-romantic dreams of
the previously mentioned film tradition (including Disney). On the other
hand, Haugen's intertextual play includes many other texts, and at the heart
of the novel is found the same theme as in many other Haugen books: the
betrayal of childhood in modern society, where lonely children have to find
a way of coping with the world on their own: maturity belongs to children,

Tormod Haugen: *Skriket fra jungelen*, 1989. Published by Aschehoug. Courtesy of
Gyldendal.

not to adults. The Jungle threatens society, but offers a shelter for the home-less and good. However, there is also a more subtle intertextual play with the Tarzan of the books—on the very first pages of the novel, Miki (Mikael), the boy hero of the novel, is with his father. The atmosphere is somehow threat-ening when Miki senses a tiger creeping on the floor. Father and son go up to the attic, a room with much the same atmosphere as Tarzan's cabin, full of relics. Like Tarzan, Miki's father opens an old wooden chest: "It was like opening a treasure chest. Mikael kept his breath. For a long time he and his father just stood there, looking into the chest, at the resting books, their sparkling spines" (Haugen 1989: 7).

Finally, his father picks up a book, *The Son of Tarzan*, and starts to read. The scene ends with Miki becoming conscious of his mission: "to live dangerously and defy the dangers of the jungle, and see to that justice be done" (Haugen 1989: 10). As I interpret this scene—on the background of Haugen's other books—it is one of few where father and son meet in a very intimate relation. In addition, I do not think the circumstances are accidental: the father is reading his boyhood favorites to his son and demonstrates both the fascination with books and reading, but also the possibility of a close relationship between father and son in what has been called the fatherless society. Haugen is, in a way, creating a myth of maleness very much in the spirit of Burroughs's first novel, combining a heroic mission with reflective literacy. I shall return to this in my final conclusion, but first we need to make a short visit to another meeting with Tarzan in an attic, and this time the reader is a young girl.

TORILL THORSTAD HAUGER: *TARZAN PÅ LOFTET (TARZAN IN THE ATTIC)*, 1993

The first-person narrator in this story confesses that she was a bookworm at the age of six. Here the "book-reading propaganda" follows the conven-tional pattern of tasty forbidden fruit: the father warns: "If you read too long at night, you'll have bad dreams and wet your bed." A younger male, who makes the young girl's heart beat, gives her the advice to drop her silly girls' books and lends her *Tarzan of the Apes* instead. Shivering, she looks at the picture of the muscular, almost naked man: "Good Lord, how handsome he was!" (Hauger 1993: 7). The retelling of Tarzan sums up all his big fights with superior animals. No mirror scenes, no books:

For a long time Tarzan believed he belonged to the apes, but one day he discovered some white people stranded on the coast of Africa. One of them was Jane. Tarzan fell in love. He protected Jane against wild animals and fetched her juicy fruits from the trees. And he kissed her. I dreamt I was Jane. (Hauger 1993: 9 [author's translation])

The reading goes on for a week. Tarzan takes the girl with him to the attic that has now turned into a big jungle with frightening animals. They greet

Torill Thorstad Hauger: *Tarzan på loftet*, 1993. Published by N. V. Damm & Sön. Courtesy of Torill Thorstad Hauger.

Sabor the lion, with great respect, and get a ride on Tantor the elephant. As it turns out, however, Tarzan also has a mission: he liberates some slaves, before he disappears with the book. Johannes, her boyfriend turns up: "Nice book wasn't it?" Her heart beats violently. "Next time I'll bring you another one," he said, and sneezed thrice, "It's called *The Return of Tarzan*" (Hauger 1993: 27).

It should be mentioned that this book came in a series of four, in which the Norwegian publisher N. V. Damm & Sön asked four authors to revisit books of their childhood. As can be seen from the drawings and the text, this retelling by Hauger is not free of irony and I think the way in which the girl is distancing herself from overromantic girl's books, and at the same time is converting the boy's book into a girl's romance, is done deliberately. In many ways, this is what Disney has done with their recent Tarzan film. The politically correct liberation of slaves could likewise find a parallel in the Disney movie, which also depicts an Africa without black Africans.

CONCLUSION

Reconstructing a childhood reading experience, whether it is in fiction or nonfiction, is risky, because pictures of the past tend to merge with pictures of the present, as in this case our aspirations for childhood, for reading, as well as for the issue of gender. I am not saying we are "falsifying" our past; on the contrary, I do not think children's literature and mainstream literature would communicate without this intuitive merging of the past with the present. However, we evidently experience very different results. Conny Svensson (1997), the Swedish professor, is conscious of belonging to a generation that experienced a childhood where it was natural to rely on books and periodicals for information as well as for entertainment. Perhaps that is also the reason why he is so reluctant to give credit to or to recognize the Tarzan of the Films in his celebration of the value of literacy. On the other hand, Bo Green Jensen's (1999) memory is more balanced between the Tarzan of the books and the Tarzan of the films. However, both seem to demonstrate a more tolerant attitude toward the old muscular male. When they do so, it is because they return to Burroughs's first novel and identify less with most of the sequels. Whether this is legitimate can, of course, be discussed.

As for the two recallings in *fiction*, I think Tormod Haugen (1989) has utilized the Tarzan mythology in a fair manner. He is very much in line with Burroughs's ambivalence toward civilization, Tarzan's quest for the father, and the attempt to restore a maleness that combines chivalry, courage, and caring. I feel more uneasy about Torill Thorstad Hauger (1993), although her self-irony is written between the lines of both the text and her own illustrations. What is her message to the young reader—what values are at stake? The value of reading? Yes, definitely. Political correctness? That too. But what of the gender question? In many ways, the changing perspective is as far from Burroughs as in the case of the recent Disney film: the romance of Tarzan and Jane foreshadows everything. Evidently, the author is recalling a young girl reader's experience of Tarzan from the 1950s that is consistent with the gendering of the time. There is a paradox, however, in the fact that the young girl is referred to as looking for an alternative to silly romantic girls' books, but then reads Tarzan in the same overromantic tradition. Such paradoxes, however, often occur in fiction, and Hauger may be said to demonstrate the very fact that you cannot always control your own story—because both present and past affect your reading memory.

BIBLIOGRAPHY

Borberg, Chr., U. Braunig, and T. Weinreich. 1980. *Tarzan. Myterne. Romanerne. Filmene. Tegneserierne (Tarzan. The Myths. Novels. Films. Comics.)*. Copenhagen: Borgen Forlag.

Burroughs, Edgar R. [1914] 1990. *Tarzan of the Apes.* Reprint, New York: Penguin.

Burroughs, Edgar R. 1930. *Tarzan apenes konge (Tarzan lord of the apes)*, Norwegian trans. Johan Saastad. Oslo: Windju Simonsens Forlag.

Green Jensen, Bo. 1999. "Handyret Tarzan" ("Tarzan the Male Animal"). In *Det Første Landskab (The First Landscape)*. Copenhagen: Rosinante.

Greystoke— The Legend of Tarzan, Lord of the Apes. 1984. Film directed by Hugh Hudson. Warner Bros.

Haugen, Tormod. 1989. *Skriket fra jungelen (The cry from the jungle)*. Oslo: Aschehoug.

Hauger, Torill Thorstad. 1993. *Tarzan på loftet (Tarzan in the attic)*. Oslo: N. V. Damm & Sön.

Morton, Walt. 1993. "Tracking the Sign of Tarzan: Trans-Media Representations of a Pop-Culture Icon." In *You Tarzan. Masculinity, Movies and Men*, ed. Pat Kirkham and Janet Thumim, 106–26. London: Lawrence & Wishart.

Romören, Rolf. 2001–2002. "The Light of Knowledge—in the Midst of the Jungle: How Tarzan Became a Man." *CREArTA: Journal of the Centre for Research and Education in the Arts* 2 (2).

Stephens, John, and Robyn McCallum. 1998. *Retelling Stories, Framing Culture: Traditional Story and Metanarratives in Children's Literature*. New York: Garland.

Svensson, Conny. 1997. *Tarzan i slukaråldern (Tarzan in the book devouring age)*. Stockholm: Rabén Prisma.

Tarzan. 1999. Animated film, directed by Chris Buck and Kevin Lima. Walt Disney.

CHAPTER 13

Spell-Binding Dahl: Considering Roald Dahl's Fantasy

Eileen Donaldson

Literature of the fantastic has been claimed as "transcending reality," escaping the human condition and constructing superior alternate worlds. From W. H. Auden, C. S. Lewis and J.R.R. Tolkien, this notion of fantasy literature as fulfilling a desire for a better, more complete, unified reality has come to dominate readings of the fantastic. (Jackson 1981: 2)

Roald Dahl's literature for children lends itself particularly well to the kind of reading that Jackson suggests has become popular in readings of fantasy; he enables his readers to transcend their respective realities through the use of the fantastic mechanisms that he writes into his books. In this way, Dahl's readers may embrace, at the very least, the illusion of a unified world. Roald Dahl concentrates on the dynamic of the dysfunctional family and the child who is at the mercy of this particular societal vice. The worlds in which he places his young characters are lonely, frightening, and often operate through relationships that have cruelty at their base. Dahl does not, however, leave his characters stranded. He injects magic into their worlds and it is inevitably through this spell weaving that Dahl binds the children into new, loving familial relationships. This is most obviously at work in the lives of the children in *Matilda* (1988), *James and the Giant Peach* (1995), *The BFG* (1982), and *The Witches* (1983).

I would suggest that it is because of this—Dahl's emphasis on the reintegration of his characters into loving, normal familial setups and hence into healthy society—that he challenges Jackson's (1981) ultimate conclusion that all fantasy is merely escapist and, hence, bad. Because Dahl concentrates on the possibilities that fantasy can bring to the "real" world, his fantasy does not necessarily encourage escapism but rather that satisfaction of the "desire for a better, more complete, unified reality" (Jackson 1981: 2).

The fact that Dahl explores this particular relationship (i.e., the relationship between parent and child) is interesting for two reasons: Dahl's own family history and the psychological stage of development of his readers. Dahl is able to write with insight into the orphaned child because of the personal experience of confusion and loss that marked the history of his own family life. Rosemary Jackson writes that,

Like any other text, a literary fantasy is produced within, and determined by, its social context. Though it might struggle against the limits of this context, often being articulated upon that very struggle, it cannot be understood in isolation from it. The forms taken by any fantastic text are determined by a number of forces, which intersect and interact in different ways in each individual work. Recognition of these forces involves placing authors in relation to historical, social, economic, political and sexual determinants. (Jackson 1981: 3)

Dahl's literary fantasies were created within the social context in which Dahl found himself having to survive; there is a very obvious intrusion of personal experiences into his writing of literature for children. Dahl's fantasy cannot be separated from the struggle that precipitated its inception; his struggle has formed the crux of his fantasy and we must, therefore, pay particular attention to that world that created both Dahl and, later, his stories.

Roald Dahl was born to Harold and Sophie Dahl in 1916, a child of his father's second marriage. When he was four, his elder sister, Astri, died of pneumonia and within the space of a month, his father followed suit. Dahl describes this event in simple terms:

Astri was far and away my father's favourite. He adored her and her sudden death left him literally speechless for days afterwards. He was so overwhelmed with grief that when he himself went down with pneumonia a month or so afterwards, he did not much care whether he lived or died. My father refused to fight. He was thinking, I am quite sure, of his beloved daughter and was wanting to join her in heaven. So he died. (Dahl 1984: 20)

The effect this must have had on a young Dahl is great; merely the change in the familial dynamic would have been enough to instill a fear of change in the child, as well as an acknowledgment of death and the instability of the world around him. Kristine Howard (2000), however, further suggests that Dahl suffered from feelings of parental rejection, having had his father choose to die to be with the favored child rather than considering his young son. This is a provocative statement that ties in with Dahl's young characters, who are certainly victims of rejection by their caregivers.

Added to this emotional aspect, the practical circumstances with which the

Dahl family had to cope after the death of the father were not easy, and would also have had serious repercussions on Dahl's formation. Dahl writes in *Boy* (1984: 21) that,

My mother had now lost a daughter and a husband all in the space of a few weeks. Heaven knows what it must have felt like to be hit with a double catastrophe like this. Here she was, a young Norwegian in a foreign land, suddenly having to face all alone the very gravest problems and responsibilities. She had five children to look after, three of her own and two by her husband's first wife, and, to make matters worse, she herself was expecting another baby in two months' time.

Needless to say, Roald Dahl, although he seems to have worshipped his mother, and she him, could not have had the attention required by a child of that age. He certainly could not have had enough to allay the fears of abandonment prevalent in children at that age, and that would have been exacerbated in Dahl's case by the early death of his father.

As well as this, circumstances at the time necessitated Dahl's being sent away to school from the age of six. He suffered terribly from homesickness. This, too, only strengthened Dahl's recognition of the instability of the family unit; we begin to see why this theme pervades most of his writing. Dahl's experiences at school did, however, introduce a new dimension to his comprehension of the unstable family unit: in the place of his loving mother, Dahl now had grotesque authoritarian figures as his primary caregivers. Howard (2002: 1) writes,

A key theme in Dahl's novels is the use of violence and cruelty by authority figures on the weak. Dahl generally depicts at least one authority in each story as incredibly cruel, sadistic and bigoted. This is a direct reflection of his experiences as a child attending boarding schools in England.

Julia Round (2002: 2) has also commented on this point. She writes,

It has often been observed that Dahl's authoritarian characters (are) inspired by his school days at Llandaff Cathedral School and Repton. Dahl often suffered systematic caning and fascistic discipline: one notable figure would be his headmaster at Repton, who administered "the most vicious beatings to the boys under his care" (Dahl 1984: 29) and yet later became Archbishop of Canterbury. Dahl saw something deeply wrong with this authority, where sheer cruelty was hidden behind a mask of Christian virtues.

Examples of these cruel characters abound in Dahl's fiction: Miss Trunchbull in *Matilda* (1988) and Aunts Spiker and Sponge in *James and the Giant Peach* (1995), as well as the witches in *The Witches* (1983).

I do not intend to pose the argument that Roald Dahl was a traumatized child. However, I do believe that his experiences as a child engendered in him an understanding of the unspoken fears of childhood: the fear of abandonment or rejection by the primary caregiver and the helpless dependency on adults for care and the satisfaction of practical needs. Jackson says that, "Fantasy characteristically attempts to compensate for that which is experienced as absence and loss" (Jackson 1981: 3). Dahl's fantasy does this. Dahl explores that which he himself experienced as loss and absence, and this is a lack to which many of his readers can relate.

The bulk of Dahl's readers are between the ages of 6 and 12, within the developmental stage of middle childhood; this is important to Dahl's exploration of the dysfunctional family. Dahl presents families in which the children are rejected or mistreated *(James and the Giant Peach, Matilda)* or in which the parents are completely absent *(The Witches, The BFG)*. These situations represent the most profound fear of middle childhood: the fear of the death of a parent.

The parent plays a pivotal role during this stage of a child's development; the child now begins to enter the larger social world around him or her and, depending on the relationship with the parent, the child will approach the world in varying manners. If the parent is either abusive or absent, the child will experience extreme difficulty in social relationships and in the development of self-esteem. This invariably causes problems well into adulthood. It is thus imperative that the child has some warm, caring, and stable relationship with an adult through whom he or she is guided into the world at large.

In his writing for children, Dahl may create a situation in which the child is the victim of a pathological relationship, but he does not leave this as the ultimate destiny of any of his characters. The child is never left at the mercy of cruelty, but finds a place where he or she is loved. This is obviously gratifying for the children who read Dahl's books. Dahl's stories are also particularly seductive in this stage of childhood for another reason. Because the children in this stage recognize their dependency on the adults in their lives, and thus the ease with which they become the victims of these adults' whims, there is a desperate need to gain some control of their own worlds. This is physically impossible in the real world in which the readers live, but for Dahl's characters, there is the means by which they are able to take control of their lives. Dahl places in the paths of each of his characters some form of magic that they, as children, are able to wield successfully and thus use to improve their situations. Dahl, therefore, both manifests the fears of his young readers and enables them to resolve their fears, vicariously, through the self-willed actions of the fictional characters.

The fact that Dahl uses magic through which to empower his readers to dissolve the shadows around them is a stroke of sorcerous genius. Dahl does not create completely fantastic worlds into which his readers can escape, the likes of Wonderland or Narnia. Instead, he roots his stories very firmly in the real worlds of the middle to lower classes, which his young readers have experienced and can easily recognize. When he then introduces his quirky brand of spell weaving into this otherwise mundane setting, Dahl makes it seem all the more possible. Magic becomes a viable option in the real world in which his readers live, and this lends his optimistic message even more power. Readers can take this "real" magic with them and make it a part of the world with which they interact, so that life is not as ordinary as it was beforehand.

As Rosemary Jackson (1981: 1) writes, "Fantasy is not to do with inventing another non-human world: it is not transcendental. It has to do with inverting the elements of this world, re-combining its constitutive features in new relations to produce something strange, unfamiliar and apparently new." Because Dahl does this, the fantasy that he creates is potent because it is seductively "real" and possible. Although each of the novels discussed below is unique, they do share the same exploration of the dysfunctional family and miraculous healing through magic.

In *James and the Giant Peach* (1995: 1), Dahl tells us that "until he was four years old, James Henry Trotter had a happy life. He lived peacefully with his mother and father"; this was before his parents were eaten by a marauding rhinoceros. It is interesting to note that the children in Dahl's novels are very young, much the same age as Dahl was when he lost his own father. After the loss of his parents, James finds himself alone and frightened in a vast, unfriendly world (Dahl 1995: 1). He is sent to live with replacement caregivers, his Aunts Spiker and Sponge, who commit all manner of atrocities against our small protagonist: "right from the beginning [they beat] poor James for no reason at all" (2) and they never called him by his real name, but always referred to him as "you disgusting little beast" or "you filthy nuisance" (2). James is given no toys, and no other children are allowed to play with him.

Dahl describes the deprivation that James suffers in terms of things to which young readers will be able to relate. Dahl has no qualms about likening James's new existence to that of a "prison cell" (1995: 8) and his emotive description of James's state of mind leaves the reader with no option but to align themselves with the sad protagonist. Dahl writes, "as time went on, [James] became sadder and sadder, and more and more lonely, and he used to spend hours every day standing at the bottom of the garden gazing wistfully at the lovely but forbidden world" (10–11).

Dahl takes care to juxtapose the worlds of Spiker and Sponge and the magic to come. His vivid descriptions of the Aunts and their actions also serve to align the readers unequivocally with James and there can be no argument that this is a dysfunctional familial setup: "Aunt Sponge had small piggy eyes, a sunken mouth and one of those flabby white faces that looked exactly as though it had been boiled. She was like a great white soggy overboiled cabbage. Aunt Spiker was lean and tall and bony. She had a screeching voice and long wet narrow lips. And there they sat, those two ghastly hags, sipping their drinks and every now and again screaming at James to chop faster and faster" (12). James works away as the Aunts primp and preen and he thinks about what other luckier children might be doing and "great tears [begin] oozing out of [his] eyes and rolling down his cheeks" (12). When his Aunts notice that James is crying, they do not offer him comfort or stop to help him; instead, they yell, "Stop that immediately and get on with your work, you nasty little beast!" (15). James effectively has no family; he is despised and, being young, is utterly defenseless.

There is no way to remedy this situation but to introduce magic; even those who are firm believers in the good of social workers must admit that a little magic is infinitely preferable and would be far more effective in any situation of this kind. Directly after Aunt Spiker's last nasty comment, James hides at the bottom of the garden where he encounters a strange little man. The man approaches James and offers a bag to him, " 'Take a look, my dear,' he said, opening the bag and tilting it towards James" (17). This is the first time in the book that James is spoken to in a relatively tender tone. The magic infiltrates James's world.

Inside [the bag] James could see a mass of tiny green things that looked like little stones or crystals, each one about the size of a grain of rice. They were extraordinarily beautiful, and there was a strange brightness about them, a sort of luminous quality that made them glow and sparkle in the most wonderful way. (17–18)

This description already smacks of heady magic but, for those children not yet able to read the signs, Dahl tells us exactly what these strange seeds of James's new life are:

Crocodile tongues! One thousand long slimy crocodile tongues boiled up in the skull of a witch for twenty days and nights with the eyeballs of a lizard! Add the fingers of a young monkey, the gizzard of a pig, the beak of a green parrot, the juice of a porcupine and three spoonfulls of sugar. Stew for a week and let the moon do the rest! (18)

The little man tells James that "marvellous things will start to happen to [him], fabulous, unbelievable things" and "[he] will never be miserable again in [his] life" (19).

James spills the crocodile tongues, which duly worm their way into the ground, into the roots of the dead peach tree in the Aunts' garden, and finally result in the phenomenal peach. James is, in the ensuing excitement, shouted at, abused, and kicked out of the house at night with no supper. In the garden, he discovers a hole in the peach and tunnels his way up into the now enormous fruit. When the Aunts discover he is missing, they are relieved because they reason that he may be missing due to an accidental death on his part. Dahl, never one to let this kind of malice go unpunished, squashes the Aunts to death when the peach falls from the tree.

Although the evil caregivers are vanquished through the power of the magical fruit, Dahl is not merely satisfied to leave James free of them. He realizes the importance of positive familial relationships. Therefore, in the peach,

James discovers new friends and a loving family composed of huge insects. Through the magic that Dahl weaves into his life, James finds a home and friends who care for him; "James Henry Trotter, who once, if you remember, had been the saddest and loneliest little boy that you could find, now had all the friends and playmates in the world" (156). In addition, Dahl invites his readers to join James; James has a little house (made from the huge peach pit) in Central Park and he invites those who have read his story to pop in and visit him. Dahl offers what he has given to James to his readers, a home. This is characteristic of Dahl, who brings fantasy into the real world for his readers, and once again refutes Jackson's declaration that fantasy can only lead to the alienation of the reader from the real world.

Unlike James, in *The BFG* (1982) we encounter Sophie, a little girl who has never had parents. She lives in an orphanage and is kidnapped by the BFG: the Big Friendly Giant. The magical reconstruction of Sophie's family unit comes about because she is a child, and therefore able to believe in the BFG and the magic he wields. Dahl uses dreams as magic in this novel. Jackson (1981: 8) writes that, "like dreams, with which they have many similarities, literary fantasies are made up of many elements combined, and are inevitably determined by the range of those constitutive elements available to the author/dreamer." Thus, dreams in this novel become the means through which Sophie and the BFG transform their worlds; they literally recombine the elements of different dreams in order to create a new entity and, through it, a new way of living together as a family.

Dahl, as the author, is also involved in this process of recombining mundane elements to create the fantasy through which he heals Sophie's world. In this story, Sophie befriends the BFG and they decide that it is their task to rid the earth of the scourge of man-eating giants who raid various countries around the world every night. The two protagonists work together and convince the Queen of England to aid them in their plight; she does and then allows Sophie and the BFG to live in a castle adjacent to Windsor Castle.

The Witches (1983) operates in much the same way as does *The BFG* (1982). In both of these stories, the expression of fantastic desire is predominantly one of expulsion rather than manifestation. Jackson (1981: 3–4) posits that fantasy, being the literature of desire, necessarily deals with the expression of desire. In some forms, we desire the manifestation of our longings; in *James and the Giant Peach* (1995), James longs for a family who will love him and this manifests in time. In other forms, we desire the expulsion of threat; in *The BFG*, Sophie and the BFG desire the expulsion of the threatening giants from society. The reconstruction of the family unit seems almost a by-product of the main dynamic of the novel, which is to expel the evil. The same is true of *The Witches;* the main plot deals with the vanquishing of the witches of the world who seek to destroy children the world over. However, the family unit receives some interesting reconstruction along the way.

In *The Witches*, Dahl does not present us with a child who is deprived of a loving caregiver. Although the little boy's parents are dead—he was present when they were killed in a car accident and he tells us that "[he] still gets shivers when [he] thinks about it" (Dahl 1983: 13)—he has a very close relationship with his grandmother. She, however, is very old and the threat of death is real.

This book seems to be the closest to Dahl's own life in that he spins much of the anxiety and the growing up of his own younger years into it; the grandmother is very old and when she catches pneumonia, there is the panic of memory tacked onto it. In *Boy*, Dahl describes his own grandmother's bout of pneumonia and the echoes in *The Witches* are remarkable. (Perhaps it is also interesting that this particular character does not have a name of his own; he could just as easily be named Roald.) In *The Witches*, the boy says,

The doctor explained to me that pneumonia is not normally a dangerous illness nowadays because of penicillin, but when a person is more than eighty years old, as my grandmother was, then it is very dangerous indeed. He said he didn't even dare to move her to the hospital in her condition, so she stayed in her bedroom and I hung about outside the door while oxygen cylinders and all sorts of frightening things were taken in to her. (48)

The little boy is made vividly aware of the fact that his grandmother does not have much time left. This situation seems more reminiscent of the dysfunction with which Dahl himself had to live than those of the other families encountered in his other books.

When the grandmother takes a holiday to recuperate, she and her grandson encounter the witches. He is able to recognize them and mask his presence through his refraining from the act of bathing, but this does not save him and he is turned into a mouse through the Grand High Witch's Delayed Action Mouse Maker. This is the magic Dahl employs in this case: "proper" spell weaving by real witches.

Through the convenience of his new mouse body, however, the grandson is able to dose all the witches with a potion and rid England of all her witches. The expulsion of evil occurs. However, in view of the reconstruction of a healthy family unit through magic, there is an interesting repercussion of the boy's mouse body. He is no longer in any danger of outliving his grandmother. The threat of death and loneliness in the future has been neutralized.

"How long does a mouse-person live, Grandmamma?"

"A mouse person will almost certainly live for about three times as long as any ordinary mouse," my grandmother said. "About nine years."

"Good!" I cried. "That's great! It's the best news I've ever had!"

"Why do you say that?" she asked, surprised.

"Because I would never want to live longer than you," I said. "I couldn't stand being looked after by anybody else."

There was a short silence. She had a way of fondling me behind the ears with the tip of one finger.

It felt lovely.

"How old are you, Grandmamma?" I asked.

"I'm eighty-six," she said.

"Will you live another eight or nine years?"

"I might," she said. "With a bit of luck."

"You've got to," I said. "Because by then I'll be a very old mouse and you'll be a very old grandmother and soon after that, we'll both die together."

"That would be perfect," she said. (196)

In the book *Matilda* (1988), a return to the dynamic of *James and the Giant Peach* (1995) is seen. Matilda's family is very obviously dysfunctional.

Occasionally one comes across parents who show no interest at all in their children. Mr and Mrs Wormwood were two such parents. They had a son called Michael and a daughter called Matilda, and the parents looked upon Matilda in particular as nothing more than a scab. A scab is something you have to put up with until the time comes when you can pick it off and flick it away. Mr and Mrs Wormwood looked forward enormously to the time when they could pick their little daughter off and flick her away, preferably into the next county or even further than that. (Dahl 1988: 10)

Dahl writes Matilda into a family who dislikes her and will never be able to give her the care she desperately needs. Her father is dishonest, arrogant, and stupid and brushes his daughter aside with little thought; he constantly tells her she is stupid and insignificant, " 'You're an ignorant little twit,' the father said. His speech was never very delicate and Matilda was used to it" (22). Matilda's mother is a useless, powdery, greasy housewife who fawns over her husband to the detriment of her children. Matilda is also the first of Dahl's characters who encounters the authoritarian figures of the English school system, in the figure of Miss Trunchbull. Matilda thus has two fronts on which she is under attack, school and home. Dahl must allow her some form of self-defense.

Dahl gives Matilda a potent form of magic; her intellectual capacity is so great that she finds she can wield it as a physical force. Matilda becomes adept at telekinesis. She uses this gift to trap the dishonest Miss Trunchbull, which results in the restoration of Miss Honey's home to her (Miss Honey being Matilda's first form teacher). This, in turn, means that when the Wormwoods are forced to flee the country, Miss Honey is able to offer to adopt Matilda. Her parents' reaction is: "I'm in a hurry," the father said. "I've got a plane to catch. If she wants to stay, let her stay. It's fine with me" (239).

Matilda's parents don't care whether they see her again or not. At this stage, however, Dahl has transplanted Matilda so firmly into the affections of Miss Honey that this cold rejection by Matilda's parents is sought after by the reader. Like James, Matilda finds her real home through the intervention of the extraordinary into her life.

Dahl uses different forms of magic in each of the pathological familial situations in which his characters find themselves; he understands the shadow world in which most children live and, because of this, he understands that the only way in which to combat shadow is to use a means as intangible as shadow to fight it. Magic in Dahl's writing can be anything from a bizarre potion cooked in the skull of a witch to the harnessing of brain power. Because he allows his readers to equate magic with powers as diverse as these, he whispers the possibility that there might be many more kinds out there waiting to be discovered by the child who looks hard enough. One has only to take the time to look under the ordinary stones to find the magic grubs wriggling, hidden in the dirt. Dahl does not try to transcend reality; he instead offers something to his readers that will enable them to cope with the alienation and rejection they may feel in the real world in which they live. Because of this, he is a master of real magic and a true friend to the children who carry his books to school, scouts, and wherever else they may be bound.

BIBLIOGRAPHY

Dahl, R. 1982. *The BFG*. London: Puffin.
Dahl, R. 1983. *The Witches*. London: Puffin.
Dahl, R. 1984. *Boy: Tales of Childhood*. London: Puffin.
Dahl, R. 1988. *Matilda*. London: Puffin.
Dahl, R. 1995. *James and the Giant Peach*. London: Puffin.
Howard, K. 2002. Available at: http://www.roalddahlfans.com. Accessed 28 December 2001.
Jackson, R. 1981. *Fantasy: The Literature of Subversion*. London: Methuen.
Round, J. 2002. "Roald Dahl and the Creative Process: Writing from Experience." Available at: http://www.roalddahlfans.com. Accessed 28 December 2001.

CHAPTER 14

"Never Lonely, Always on the Go": The Merry-Go-Round as Kinetic Metonym, in Text and Illustration, in Tove Jansson's Short Story, "The Hemulen Who Loved Silence"[1]

Sirke Happonen

This chapter explores the spatial representation of the tension between solitude and togetherness, the individual and the others, in an illustrated short story by Tove Jansson (1962), "The Hemulen Who Loved Silence" (original title, "Hemulen som älskade tystnaden," published in a collection called *Det osynliga barnet*, [*Tales from Moominvalley*]). The idea of the merry-go-round, or carousel, is central to this narrative and also to Tove Jansson's entire production, not only because it is directly presented or referred to in several of her pictures and texts, but because it works as *kinetic metonym*. In the whirl of the merry-go-round, one is together with other people, in a definite movement with no destination, while the space between the "passengers" is fixed—they are together, moving at the same speed and in the same direction, but still alone, isolated by the monotonous distance.[2]

In this short story, the metonym of the merry-go-round has a variety of meanings. During the narrative, the merry-go-round will be destroyed, broken into pieces, rejected, rescued and collected, and finally reconstructed. The rebuilt merry-go-round, however, is significant in a different way, because its fixed, whirling flow is disrupted, enabling a more personal flow of movement and a freer way of sharing space between the protagonist and others.

The story begins with the Hemulen, the protagonist, working in a pleasure-ground (amusement park) owned by his hemulen relatives. The protagonist, however, yearns for solitude and silence and would like to be pensioned from the jangle of the pleasure-ground. He does not manage to express this desire before a great rain destroys the ground. He gets keys to an overgrown park in which he can happily start living on his own. The children have, however, collected the remains of the amusement park in front of his gate. Unwillingly, the Hemulen starts to pull the junk in and rebuilds the park, first alone and then together with the children. The new amusement park is a collage from the earlier version, and both the children and the Hemulen begin to love it. According to the Hemulen's wish, the park will, however, remain silent and accessible by children only. The Hemulen himself lives in the merry-go-round.

The merry-go-round, on which Jansson's story pivots, imbricates the ideas of self, individuality, and subjectivity, central to the modern tradition of philosophical and psychological studies that more recently have been questioned by poststructural scholars such as Althusser, Lacan, and Foucault. In this story, the first phase is directed toward the modernistic self and identity as a core that is both unique and essential (Culler [1997] 2000: 104–5). The protagonist steps out of the role into which he has been interpellated by his relatives and starts to look for his own identity in a park of solitude surrounded by high walls.[3]

The next phase of the story involves the development of a more intersubjective space: as the Hemulen reconstructs the remains of the merry-go-round in cooperation with others, there emerges a freedom for both individuality and togetherness. This second phase is closer to the idea of constructed subjectivity, and subjectivity that is not specific to the individual but arises intersubjectively—that is, in interrelationships with others—and recognizes others as subjects, not objects (McCallum 1999: 3, 20n, see also Benjamin 1995: 29–30).

How are these spaces—individual and intersubjective—constructed in this story? The sense of space is characteristic of both Jansson's texts and her pictures. She uses space to convey physical, imaginative, compositional, and metonymic meanings: the sea, forests, and islands signify actual phenomena, but also represent individuality, subjectivity, and interrelationships. This short story pivots on the *shape of the merry-go-round*, whose form and direction will undergo several changes. In this chapter, I focus briefly on four basic shapes linked with the idea of the carousel and explore how these "moving" shapes are constructed by various viewpoints and voices presented in the illustrations and the text. I draw on Bakhtin's (1981) notion that dialogic construction of subjectivity has its analogue in the polyphonic form of the novel. Bakhtin sees the novel as an inherently many-voiced narrative form, in which the internal dialogism of the prose discourse grows out of a stratified language (ibid.: 315, 324–26). Thus, the representation of intersubjectivity depends on the dialogic orientation of focalizing and narrational positions, and multivoiced narratives use two or more character focalizers or narrators (see McCallum 1999: 25, 23).

Tove Jansson's Moomin books, written between the 1940s and 1970s, are not structurally polyphonic. For instance, in comparison to many of the contemporary children's novels and picture books that apply narrative strategies such as metafiction and multiple narrators, Moomin books are not overtly many-voiced narratives. In a Bakhtinian sense, nevertheless, they convey a multiplicity of voices because they imply a variety of *ideologues* by means of the various characters living in Moominvalley. Each species living in this fantasy world represents its own "ideological discourse" or "language world view" (Bakhtin 1981: 332–33). Further, as Robyn McCallum (1999) argues, polyphony can be more or less implicit. I believe that discussing this particular short story as an "implicitly multivoiced" narrative can offer a framework to look at both narrative and pictorial strategies that express the ideas of individuality and subjectivity.

In Jansson's books, these ideas are actually spatial representations, and are constructed by focalization, viewpoint, and the use of frame and distance. In various parts of the narrative, the idea of the merry-go-round as an interpersonal space is structured by voices and views that are expressions of character thought, speech, and worldview. It is a space constructed by narratorial ideology and positions offered for the reader/viewer.

By means of this framework, I see the story of the Hemulen structured by various tensions. First, there are thematic tensions among solipsism, interpellation, individuality, and intersubjectivity, culminating in the metonym of the merry-go-round. Second, there are tensions between various viewpoints: the protagonist's and the narrator's, the protagonist's and the other hemulens', and the protagonist's and the children's. Third, there is an ulterior tension between childhood and adult discourses, a dichotomy that arises during the reading process and results from the context of children's literature. Fourth, the tension is representational, originating from the diverse characteristics of how pictures and words convey meaning.[4]

FOUR SHAPES OF THE MERRY-GO-ROUND

Whirl: Fixed Movement between the Characters

The first shape of the merry-go-round, the whirl, expresses the unvaried interaction between the impersonal characters. It is created by voices that speak for and against its movement. The resisting voices and views are constructed in an ambivalent relation between the verbal-visual narrator and the protagonist:

He had terribly many relatives, a great lot of enormous, rollicking, talkative hemulens who went about slapping each other's backs and bursting into gigantic laughs.
    They were joint owners of a pleasure-ground, and in their spare time they blew the trombone or threw the hammer, told funny stories and frightened people generally.
    But they did it all with the best of intentions. (Jansson 1963: 78–79)[5]

The text employs a third-person narration, and despite the direct impression of a narration conveyed by an extradiegetic narrator, the focalizer here could also be the protagonist Hemulen, because the perceptual and attitudinal point of view is his (see McCallum 1999: 31, Stephens 1992a: 27). However, the ironic comment "but they did it all with the best of intentions" seems to imply the attitude of the narrator, who sympathizes with the Hemulen but has more experience and wants the audience to understand that the Hemulen's relatives are not really evil. A pause caused by presenting this sentence alone in a separate paragraph[6] might also imply the change of focalizer. A similar observation is possible in the very beginning of the story: "Once upon a time there was a hemulen who worked in a pleasure-ground, *which doesn't necessarily mean having a lot of fun*" [Jansson 1963: 78; italics added].

The story begins with an omniscient narrator perspective, but also with an immediate comment: already, the narrator expresses his or her attitude toward working in a pleasure-ground. In addition, the narrator reveals (or warns) in advance that this is not going to be a story about the funny aspect of amusement parks. With regard to the dichotomy between childhood and adult discourses, this detail is quite interesting: amusing children do not necessarily make adults happy—in fact, children's fun might be tragic for adults. The narrator announces in the very beginning that he or she is going to support the Hemulen—the adult, not the children.

The opening vignette for "The Hemulen Who Loved Silence." © Moomin Characters, Tove Jansson

The first vignette above the title of the story draws a third dimension to the narrational positions presented in this short story.[7] The illustration is a medium long shot of the protagonist Hemulen depicted from far social distance (see Kress and van Leeuwen 1996: 130–31). He gazes at the reader/ viewer directly, with his arms hanging inertly at his sides, his coat hanging loose as well. Behind him is the merry-go-round and the swarming crowd of dancing creatures with their extended limbs pointing energetically in various directions. In contrast to them, the Hemulen's posture is heavy and powerless, and lacks purpose. His gaze, however, is the only reciprocal gaze presented in the illustrations during the narrative, and considering Jansson's work in general, there are only a few gazes like this [Kress and Van Leeuwen (1996: 121–26), term this a "demand image"]. It addresses and challenges the viewer to enter an imaginary relation with the Hemulen, the subject presented in the picture. What does the Hemulen "demand" of us? The sad look might ask for empathy, but, at the same time, his body is turned away from the viewer as if he would like the viewer to maintain a distance. Perhaps he is afraid that the viewer's position is coextensive with that of the noisy and forever happy hemulens.

The voice of the hemulens as a collective that keeps the whirl going on is presented in a dialogue between the protagonist and other hemulens.

"You are lonely and have nothing to do," the other hemulens used to tell him in their friendly way.

"So it might cheer you up a bit to lend a hand and be among people."

"But I'm never lonely," the hemulen tried to explain. "I can't find time to be. There is always such a lot of people who want to cheer me up. If you don't mind, I'd like so much to. . . . "

"Splendid," the relatives said and slapped his back. "That's the thing. Never lonely, always on the go." (Jansson 1963: 78–79)

The last sentence of the dialogue, "Never lonely, always on the go," is not commented on by the narrator. Leaving the commentary out and going on with the story makes the Hemulen's viewpoint even clearer and emphasizes the tragedy (or tragicomedy) of the relationship. The voice of the hemulens is solipsistic because it responds only to itself and cannot perceive another as a separate self, and thus occupying a different subject position (see McCallum 1999: 7). The hemulens' conception of interrelationships is the merry-go-round, in which everybody can be merry and go round, wildly screaming and never meeting each other.

This nonencountering has a compressed expression in the narrator's inquit-tag following the hemulens' lines: "the other hemulens used to tell him in their friendly way" (Jansson 1963: 79). Whose voice is actually represented in the descriptive word "friendly"? It reveals the narrator's ironic attitude to the conversation between the very different characters by linking the tag simultaneously to two separate voices: to the hemulens who see themselves as being friendly, and to the opposite effect that their gesture produces in the protagonist. Further, this double meaning is paralleled in the inquit-tag: "slapped his back" (Jansson 1963: 80), which stifles the protagonist's speech and oppresses him both physically and mentally.

This ideological stance (action-based nonstop happiness) is also implied in the hemulens' visual shape. In this picture, the viewer can look at the hemulens from outside and as objects (Kress and van Leuuwen 1996: 124). However, the illustration may also convey the viewpoint of the protagonist Hemulen, and present a form of visual first-person narration (see Nikolajeva and Scott 2001: 124–32, Nodelman 1991). The Hemulen himself is not depicted in the picture and the viewer is more or less on the same level. I find it possible to consider Hemulen himself as the visual focalizer in this picture: how he sees his relatives laughing at his dream.

When depicting the laughing hemulens, the illustrator has broken the contour line to express the trembling movement caused by heavy guffawing. Slapping each other's backs might also have a connection to the hemulens' visual shape as a species living in Moominvalley: in terms of modern dance, their upper back has become curved by a constant contraction.[8]

According to the text, the laugh of the hemulens makes the protagonist Hemulen "shrink inwardly" (original, *"krympa ihop invärtes"*; Jansson 1962: 83) and thus actually take a similar posture to his relatives. This contraction, expressed now verbally, implies pain instead of laughter and joy. When we think that the original impulse for contraction is the feeling of pain in the stomach, in this story, contraction has two contradictory meanings: joy and

The relatives of the Hemulen. © Moomin Characters, Tove Jansson

pain. Interestingly, while riding a merry-go-round, it is usual to experience a painlike feeling in the stomach, and some people like it, some don't. When the Hemulen later in the story realizes that the merry-go-round might try to intrude upon his park, the text expresses that "a horrible suspicion began burrowing in his stomach." Hence, this moment condenses the bipartite, two-edged meaning that Jansson has built on the ideas of circled movement and the feelings it raises. Further, the story also includes two parallel metonyms for the merry-go-round: a barrel organ and a skating rink, both of which combine the circling movement, jangling or screeching sound, and an entertaining purpose.

Pause: Streams of Broken Merry-Go-Rounds

The second shape, pause, is the destruction of the merry-go-round, which floats away in bits and pieces. It is created by the voice of children who have lost their amusement park. This voice is actually a multimodal presentation constructed by the layout. Similar to the vehicles that are said to loosen from the whirling spin, separate, and sail away, the figures of children are depicted dispersed and separated in the double page of the book. The use of air frame—

För att säga sanningen höll regnet på i åtta veckor i ett kör och ingen hade nånsin hört om något liknande.

Nöjesfältet vissnade ner och tappade färgen som en blomma. Det sjönk ihop, bleknade, rostade, krympte — och eftersom det var byggt på sand började alltsammans småningom glida sin väg.

Berg-och-dalbanan satte sig med en suck och karusellerna gled runt runt i stora gråa pölar och åkte sakta klingande ner i de nya floderna som regnet hade grävt. Alla små ungar, knytt och skrott och homsor och mymlor och allt vad de hette satte nosen mot rutan och såg hur juli regna bort och färgen och musiken segla ifrån dem.

Spegelsalen rasade i miljoner våta skärvor och ljusröda blöta pappersrosor ur mirakelhuset simmade bort över åkrarna. Och över hela trakten steg ungarnas jämmersång.

De höll på att driva sina pappor och mammor till förtvivlan för de hade ingenting att göra och bara sörjde över det förlorade nöjesfältet.

I träden slokade vimplar och tomma ballonger, lustiga huset var fullt av gyttja och krokodilen med tre huvuden gav sig av mot havet. Två huvuden lämnade han efter sig för de var fastsatta med lim.

Hemulerna hade förfärligt roligt åt alltsammans. De stod i sina fönster och skrattade och pekade och dunkade varann i ryggen och skrek:

Titta! Där åker ridån för Arabiens Hemlighet! Där seglar dansbanan! Där sitter fem läderlappar ur skräckhuset på Filifjonkans tak! Är det inte storartat!

De beslöt med gott humör att starta en skridsko-

6

81

The suffering chorus constructed by the layout. © Moomin Characters, Tove Jansson

total absence of background—emphasizes the collective power of their grieving. The suffering chorus surrounds the text from various sides and creates an impression of emptiness and cessation. However, this is not only a "voice" in a Bakhtinian sense, but also in a Brechtian sense: for a paragraph, children are the focalizing agents in this part of the story, and, in addition, their visual presence creates a dramatic, estranging effect.

Rotation around the Self: Hemulen Framed by His Private Park—and by the Gaze of Children

The third shape of the merry-go-round is the new park of the Hemulen, which expresses individuality as a monadic space, the individuality that is later threatened and framed from the outside. Although the carousel is absent and excluded from his park, the park itself is a shape framed by a wall that goes around it, as described in the text.

When the Hemulen explores the overgrown park, he is the focalizer in the text, which is full of symbolic language traditionally connected with the ideas of the self. Already the neglected park surrounded by walls can be seen as a metaphor for the untended individuality of the Hemulen. Among the representations of the self and subjectivity, this part of the story illuminates the traditional and modern individual, and his desire for self-fulfillment.[9] This self is to be found in privacy, inside the high walls of the park. The Hemulen falls in love with his "wide and mysterious" park; he wanders all around it and gets lost, but is not worried because in this park "one could lose one's way in it and still be at home" (Jansson 1963: 89). In the new space, the self is the mysterious core to be found, and from the other hemulens, the solitary Hemulen accepts nothing more than a dinner left outside the gate.

The verbal narration describes the glittering secrecy of the Hemulen's park with the Hemulen as the focalizer and with such a beauty that the reader can do nothing but allow the Hemulen to melt into his paradise. The new space of solitude is described in concrete, physical language:

The hemulen threw himself headlong into the green, friendly silence, he made capers in it, he wallowed in it and he felt younger than he ever had before. Oh how wonderful to be old and pensioned at last, he thought. How much I like my relatives! And now I needn't even think of them. (Jansson 1963: 87)

The illustration with the Hemulen wandering in his park differs from the earlier illustrations in the sense that it has a detailed depiction of a background, whereas most of the illustrations in this story are sketchlike portraits of the characters with only an air frame. The frame has been described as the gate between the viewer's world and the world of the fantasy. In this narrative, it is interesting to see how two of the most beautiful moments—both depicting the park of silence—are framed and thus distanced from the viewer. More important than distancing, I think, is the idea of the frame giving an illusion

The Hemulen in his private park. © Moomin Characters,
Tove Jansson

of another world, which here is a paradise, implying—sadly—that this beautiful scene might be less real than the one of the laughing hemulens or the baby-sitting Hemulen. The Hemulen is depicted from a distance, it is a long shot, and the viewer peeks at him between the branches. The Hemulen looks superior, because he is situated centrally, his open posture presents a "release"—an opposite movement from the former contraction—and the negative space around him emphasizes his feeling of lightness, freedom, and strength.

Among the sketches is a draft version of this scene with the possible viewer situated at a lower angle, so that the viewer is almost swimming in the river. The shape of the Hemulen cuts the circle of the sun, which in turn surrounds him by almost a majestic halo. In the realized version, the egoistic illumination is not so underlined: the high vertical space over the Hemulen implies that there is still a lot to be explored.[10] The halo of the sun above him suggests a rotating movement, which is accentuated by the curved forms of the branches of the trees. Is this rotation an indication of the merry-go-round, or a rotation of one becoming entangled in himself while walking around his or her paradise?

In the story of the Hemulen, his happy solitude is encroached upon by a Whomper—a child figure who tinkles at his gate one morning. Remarkably, the peace is first broken by means of the layout in the double page. When turning the page after the beautiful paradise picture, the reader immediately encounters a drawing of a child figure in the upper part of the opening; in the verbal text he does not surprise the Hemulen before the next page. The dialogue between the Whomper and the Hemulen enables the reader to switch between two different subject positions:

"Go away," the hemulen called anxiously. "This is private ground. I live here."

"I know," the small whomper replied. "The hemulens sent me here with some dinner for you."

"Oh, I see, that was kind of them," the hemulen replied willingly. He unlocked the gate and took the basket from the whomper. Then he shut the gate again. *The whomper remained where he was and looked at the hemulen. There was a moment of silence.*

"And how are you getting on?" the hemulen asked impatiently. He stood *jiggling his feet* and longed to be in his park again.

"Badly," the whomper replied honestly. "We're in a bad way all of us. We who are small. We've got no pleasure-ground any more. We're just grieving."

"Oh," the hemulen said, staring at his feet. (Jansson 1963: 89–90; Jansson 1962: 87 [italics are my translation; otherwise translation is by Thomas Warburton])

The description of the Hemulen's nonverbal behavior (closing the gate and jiggling his feet impatiently) expresses for the first time the antisocial traits of the Hemulen from a more outside point of view, the Whomper and the Hemulen both presented as equal participants in the scene. The Whomper's power is in his silence, how he *looks at* the Hemulen. The narrative description "The whomper remained where he was and looked at the hemulen" marks a point where the Whomper and other children slowly start to exercise what I would call a *focalizing effect* on the Hemulen: the protagonist feels he is surrounded by the gaze of the children. A single paragraph expresses the almost horrifying presence of this gaze: "The children were sitting on the high, ragged wall around the hemulen's park. Just like grey sparrows, but quite silent" (Jansson 1962: 91 [my translation]).

From here on, the Hemulen is still the principal focalizer in the verbal text, but the illustrations present him in various actions depicted from above. He is no longer framed by impersonal walls protecting his private individuality, but from now on his new subjectivity becomes framed by the children and their wish to help both themselves and the "lonely" hemulen (all the tragedy of being well meaning!). Finally, the Hemulen cannot escape from being a hemulen. After a short monologue in which he tries to convince himself that he is pensioned and has learned to say *no*, the text relates how he, unwillingly, starts to pull the remains of the pleasure-ground—signs of his former life— that the children have collected outside his gate, into his park. The first vehicle he begins to build in the very center of his park of silence is, instead of the hermit cottage, the merry-go-round.

The illustrations depict the Hemulen reconstructing the pleasure-ground and the carousel. Now, the angle is slightly from above and could imply the children as visual focalizers, sitting up on the wall and looking at the angry Hemulen. Compared with the previous relationship between the protagonist and the other hemulens, the relationship between the protagonist and the children is more reciprocal: although the Hemulen, again, has been interpel- lated into a role he dislikes, he now has someone to whom he can address his frustration. The Hemulen's aggression is loud, and the children who sit on the wall, not allowed to help him, are his silent but supportive audience as he complains about the tragedy of his life.

This situation portrays the paradox of subjective agency: in order to have agency, one has to resist the overarching discourse and ideology, which in this case is the ideology of the merry-go-round (see Smith [1988] 1999: xxxiv– xxxv). In other words, only by means of another interpellation can the He- mulen begin to possess subjective agency, because he now can read and resist this ideology (and his interpellation into it). In the private park of silence, which represents the modern individuality—individuality that, according to Paul Smith ([1988] 1999), is always an illusion, a false impression of a free and self-determining personal organization, he cannot truly discern his agency. Also, building a new space out of the old waste cannot be achieved by a subject without a relation to other subjects—just as there is no sense of identity without interrelationships with others, which leads to the idea of intersubjectivity unfolding in the consequent phase of the Hemulen's park.

Free Flow and Reconstruction: Toward an Intersubjective Paradise

The last shape of the merry-go-round is a wild and imaginative collage, a reconstruction of ruins that is filled with interpersonal distances and individual movement. When the children jump down from the wall, they break the "frame of gaze" around the park, and start building together a space that will be a compromise between the wishes of both the children and the Hemulen. In this space, one can find numerous secret, private places or places in which one can decide to be together with others. Even the Hemulen starts slowly to give up his principle of silence in the park:[11] "[T]omorrow, thought the hemulen, tomorrow I'll tell them they may laugh and possibly even hum a little if they feel like it. But not more than that. Absolutely not."

It is another paradox that this space implies both silence and invisibility and, at the same time, freedom: a multitude of silent voices anywhere in the park, and a multitude of creatures hiding happily in the glimmering and dusky paradise. The illustration that accompanies the text in this section is in full-page format, and, like the picture of the Hemulen wandering privately in his park, has a frame that emphasizes the secrecy and dreamlike fascination of the scene.

On the cover of the short story collection that contains "The Hemulen Who Loved Silence," is a gouache version of the same motif. Here, the il-

Cover illustration for *Tales from Moominvalley* (original title, *Det osynliga barnet*). © Moomin Characters, Tove Jansson

lusion of depth is stronger; furthermore, a peritextual element adds another dimension to the beauty of this paradise—the invisible child. "The Invisible Child" is the name of another, completely different short story in this collection after which the whole book was named. In that story, invisibility indicates leaving somebody without personal attention. In the story of the Hemulen, in turn, Jansson has outlined invisibility as a state of happiness and hiding, an exciting form of privacy that can be interrupted whenever one desires.

Just as the whirl of the merry-go-round was constructed by contradictory voices (Hemulen/narrator versus solipsistic hemulens), its reconstruction is shaped by two opposing voices and views. The very last vignette and the small epilogue implies that not everybody can enter this intersubjective space: the Hemulen's uncle tries to peek in, but does not see anything. The ideas of space and sound, or view and voice, have united. This hemulen does not see, because he does not hear anything. "Doesn't sound as if they had much fun," he thinks (Jansson 1963: 102). In the illustration, the white space behind the bars indicates the uncle's interpersonal blindness and although he is the focalizer in the last paragraph of the verbal text, the reader finds him an unre-

The closing vignette: The Hemulen's uncle at
the gate. © Moomin Characters, Tove Jansson

liable one. The reader has seen more, both of the park of silence and of the spaces of solitude and togetherness. This knowledge creates a feeling of irony in relation to this complete outsider. The narrative space of merry-go-rounds is closed by this ignorant glance, whose viewer also takes the final sign of a possible whirl, the barrel organ, away from the gates of the paradise.

CONCLUSION

In the story of "The Hemulen Who Loved Silence," Tove Jansson spins complex existential and social ideas in the reshaping movement and form of the merry-go-round, which can be seen as a metonym of interpersonal patterns and distances. During the narrative, the Hemulen experiences first interpellation, then individuality that develops to a solipsism, again interpellation, and finally intersubjectivity—or at least a possibility of it when he builds the park together with children. Jansson's short story shows how these phases of subjectivity are shaped by different voices and views that are representations of various character and narrator worldviews. For different characters (the protagonist, the hemulens, and the children as a collective), the merry-go-round signifies different ideas. It is not always clear who is the focalizer, who views the situation presented in words or pictures. The subtle interventions of a narrator, who sympathizes with the protagonist but also regularly offers subject positions that convey the vantage point of other characters, builds bridges among this many-voicedness, allowing the reader to become aware of the very different interpretations and meanings that the four phases of the merry-go-round can have at the same time. In viewing the nonmeeting of the characters, this voice of the narrator seems both ironic and tolerant, pessimistic and optimistic, alternatively making an appearance in the small tags between the different speakers or focalizers, or being conveyed by more obvious narrator's commentary.

The merry-go-round seems unavoidable. The dream of individualism is overrun by the social feelings of responsibility and empathy, which make the Hemulen choose to be interpellated by the gaze of children. His desperate glance between the hermit cottage and the "lost, motley world" (Jansson 1962: 90 [my translation]), the ruins of the amusement park, exposes the basic tension between the modern individual and the more postmodern ideas of collage, deconstruction, and reconstruction. However, at least in Jansson's story, these ideologies can include each other. The glimmering dream of a self as a center living in a hermit cottage is actually present in the final shape of the merry-go-round. The Hemulen lives in the core of the halted merry-go-round, surrounded by the zigzagged, almost invisible and inaudible movement of the children. Actually, from his viewpoint, he has become the center of the kinesis of the merry-go-round. After lighting the artificial moon he still looks at the stars, although now through a hole in a ceiling—is this the portion of a social, interpellated individual?

NOTES

1. Tove Jansson (1914–2001), the Finnish artist and author, was best-known as the creator of Moomin books—nine small novels and three picture books, which she illustrated herself. In addition, she did numerous cartoons on Moomins, not to mention her work without these fantasy creatures: paintings, caricatures, and novels and short stories that she wrote for an adult audience. For her entire work for children, she received the Hans Christian Andersen Award in 1966. Jansson's imaginative fantasy world, Moominvalley, consists of books which have been translated into 35 different languages (2000). Their original language is Swedish, the writer being a member of the Swedish-speaking minority in Finland. The Moomin books generally speak to a dual audience, but there is also a more recent, commercialized, and single-voiced Moominworld, which most Finnish and Scandinavian children encounter by means of a television series based on Jansson's books but reworked by Japanese and American script writers.

2. A metonym is a figure of speech that has a literal and a figurative function that overlap. Metonymy draws attention to the "depth of significance lying behind seemingly ordinary things" (Stephens 1992b: 67; see also 131–32). In the story about the Hemulen, the merry-go-round has a literal meaning (vehicle situated in the pleasure-ground in the setting of the narrative), but it also conveys a figurative function in presenting interpersonal relationships in the world the Hemulen inhabits.

3. According to Althusser (1971: 162) all ideology "hails or interpellates concrete individuals into concrete subjects by the functioning of the category of the subject." I've applied this in regard to the "ideology of the merry-go-round or the pleasure-ground" because the movement of the merry-go-round (whirl, pause, whirl again) parallels the phases of interpellation in this story. As the ideology "calls" the protagonist of this story, he thinks he recognizes his own self (although he is actually being told what he is)—a Hemulen who enjoys a particular kind of lifestyle and social interaction.

4. In regard to picture books there has been a lot of discussion about the various forms of interaction between words and pictures (see for instance Nodelman 1988, Rhedin 1992, Stephens 2000, Nikolajeva and Scott 2001), but in relation to children's novels and short stories in which illustration plays a significant part in the story-telling process the argumentation is abridged and occasional. To support my focus on both illustration and the verbal text, I build on Gérard Genette's idea of paratextuality (1997), especially peritext, which implies that all books are also physical objects and their materials, paper, covers and illustrations, to name a few qualities, have a significant importance in the reading experience. Further, Ulla Rhedin's (1992: 170) argument about the picture book layout either supporting or resisting the dynamics of a picture book story, does not only, I think, apply to picture books but affects the reader/beholder in illustrated literature in general. It seems especially worth attention in the case when the author and the illustrator is the same person, and has been involved with designing the book.

5. Unless otherwise indicated, the text is cited in Thomas Warburton's translation from 1963.

6. This does not appear in the English translation printing by Penguin. In the citations of Jansson's text, I have, however, followed the original paragraphing of the Swedish-speaking version.

7. In the English paperback version the order of the illustrations is changed in parts and thus has a different effect on the reader/viewer. The vignette above the title in the original version has been placed in the English paperback (Puffin) as the second illustration of the short story. In the same version, the last vignette (which will be discussed later in this chapter) is situated in the middle of the story and, because of the relaying, complementary relation between pictures and words (Barthes [1982] 1991: 30), the vignette actually seems to portray another hemulen—another character—than in the original layout.

8. Contradiction and its opposite movement "release," introduced by Martha Graham in the 1940s, are central to the movement language of modern dance. Jansson's Moomin books present several contradiction-like expressions both verbally and visually (see Happonen 2001).

9. The ideological tenet inscribed especially in picture books, as Stephens points out, is the belief that people "must assert their own individuality and fulfill their innate capacities," which in turn can result in a social conflict with authority (1992a: 177, 199).

10. In some cases the vertical space can be seen as an existential space. In the art of illustration, especially picture books, vertically rectangular pictures are most suitable for representing portraits or existential dimensions of the characters, whereas horizontally rectangular pictures offer wider opportunity to represent action and relationships between characters (see Nodelman 1988: 46; Rhedin 1992: 156).

11. What happens with the park in the long run and with the intersubjective space it is starting to resemble is not revealed by this story (although I doubt that the Hemulen immediately considers the children as subjects instead of objects). The illustration, however, extends the idea of this paradise.

BIBLIOGRAPHY

Althusser, Louis. 1971. *Lenin and Philosophy and Other Essays*, trans Ben Brewster. London: New Left Books.

Bakhtin, M. M. 1981. *The Dialogic Imagination: Four Essays*. Reprint, Austin: University of Texas.

Barthes, Roland. [1982] 1991. *Responsibility of Forms: Critical Essays on Music, Art, and Representation*. Reprint, Berkeley: University of California Press.

Benjamin, Jessica. 1995. "Recognition and Destruction: An Outline of Intersubjectivity." In *Like Subjects, Love Objects: Essays on Recognition and Sexual Difference*, 27–48. New Haven, Conn.: Yale University Press.

Culler, Jonathan. [1997] 2000. *Literary Theory: A Very Short Introduction*. Reprint, Oxford: Oxford University Press.

Genette, Gérard. [1972] 1980. *Narrative Discourse. An Essay in Method*. Reprint, Ithaca, N.Y.: Cornell University Press.

Genette, Gérard. 1997. *Paratexts: Thresholds of Interpretation*. Cambridge: Cambridge University Press.

Happonen, Sirke. 2001. "Choreography of Characters. Movement and Posture in Illustrated Texts for Children." *Reading Literacy and Language* 35 (3): 99–105.

Jansson, Tove. 1962. *Det osynliga barnet och andra berättelser (The invisible child and other stories)*. Helsinki: Schildts.

Jansson, Tove. 1963. *Tales from Moominvalley*, trans. Thomas Warburton. London: Ernest Benn.

Kress, Gunther, and Theo van Leeuwen. 1996. *Reading Images: The Grammar of Visual Design*. London: Routledge.

McCallum, Robyn. 1999. *Ideologies of Identity in Adolescent Fiction: The Dialogic Construction of Subjectivity*. London: Garland.

Nikolajeva, Maria, and Carol Scott. 2001. *How Picturebooks Work*. London: Garland.

Nodelman, Perry. 1988. *Words about Pictures. The Narrative Art of Children's Picture Books*. Athens, Ga.: University of Georgia Press.

Nodelman, Perry. 1991. "The Eye and the I: Identification and First-Person Narratives in Picture Books." *Children's Literature* 19 (2): 1–30.

Rhedin, Ulla. 1992. *Bilderboken. På väg mot en teori*. (*Skrifter utgivna av Svenska barnboksinstitutet* 45). Stockholm: Alfabeta.

Smith, Paul. [1988] 1999. *Discerning the Subject*. Reprint, Minneapolis: University of Minnesota Press.

Stephens, John. 1992a. *Language and Ideology in Children's Fiction*. London: Longman.

Stephens, John. 1992b. *Reading the Signs: Sense and Significance in Written Texts*. Kenthurst, N.S.W: Kangaroo Press.

Stephens, John. 2000. "Modality and Space in Picture Book Art: Allen Say's 'Emma's Rug.'" *CREArTA: International Journal of the Centre for Research and Education in the Arts* 1 (1): 44–59.

CHAPTER 15

The Beginning of All Poetry: Some Observations about Lullabies from Oral Traditions

Anne de Vries

Lullabies are the beginning of all poetry, in the life of each individual and probably also in the history of mankind. It seems obvious that the poets of the first epic poems and the first hymns were rocked and lulled to sleep by their mothers. I owe this idea to Desmond Morris. In an episode of his TV series *The Human Animal* (1994) he showed how much the treatment of new-born babies differs in different parts of the world. But when babies start to cry, the reaction is the same everywhere: they are picked up and rocked in the arms, accompanied with a soothing humming or singing. According to Morris, we were already acquainted with the rhythm of rocking and lulling before we were born: it repeats the heartbeat we heard in the womb. So, one could say, our first literary activities have a biological background.

As researchers from all over the world, we all share this experience. It has often struck me that our common frame of reference is very restricted, because there is no worldwide canon of children's literature. But when speaking about lullabies, there is common ground. Songs from other cultures, even from other continents, are often quite recognizable.

I have been collecting lullabies from oral traditions all over the world. My main sources were books that I could find in the Netherlands: collections of songs, or folklore in general, that contained lullabies in the original language with an English translation. Only in a few cases I used oral sources. I currently have about 150 lullabies from 30 countries or regions in four continents. Even this relatively small corpus contains examples of a fascinating process of change and renewal. At the 2001 Congress of the International Research Society for Children's Literature, the theme "Change and Renewal" was discussed as a contemporary process, but it has been going on from the beginning of poetry. When looking forward, we should not forget that we are standing on the shoulders of previous generations.

In this chapter, I restrict myself to short observations, illustrated with many examples. If the texts of the lullabies are observed closely, it is possible to obtain a picture of the development of the genre, resulting in an increasing complexity of its function and its literary character.

The elementary forms of the genre are universal. More elaborate songs reflect cultural differences, but they also contain common elements, even on different continents. The most elementary form in my collection comes from a study about Chinese folk songs in southern Jiangsu. It contains only two small references to lullabies. The first one reads: "Cradle songs were a very common genre—still much in evidence today but limited in scope. The lullabies I heard in the Wu area were mostly textless melodic hums" (Schimmelpenninck 1997: 94). The second one reads: "Many lullabies in Jiangsu are just wordless hums. Some contain a few words or simple lines. . . . One singer remembered a line that his mother used to sing for his younger sister: "Hush, my darling, little one, sleep softly, hush-a-bye" (Schimmelpenninck 1997: 180–81).

The first reference shows the archetype of the lullaby, the most primitive form in a literary sense; it is just rhythm, the heartbeat of poetry. It is safe to assume that this is also the oldest form, although it is still alive all over the world: *Mm-mm, mm-mm, mm-mm.* It seems to be a tune we could all hum. But we have to be careful: humming is already an interpretation, which may be colored by our cultural background.

In the second reference, the words most common in lullabies appear: "hush," "sleep," "my darling," and "little one." These words are universal in my material from four continents. But lullabies are meant to be sung, and their sound may be less universal. I want to illustrate this with a Native American lullaby, from the Cheyenne people (Giglio 1994: 44–45). The content is very simple:

A ma ho,	Hush, Hush
baby da hii sso	little baby,
no gi yo zi	you are alone to sleep
ni o zi	Go to sleep.

The text as it is sung is much longer, thanks to a repetition of text elements, which is unique in the material I have collected thus far:

A ma ho o o o o
baby da hii sso hi yi
no go yo zi yi
nau o zi yo zi yi yi yi
a ma ho o o o

nau o zi yo zi yi
baby da hii sso hi yi
nau o zi yo zi yi yi
a ma ho o o o
baby da hii sso hi yi

I found this lullaby in Virginia Giglio's *Southern Cheyenne Women's Songs*, a book that comes with an audiocassette. When I listened to it for the first time, I was really surprised. The sounds were familiar, but they were not even close to my expectation of lullabies: they reminded me of Native American songs in movies, songs that accompanied dances. So, although the content is universal, the sound is colored by the Cheyenne language and the Cheyenne singing culture.

In origin, lullabies are a "pragmatic" genre. They are meant to obtain a concrete result: soothe the baby and make him or her go to sleep. The themes of the basic forms are closely connected to this pragmatic character: reassuring the child: "mother is here," "mother is carrying you"; comforting the child: "I will rock you," "I will sing you a song"; caressing the child: "my dearest one" or—as I found in a Spanish cradle song—*lucerito de la mañana*, "my little morning star."

Of course, this last theme is not completely pragmatic: it reflects the mother's feelings, so it is a lyrical element; but at the same time, it is caressing, and therefore soothing, depending on the age of the child. For babies, the really soothing elements are melody and rhythm; they don't understand the words. You could even use aggressive words, as long as they are sung in a sweet tone. This means that the words are in fact for the mother, or have a magical function, as if they could charm the baby to sleep (you can test this theory with your dog: say "Bad dog!" in a kind tone or "Good dog!" in an angry tone).

An important theme is persuading the child to go to sleep. In some songs, we find the argument that it is time to go to sleep, or the observation that the child is sleepy. A wonderful example is this song from Surinam, in Sranan Tongo, a Creole language (Harris 1998):

Doy doy pin-pin.	Sleep, sleep, baby.
Pin-pin wanni doy doy.	Baby wants to sleep.
Neti doro mofodoro,	The night is coming,
sribi e kon moromoro.	and you're getting very sleepy.
Doy doy pin-pin doy doy.	Sleep, sleep, baby, sleep, sleep.

In this song, the baby is charmed to sleep. In a number of French songs sleep is called on, a form of magical thinking that is typical of young children. In an Estonian song the dream is invoked (László and Enikö 1985: 126–27):

Tule, tule, unekane,	Come, come little dream,
käü lapse kätkü pääle,	Come into baby's cradle,
kuku lapse, kulmu pääle,	fall upon his eyebrows,
sihi silma laua pääle.	watch his eyelids.
Tule, uni, ukse-esta,	Come, come in the door,
lingu-langu seppänestü,	slip in by the smoke hole,
tule, uni, ulnutamma,	Come to lull him to sleep
une-lekka saumitauma.	to caress his long hair.

Even magic, however, has little effect if a child has an empty stomach. Therefore, the most common means to humor a child is food. All over the world, it is the most frequent theme in lullabies. An example is this Swahili song (Knappert 1990: 132):

Lala kijitoto	Sleep, little child,
mamako yu mato.	your mother is awake.
Ule tototo	Eat your porridge,
ubwabwa wa moto	your hot gruel,
ota njema ndoto	dream sweet dreams,
fumba yako mato	close your eyes,
lala changu kito.	sleep my jewel.

If food is not immediately available, the child is comforted with promises, as in this song from Beauce, France (Chapiseau 1902: 29):

Fais dodo,	Go to sleep,
Colin mon p'tit frère;	Colin, my little brother,
fais dodo,	go to sleep,
t'auras du lolo.	you will get milk.
Papa est en bas,	Daddy is downstairs
maman est en haut,	mummy is upstairs,
qui fait la bouillie	she makes the porridge
pour l'enfant qui crie.	for the crying child.

Most people promise the child more than milk and porridge if he or she goes to sleep, as in this example from the same region (Chapiseau 1902: 29):

Dodo, l'enfant do,	Sleep, child, sleep,
l'enfant dormira bientôt.	the child will sleep soon.
Une poule blanche	A white chicken
est là dans la grange,	is in the barn,
qui va faire un p'tit coco	it will make a little egg
pour l'enfant qui va faire dodo.	for the child that is going to sleep.

Both lullabies start with a direct address of the child, then other elements appear—for example, the objective information that mummy is upstairs, making the porridge. The information in the second lullaby, that a chicken will make an egg for the child if he or she will go to sleep, is something else entirely: here we are entering the world of fiction, a world full of promises. A well-known example of this type of lullaby is "Hush little baby, don't say a word,/Papa's gonna buy you a mocking bird," and even a diamond ring, a dog named Rover, and finally a horse and cart (Donlon and Glas 1991: 18). Again, the little baby doesn't understand a word of these promises. They are simply an expression of pure joy and the mother's love and good intentions. On the surface, however, they still have a pragmatic character: if the baby won't be quiet, he or she won't get anything. In other words: the song has kept the traditional pattern, but it is used for literary play.

The chicken that was introduced in the second song from Beauce is not the only animal in the barn. In Western Europe, lullabies are crowded with cows and sheep: quite comforting images, because they provide milk and wool, food and warmth. The most common Dutch lullaby shows a sheep as an example for the child (Troelstra-Bokma de Boer and Pollmann 1936: 3):

Slaap, kindje, slaap!	Sleep, baby, sleep!
Daar buiten loopt een schaap,	In the Meadow is a sheep,
een schaap met witte voetjes,	a sheep with little white feet,
dat drinkt zijn melk zo zoetjes.	it drinks its milk so sweetly.
Schaapje met je witte wol,	Sheep with your white wool,
kindje heeft zijn buikje vol.	baby has drunk a belly full.

In this lullaby, the fictional character becomes even stronger. There is no concrete connection between the baby and the sheep: it is a parallel story, and the sheep is a metaphor for the baby. Other common metaphors concern the cradle. In an Indonesian lullaby from the Island of Flores, the cradle is a little boat in which the baby sails away (Heerkens 1930: 138–39):

Ndeeng, ndeeng, ndeeng, kon-deeng,	Rock, rock, rock-a-bye,
ndeen-ke, ndeen-deeng.	rock-a-bye, rock.
Nial 'akoe panging	Where shall I Look?
panging sili taatsiek	Look at the sea!
nial'ak oe ladjar	Where shall I sail,
ladjar sili wangka,	sail with the prau?
wangka dionchio sili lobonio	Whose prau is there near coconut
teenda rembongbong.	trees?
	Such a nice cradle! . . .

Who wouldn't be lured to go on such a wonderful sailing trip?

Let's go back to a theme that seems to be more pragmatic. Promises have their counterpart in threats. In a long Iranian lullaby, over a hundred lines, there are several references to the wolf that will come if the child doesn't go to sleep, in a constant alternation of threat and appeasement (Vahman and Asatrian 1995: 63):

Lålå, lålå, lålåhī!
arax kèrdī, šåla rūdum na-čoihī.
gurg iyå ixurat,
na, na, bač'um na-xurī,
hama'sa na-xurī!
sarasa b'ēl, mama'sa bixur.
hai gurg, beyau biweras!
na, na, nēhåhī! Bač'um ixausē,
Dungē nē- idē.
àl-illå, dindūnī, gurg avēd, xud
     dūnī.

Hush, hush, hush-a-bye!
You are all in sweat, my child,
God give you won't catch cold.
The wolf is coming and will eat
     you.
No, no, don't eat up my child,
don't eat all of him!
Leave his head, eat his nipples.
O wolf, come and carry him off!
No, no, don't come! He is asleep,
he doesn't make a sound.
O God, the fellow with the long
     teeth,
the wolf has come, you know it
     yourself.

In a song from Mauritius, children who won't sleep are a nice morsel for the wildcat (Baissac 1888: 452); in an English song the Giant Bonaparte will come and get them (Opie [1955] 1991: 20). In Spanish lullabies one finds all kinds of bogeymen: one of them is El Coco, a black devil. In an Argentinian song with an African Argentinian background—written around 1850 and then welcomed into the oral tradition, even in Spain—its counterpart appears: the white devil (Blanker 2000). In a song from Curaçao (Dutch Antilles), the bogeyman is the white cow (Blanker 2000):

Drumi juchi, drumi juchi.
Si juchi no ta drumi,
baka ta bin kwe juchi.

Sleep baby, sleep baby.
If you won't sleep,
a cow will come and take you away.

Compared with that, there is only a small distress in this Indonesian lullaby (Blanker 2000):

Nina bobo, ohoh nina bobo,
kalau tidak bobo,
digigit nyamuk.
Marilah bobo nonaku sayang,
kalau tidak bobo,
digigit nyamuk.

Baby sleep, baby sleep,
if you won't sleep,
a mosquito will bite you,
Go to sleep, my dear girl,
if you won't sleep,
a mosquito will bite you.

Much worse is the fate of Bodo children (in Assam, North-East India): if they won't quiet, the "Harsa" (non-Bodo) will snatch them away (Brahma 1960: 7). Political education starts in the cradle; we drink it in with our mother's milk. Some of these threats may seem to lack political correctness, but a philologist should not judge, but try to understand by discovering the background.

If you have ever carried around a crying baby in the middle of the night, you are aware of the despair that pushes people to make threats or promises. It is not always clear how seriously we have to take the former. The alternation of threat and appeasement reflects the parent's mixed feelings of love and irritation. And in some examples, threatening seems to be merely an element in a play, which ends with comforting, cuddling, and hugging.

Threats can also be a means to keep dangers away. If the wolf is already there, eating the best parts, the child has become worthless for other dangerous elements, such as fairies who steal children. In her exciting book *No Go the Bogeyman*, Marina Warner suggests that naming evil forces can undo and banish them, as in the fairy tale "Rumpelstiltskin":

The cradle blessings over Baldur the beautiful list the metals and woods and materials that might harm him, but fail to include mistletoe—and so it is with a mistletoe arrow that he is killed. Lullabies dip infants prophylactically in the imaginary future of ordeals and perils; nightmares are uttered in order to chase them from the impending dream-world—a maneuver akin to a blessing in the form of a curse: as in "Break a leg." (Warner 1998: 201).

Lullabies are just as much parents' songs as children's songs. The mother's feelings are expressed directly in quite a few songs, for instance in this Swahili song (Knappert 1990: 132):

Mwana huyu ana nini?	What ails this child?
Anidhiki roho yangu	He makes my soul suffer,
usiku kucha hulia	he cries all night long,
anakata ini langu	it cuts into my heart.
Mwana wako akilia	When your child cries,
mubembeleze alale	rock him that he may fall
ayanywe na maziwaye	asleep,
azile na sukaria	let him drink his milk,
	and let him eat his sweets.
Mwana wako akilia	When your child cries,
umwimbie nyimbo mia	sing a hundred songs for him:
mwana wangu wa lilanji	"My child of orange blossom,
mwana dhahabu wa ranji	lmy golden coloured child."

This is a remarkable song, showing both a change of perspective and a change of addressee. The first stanza expresses the mother's despair at her baby's crying. In the last two stanzas, advice is given from a different point of view: the lullaby is used to pass on the experience of previous generations. It is both lyrical and didactic. Even the lyrical part, in the first stanza, is didactic, because it shows the burden of motherhood to the bystanders.

Another reason for despair is found in the following song from South Uist, in the Scottish Hebrides, which may go back to the time of the potato famine in 1848 (Shaw [1955] 1977: 143):

Bà, bà, mo leanabh beag,	Bà, bà, my little babe,
bidh tu mór ged tha thu beag,	you will be big although you're wee,
bà, bà, mo leanabh beag,	bà, bà, my little babe,
cha n-urrainn mi'gad thàladh.	I am not able to soothe you.
Dé, a ghaoil, a nì mi riut,	What, love, will I do for you,
gun bhainne cìche agam dhut?	for I have no breast milk for you?
Eagal orm gun gabh thu crup	I fear that you will get the croup
le buigead a' bhuntàta.	from the softness of the potatoes.

Many lullabies from South Uist are really sad. One of the reasons is ill fate in love: in one song the mother curses her rival who lured the baby's father; in another, she is distressed because the baby's father says the baby doesn't belong to him.

Doubt about fatherhood is also found in a lullaby from Surinam, but in this case, it is not presented as a terrible problem. It is supposed to be sung by a Chinese father, but it can also be read as being sung by the mother (Pengel-Wong 1999):

Doi, doi mi pikin	Sleep, sleep, my baby,
sonte, chinese pikin	perhaps you are the child of a Chinese,
sonte blakaman pikin	perhaps you are the child of a black man,
sribi switi, blakaman pikin	sleep well, my black baby.

As these examples show, lullabies often reflect social circumstances, and it is there that the biggest differences can be found. Let us look at two examples. The first is a lullaby from Argentina, which contains most of the themes I have discussed above (Blanker 2000):

Duerme, duerme negrito,	Sleep, sleep, black baby,
que tu mama está en	your mother is in the field, black baby.
el campo negrito.	Sleep, sleep, Lumila,
Duerme, duerme Lumila,	your mother is in the field, Lumila.
que tu mama está en el	
campo, Lumila.	

Te va a traer cosa rica para ti,	She will bring you nice morsels,
te va a traer rica fruta para ti,	she will bring you nice fruits,
te va a traer carne de cerdo para ti,	she will bring you pork,
te va a traer mucha cosa para ti.	she will bring you bits of everything.

Y si el negro no se duerme,	If the black baby won't sleep,
viene el diabolo blanco	the white devil will come
y chac te como la patita.	and snap! he'll eat your leg.
Chica pumba, chica pum,	chica boom, chica boom,
chica pumba, chica pum.	chica boom, chica boom.

Duerme, duerme negrito,	Sleep, sleep black baby,
que tu mama está en el campo negrito.	your mother is in the field, black baby,
trabajando, trabajando duramente,	working, working hard, working.
trabajando.	

Y va de luto, trabajando si, trabajando.	She is in mourning, working yeah, working
No se pagan, trabajando y va trabajando,	They don't pay her, but she's working
trabajando si.	and working, working yeah.
El negrito chiquitito, el negrito si,	Little black baby, black baby, yeah,
trabajando si.	working yeah.

Duerme, duerme Lumila,	Sleep, sleep, Lumila,
Que tu mama está en el campo negrito.	your mother is in the field, black baby.

My last example, from Surinam, goes back to the slavery period. The children of owners were lulled to sleep by one of the female slaves. If they were not present, their mistress had a problem. This is ridiculed in the song, which enumerates all female slaves with their traditional African names[1] (Pengel-Wong 1999).

Tantiri, o, tantiri, vu yu ba,	Keep quiet, o, keep quiet, my baby.
efu Yaba ben de, a ben sa doi, doi yu,	If Yaba were here, she would soothe you,
efu Abeni ben de, a ben sa doi, doi yu,	if Abeni were here, she would soothe you,
efu Kwasiba ben de, a ben sa doi, doi yu,	if Kwasiba were here, she would soothe you,
efu Adyuba ben de, a ben sa doi, doi yu,	if Adyuba were here, she would soothe you,

efu Akuba ben de, a ben sa doi, doi yu,	if Akuba were here, she would soothe you,
efu Amimba ben de, a ben sa doi, doi yu,	if Amimba were here, she would soothe you,
efu Afiba ben de, a ben sa doi, doi yu.	if Afiba were here, she would soothe you.

According to the text, it seems to be sung by the mother. In reality it was probably sung by the nanny, who was mocking her mistress. With this social satire, we have come a long way from the wordless humming to lull a baby to sleep. Over the centuries, a pragmatic form of communication developed into lyrical poetry. In that process, lullabies went through a remarkable process of change and renewal. The songs I have presented here show an increasing complexity. On the surface they remain soothing songs for the baby, with a simple monotonous rhythm. However, lyrical elements, fiction, metaphors, and satire add other layers to the texts, which raise them above the pragmatic archetype of the lullaby. These layers address another public over the head of the baby. Generally, and just as remarkable, this public will consist only of the singer, mostly the mother, expressing her feelings and entertaining herself with literary play.

NOTE

1. The traditional African names refer to the day of the week on which a person was born. For women the names are Kwasiba (Sunday), Adyuba (Monday), Abeni (Tuesday), Akuba (Wednesday), Yaba (Thursday), Afiba (Friday), and Amimba (Saturday).

BIBLIOGRAPHY

Baissac, M. C. 1888. *Le folk-lore de l'Ile-Maurice (The folklore of the Island of Mauritius)*. Paris: Maisonneuve et Ch. Leclerc. (Les littératures populaires de toutes les nations: tome 27)

Blanker, Gracia. 2000. Unpublished personal interviews and oral sources.

Brahma, Mohini Mohan. 1960. *Folk-Songs of the Bodos*. Gauhati: Gauhati University.

Chapiseau, Félix. 1902. *Le folk-lore de la Beauce et du Perche (The folklore of the regions Beauce and Perche)*. Tome II. Paris: J. Maisonneuve. (*Les littératures populaires de toutes les nations;* tome 46)

Deetman, Huib. 1977. *Uit de zak van de Tjelana Monjet: Vijftig Indische and Indonesische liedjes (From the sack of Tjelana Monjet: Fifty Indonesian songs)*. Alkmaar: Blimbing.

Donlon, Pat, and Maddy Glas. 1991. *Moon Cradle: Lullabies and Dandling Songs from Ireland with Old Childhood Favourites*. Dublin: O'Brien Press.

Giglio, Virginia. 1994. *Southern Cheyenne Women's Songs*. Norman/London: University of Oklahoma Press.

Harris, Ann. 1998. *Sribi kino*. Den Haag: Centrum voor Amateurkunst.

Heerkens, Piet. 1930. *Flores: de Manggarai*. Uden: Missiehuis.

Knappert, Jan. 1990. "Swahili Songs for Children." *Afrika und Übersee* 73: 129–43.

László, Vikár, and Sz'j Enikö. 1985. *Songs of the Forest: 100 Folk Tunes of the Finno-Ugric Peoples*. Budapest: Corvina.

Morris, Desmond. 1994. *The Human Animal*. Six one-hour television programs on human behavior, BBC1.

Opie, Iona, and Peter Opie. [1955] 1991. *The Oxford Nursery Rhyme Book*. Thirteenth impression. Oxford: Oxford University Press.

Pengel-Wong, Nathalie. 1999. Unpublished text from oral sources.

Schimmelpenninck, Antoinette Marie. 1997. *Chinese Folk Songs and Folk Singers; Shan'ge Traditions in Southern Jiangsu*. Leiden: n.p.

Shaw, Margaret Fay. [1955] 1977. *Folksongs and Folklore of South Uist*. Second edition. Oxford: Oxford University Press.

Troelstra-Bokma de Boer, S., and Jop Pollmann. 1936. *Het spel van moeder en kind: Oude kinderrijmen voor jonge ouders (The play of mother and child: Old rhymes for young parents)*. Heemstede: De Toorts.

Vahman, Fereydun, and Garnik Asatrian. 1995. *Poetry of the Baxtiaris: Love Poems, Wedding Songs, Lullabies, Laments*. Copenhagen: Munksgaard.

Warner, Marina. 1998. *No Go the Bogeyman: Scaring, Lulling and Making Mock*. London: Chatto & Windus.

CHAPTER 16

Change and Renewal: Translating the Visual in Picture Books

Riitta Oittinen

Children's books are often illustrated and often meant to be read aloud. The relationship between verbal text and illustration that we see in picture books is important in the modern/postmodern world that is so markedly influenced by the visual. However, the problems of the visual seem to appeal to few scholars within translation studies, even though translators increasingly have to deal with the visual in literary, technical, and media translation (see, e.g., Tabbert 1991: 130–48, Vermeer 1986: 304).

In my books—especially in *Translating for Children* (Oittinen 2000)—I deal with issues that concern the translating of books for children: reading aloud and the dialectics of texts in writing and in illustration. In my Finnish-language book, *Kuvakirja kääntäjän kädessä* (*Translating picture books;* 2004), I concentrate on the problem of translating picture books. This article is based on these two books, with the starting point being that picture books are icono-texts that involve the interaction of two semiotic systems—the verbal and the visual. Picture books are unities formed by words, images, and effects and have a special language of their own (see also Oittinen 1990, Oittinen 1996).

As iconotexts, picture books and comics share many features—for example, they are both based on a series of images and have a serial character. Instead of frames, however, picture books have pages that are turned—but what is a picture book really? The American artist Uri Shulevitz (1985: 15–16) makes a clear separation between picture books and storybooks:

A "story book" tells the story with words. Although the pictures amplify it, the story can be understood without them. . . . In contrast, a true "picture book" tells a story mainly or entirely with pictures. A picture book says in words only what pictures cannot show.

It is often very difficult to tell a picture book from a storybook or an illustrated book. Moreover, if we consider the postmodern picture book—for
example, books by David Macaulay and Anthony Browne—the task of defining picture books becomes even more difficult. As David Lewis (2001: 27, 90)
points out, what is distinctive of picture books is their diversity: canons and
boundaries have faded, and there is "mixing of forms . . . parody and pastiche."
This is why I am reluctant to compare picture books with storybooks, but
rather use the term "picture book" in the sense of Perry Nodelman (1999:
69–70): picture book is the "province of the young child"; picture book is also
a "polyphonic" form which absorbs and uses many codes, styles, and textual
devices, and which frequently pushes at the borders of convention."

Barbara Bader (1976, as cited in Lewis 2001: 137) goes even further and
places picture books within a wider frame: "A picturebook is a text, illustrations, total design; an item of manufacture and commercial product; a social,
cultural, historical document; and, foremost, an experience for a child." I also
argue that the picture book is a polyphonic art form with many different
voices—voices that are both heard and seen.

As for the translation of picture books, my starting point is that translation
always implies change and renewal: translating involves rewriting for target-
language audiences in target-language contexts. Translations are never the
same as their originals, but every time a book is translated, it takes on a new
language, a new culture, new readers, and a new point of view. Therefore,
although we acknowledge "original" literature written for child readers, we
should also acknowledge translating for children. Translators always bring
along their own child images: anything that is created for children—whether
it involves writing, illustrating, or translating—reflects the creator's views of
childhood. Children's culture has always reflected all of society, adult images
of childhood, the way children themselves experience childhood, and the way
adults remember it (see Oittinen 2000: 41).

My thinking is influenced by the Russian philosopher Mikhail Bakhtin and
his views about dialogics (see Oittinen 2000: 29–32). I am also inspired by
semioticians such as Charles S. Peirce (1932) and Dinda L. Gorlée (1994)
who have applied semiotics to translation studies. In addition, picture theories
and research on comics have proved very helpful (see Arnheim 1974, Gombrich 1998, Kress & Van Leeuwen 2000). In other words, I use hermeneutics
as a wider frame for my research and use the tools of semiotics and picture
theory in analyzing illustrations along with words.

DIALOGUE AND SEMIOSIS

Translators always begin their work as readers. We can understand "reading" as being applicable not just to the verbal, but also to the visual. However,
we must not forget the use of children's books: children's books are being
read; they are "performed" for child audiences, especially for children who

cannot read. The visual (e.g., typography and layout) also influences the readability of texts. However, even though performance is another aspect of translation and illustration, my focus is on the visual in this chapter (see Oittinen 2000: 100–14).

Throughout his writings, Mikhail Bakhtin stresses the importance of "unfinalizability." He makes a clear distinction between "the given" and "the created." "The given" is "the material," the resources with which we speak and act—that is, concrete words and illustrations. "The given" also comprises language, culture, and the person's background. However, no utterance—no word, no work of art, no original or translation—is only a "product" of what is given; something new is created in the process of understanding and interpretation, when different material worlds meet with human beings (see Bakhtin, as cited in Morson and Emerson 1990: 130–31, 170–71; see also Bakhtin 1990: 292–93, 352).

Dialogue is not far removed from what Bakhtin calls heteroglossia. "At any given time, in any given place, there will be a set of conditions—social, historical, meteorological, physiological—that will ensure that a word uttered in that place and at that time will have a meaning different than it would have under any other conditions" (Bakhtin 1990: 428). To divorce word and dialogue, word and context, would be artificial, because words are heteroglot: they are situated in time and place and born between the known (the source culture) and the alien (the target culture) (see Oittinen 2000: 30). Illustrations are also part of the context of the words, just as words are part of the illustrations. Detached from its context, a word or a picture is different from what it is within a context: for example, when I placed a picture from Maurice Sendak's *Where the Wild Things Are* on my kitchen wall, the picture became detached from its context and took on different meanings from those that the picture had as a page opening in the book.

Translating the verbal and the visual of picture books may also be understood as a semiotic process. Like Bakhtin, Peirce (2001) describes semiosis as an endless process of interpretation and human cognition involving signs. From the viewpoint of picture books, a word, an image, a page, and even an entire book may be seen as either a sign or a collection of signs. Everything in a book is of importance, every detail carries meanings, all of which are available for translation. Translators need to be aware of many different visual (and cultural) signs, such as the reading direction, the symbolism of colors, and facial expressions. For instance, the change in reading direction causes many problems in translating comics from English into Arabic (see Zitawi 2004, and later in this article).

Peirce (2001) introduces three orders of signs: icon, index, and symbol. Icon is a sign of likeness; like a photograph, it resembles the thing to which it is referring. Index is something that is in a causal relationship to its referent, like smoke implying fire. Symbol is an artificial sign: words are symbols referring to things in the real world just by agreement. There is no logical connection between meaning and the symbol itself; rather it's something that has to be learned (see Peirce 2001: 415–40). All of these different signs can be found in a picture book. A picture is an icon; a picture of a girl resembles a real girl. A word in a picture book is a symbol based on agreement, and there is an indexical relationship between the words and the images. It is this relationship that influences the translator's choice of words and his or her idea of the whole book. In semiotic terms, translating picture books is intersemiotic translation (see Gorlée 1994: 162–65).

Peirce (2001) also introduces three different phases of semiosis (that is, the process of interpretation): Firstness, Secondness, and Thirdness. Firstness is feeling that does not need rational explanation; Secondness is action; and Thirdness is systemizing, ordering, making sense, and thinking of the future. At the stage of Firstness, the translator of a picture book gets the first impression of the story told in words and images and breathes them in. At the second stage, Secondness, the translator starts reading the original more closely and draws conclusions from the verbal and the visual of the story. At the stage of Thirdness, the translator gives his or her new interpretation for new target-language readers (see Peirce 2001: 415–40; see also Gorlée 1987: 45–55).

THE VERBAL AND THE VISUAL

When reading the visual and interpreting images, we need to know a number of conventions. John Spink, the American scholar of children's books, has studied children as viewers of illustrations. According to Spink (1990: 60–62), we need to be aware of conventions like "scaling down [for example, a picture is smaller than the thing in itself], . . . indicating three dimensional objects in a two dimensional medium, indicating colour in monochrome, stylized indications of mental processes and mental states, frozen action (indicating motion), and a part implying the whole." Moreover, the visual appearance of a book always includes the illustrations as well as the actual print, the shape and style of letters and headings, composition, and picture sequence. Even the elements of the layout and typography can be strictly culture bound. As Joseph Schwarcz (1982) points out, in picture books, letters and words may have various tasks and forms: letters may be personified or words may represent themselves or be three-dimensional objects. Letters may also be signs of big or small sounds by growing bigger or smaller. A picture book is a combination of the verbal, the visual, and also the effects—such as speech bubbles or movement lines, which also add to the contents of the story.

The Finnish scholar, Juha Herkman (1998), divides the visual into four functions. An illustrated text may be based more on pictures than on words, or the other way around; there may also be collaboration of the verbal and the visual, or the visual may tell quite a different story than the verbal. In other words, illustrations affect the reading experience through congruency and deviation. Deviation may also be called irony: when the visual is telling something very different from what the words are stating, the reader stops believing in what he or she is being told and starts putting words and images in quotation marks. Nodelman even claims that words and pictures always have an ironical relationship because they never really tell the same thing (see Nodelman 1988: 221, see also Lewis 2001: 90).

We might also say that illustrations domesticate and foreignize. Illustrations may bring the text closer to the story told in words. By domestication, keeping close to the text in words, they add to the smooth entity. By telling a different story than the text in writing, illustrations may also foreignize or bring something unclear into the text, something difficult for the reader to understand. When domesticating the text, translators need to pay special attention to the visual. If, for instance, a story is situated in Paris, France, and the illustrator shows the Eiffel tower and other landmarks of the city, the end result may be strange, if, in the Finnish translation, the story is situated in Helsinki. In this case, by domesticating the text and ignoring the visual, the translator may paradoxically foreignize the story. Of course, illustrations may also domesticate or foreignize by bringing the story closer to or further away from the target culture.

THE VISUAL AND THE TRANSLATOR

Translators interact with illustrations in many ways. On the one hand, translators try to make the text in words and illustrations match each other; on the other hand, translators have—either consciously or unconsciously—internalized the images from their reading of the words and illustrations. When solving the problem of the verbal and visual, translators may choose different strategies. In his *Memes of Translation*, Andrew Chesterman (1997: 172) points out that translators' strategies are governed by different norms, which promote certain values: "A norm is a norm because it embodies certain values." Norms place restrictions on the translator, but they also give the translator freedom. Dirk Delabastita (1989) has listed strategies for film translation: *transmutatio* (reordering), *adiectio* (addition), *repetitio* (repetition), *detractio* (visual manipulation), and *deletio* (omission). Jehan Zitawi (2004) has applied these strategies for translating the visual in comics.

Reordering the visual in picture books is not very common in the Western world. However, Zitawi (2004) points out that reordering of frames is natural in the translation of comics from English into Arabic, because Arabic is read from right to left. Translators may also add things like footnotes to explain and clarify some culturally specific details. At best, this helps the reader to understand and enjoy the book better; at worst, the translator may destroy the pleasure of the reading experience. The translator needs to be able to recognize the gaps left in the text by the author and the illustrator. Sometimes the translator may feel tempted to explain the story told in words on the basis of what he or she sees in the illustration. However, this may change the in-dexical relationship of the verbal and the visual altogether, resulting in dull, overexplanatory texts that leave no room for the reader's own interpretation. Emer O'Sullivan presents a good example of this with regard to Michel Gay's *Papa Vroum*. In the American edition of the book, the translator has filled in the gaps left by the author, which has led to a story where everything is explained away so that there are no surprises for the reader (O'Sullivan 1999: 168–70, O'Sullivan 2000: 287–90). The strategy of explaining and adding has changed the dialectic and indexical relationship of the verbal and the visual: the narrative is changed and a relationship of deviation has become that of repetition. Moreover, filling in the gaps is quite close to what Bakhtin calls passive understanding and authoritarian discourse, which is an alien object given beforehand and from above: the target language reader is suppressed and deprived of his or her recreating role (see Bakhtin 1990: 282, 342; Oittinen 2000: 29–32).

Some details, like onomatopoeic expressions or inscriptions (labels and posters) in the verbal or the visual, may be repeated (Kaindl 1999). Zitawi (2004) presents an example: in one panel of the Arabic translation of Mickey Mouse, there is an inscription on a blackboard "2 – 1 = 1," which the trans-lator has kept in the English form. Visual manipulation seems to be quite usual in translating from English into Arabic, as is shown, for example, in another panel of Mickey Mouse, in which the pig characters have been ma-nipulated: their nostrils have been removed, perhaps due to religious reasons ["Islam prohibits the eating of pigs," Zitawi (2004) points out]. In the Western world, visual manipulation is not usual, especially not in co-prints, where translations into different languages are printed at the same time. Sometimes illustrations may be censored, as was the case in one scene in the Finnish picture book series, Aino, by artist Kristiina Louhi, in which the little girl Aino's little brother is naked and about to get dressed. The British publisher asked the illustrator to draw some clothes on the boy on the book cover before publishing the book in Great Britain (Jurvelin 1990). Omissions are not un-usual in translations into Arabic either, as Zitawi (2004) describes: they may be details added to the text using sound bulbs or bolding or italics.

Whichever strategy the translator chooses, and for whatever reason, illus-trations may help him or her in many ways: they show the time and place in which the story is situated. They also show the physical appearance and the relations of the characters in the story. As a whole, illustrations provide all kinds of hints to the reader: for example, placing one character higher than the others is often a sign of a higher status. Sometimes the text in words does not give this kind of information, and yet it can be found in the pictures.

Although illustrations may help the translator, they can also make his or her task very difficult. By showing details, illustrations restrict the translator's solutions. Sometimes pictures are heavy-weight opponents, like when I trans-lated one book by the South African author and artist Niki Daly. In one of the scenes of the book *Jamela's Dress* (1999), I encountered a problem concerning the visual. In the scene, the little girl Jamela and her mother are playing games and singing while waiting for a fabric to get dry. Then Jamela asks her mother: "Let's do teapots, Mama!" and teaches her mother how to do "a little song about a teapot with a spout. They dipped and tipped and the tea poured out" (Daly 1999). In the Finnish culture, we don't have anything quite similar, so I decided to read the illustration more closely and tried to find a song game that matched the illustration. After a long hunt, I found the Finnish song "Aamulla Herätys, Sängystä Pois," which tells about what people do in the morning when they wake up (see Daly 2001). In the end, the solution seemed successful, because the tune is international ("Lou, Lou, Skip to My Lou") and the way the song is played in Finland is very close to Jamela's and her mother's hand and body movements.

Another example of how illustrations influence the translator's work involves the book *To Every Thing There Is a Season* (1998) by the American artists Leo and Diane Dillon, which I translated quite recently. The passages in the book are from the Book of Ecclesiastes, the King James version of the Bible. On every page opening there is one line of the book with an illustration depicting different cultures and different periods of time. After reading the book a few times, I decided to use an existing translation: the newest Finnish translation of the Bible from 1992. However, my decision proved to be problematic in one passage that goes like this: "A time to embrace, and a time to refrain from embracing." The translators of the 1992 Finnish version had a different point of view than the translators of the King James version. The 1992 version reads: *"Aika on syleillä ja aika olla erossa,"* which can be rendered into English: "Time to embrace and time to be separated." Thus, this translation introduced an unwanted contradiction between the story told by the verbal and the story told by the visual. On the left-hand page, the family is shown in a private home, embracing and leading a cozy family life. On the right-hand page, the family is shown working together; they are probably tradespeople because there are coins and a pair of scales on the table. The family is not embracing, but they are still together and certainly not separated. To solve the problem, I decided, in this one instance, to use an older Finnish translation from 1933, in which the translator's solution is very close to the King James version: *"Aika on syleillä ja aika olla syleilemättä"* ("A time to embrace and a time to refrain from embracing"). Otherwise, I used the newer 1992 version. There were forewords in the book, so it was easy for me to add a comment on my solution, which was, in its entirety, based on the iconotext, the indexical relationship of the words and the illustration.

From the perspective of semiosis (Peirce 2001), at the stage of Firstness, I read the verbal and the visual of the original and I enjoyed my reading. That was the first encounter with the text. At the stage of Secondness, I started thinking of the interaction of the verbal and the visual. I started pondering the message of the book and the future readers as well. I wondered whether the book was directed toward both adults and children or children alone. At the stage of Thirdness, I started writing my translation and addressing the future readers of the text and my translation was largely based on existing translations, and my process of understanding was not the final solution, but part of a long chain of interpretations.

HYBRIDS

Placing existing translations with new illustrations may also be problematic. In *Translating for Children*, I presented an example of one Finnish translation of Lewis Carroll's *Alice's Adventures in Wonderland*. There were four Finnish translations of the book, and three of them first appeared along with John Tenniel's illustrations. The first translation by Anni Swan was published in 1906 (Carroll 1958). Later, the same translation appeared with Tove Jansson's illustrations (Carroll 1983).

Jansson's illustrations were first published in Sweden, along with Åke Runn-quist's Swedish translation (Carroll 1966). Bonniers, the Swedish publisher, asked Jansson to do the illustrations. She agreed when Bonniers gave her a free hand in her illustrations to criticize the bureaucracy of the (Swedish) grown-up world. Because the Finnish publisher, Werner Söderström Osake-yhtiö, wanted to participate in co-printing the book, they needed to act promptly, which was probably why they published Jansson's new illustrations with a translation whose rights they already had: the Finnish version by Swan. The publication of this hybrid, disregarding the radical views of Runnquist's Swedish translation, resulted in many awkward solutions.

The poem "Father William" presented special problems because Åke Runnquist's translation into Swedish, which was the basis for Jansson's illustration, had a different starting point: Runnquist had abandoned Tenniel's illustrations and created a totally new version of the original. For instance, the main figure in the poem, Father William, became Pappa Kantarell (Father Chanterelle); thus, Jansson, in her illustration, drew the figure as a mushroom. Swan's Finnish translation, however, was created with the illustrations of John Tenniel in mind, so her more traditional translation of this poem, "Father William," could not be used in the book illustrated by Jansson (Carroll 1983). The task of writing the poem in Finnish was therefore given to another translator, Panu Pekkanen, who did not pay any attention to the interaction between the text in words and the illustration.

Although Runnquist's Swedish translation mocks the grown-ups' urge to improve the child, Pekkanen's translation ends in scolding the young reader: be a good child and be careful with matches! With this solution, the publisher showed no respect for Jansson's illustrations or for the Finnish readers of the book, and of course showed nothing but disrespect for Lewis Carroll, the author of the original. The publisher seems to have believed that an original work and all its translations are interchangeable.

Sometimes changing the wording in translations—due to a new illustration—is a success. This was the case when Anthony Browne's illustration of "Alice" was published in Finnish (Carroll 1988). The publisher, having decided to use an existing translation by Kirsi Kunnas and Eeva-Liisa Manner (first published in 1972; Carroll 1972), contacted the translators and asked them to check the verbal to make sure that it went together with the visual. In the end, the wording was changed here and there, because some scenes shown by the illustrator radically influenced the interpretation of the story.

The translators had domesticated their translation for Finnish child readers and thus omitted some allusions to British culture that might have seemed too strange to Finnish child readers. Consequently, they had omitted a reference to Shakespeare, which was no problem at all as long as the translation was placed beside Tenniel's illustration: he does not present a picture of Shakespeare. However, with Browne's visual interpretation, the situation was different altogether because he actually showed Shakespeare in his illustration. Unless the translators had changed their wording, the picture of Shakespeare presented by Browne would have been uncontextualized and unmotivated.

CONCLUSION

Translators of picture books translate whole situations including the words, the illustrations, and the whole (imagined) reading-aloud situation. When reading a picture book, readers participate in a dialogue between themselves and the story told by the author and the illustrator with words and pictures. However, the verbal, the visual, and their dialectical and indexical relationship are also part of a greater whole: the original work and its translations and the various individual readers in different cultures.

Translating picture books may also be compared with theater translation. As in drama translation, translators of picture books need to pay attention to the readability of the verbal text: the text is "performed" for the child and it must flow while being read. In addition, the illustrations are a kind of set design for the text: as in the theater, they have an effect on the audience. Like theater translation, picture book translation is a stage for a multitude of voices. Translation and performance always go together: translators need to know and take into consideration which media—which senses—they are translating for. Along with verbal elements, translators of picture books need to be able to read graphic elements such as illustrations. Translators of picture books need to be specialists in reading the visual, which is a special field requiring special skills and knowledge.

BIBLIOGRAPHY

Arnheim, Rudolf. 1974. *Art and Visual Perception: A Psychology of the Creative Eye.* Berkeley: University of California Press.

Bakhtin, Mikhail. 1990. *The Dialogic Imagination: Four Essays*, ed. Michael Holquist, trans. Caryl Emerson and Michael Holquist. Austin: University of Texas Press.

Bassnett, Susan. 1991. *Translation Studies*. London: Routledge.

Carroll, Lewis. 1958. *Liisan seikkailut ihmemaailmassa (Alice's Adventures in Wonderland)*, illus. John Tenniel, Finnish trans. Anni Swan, 1906. Porvoo: WSOY.

Carroll, Lewis. 1966. *Alice i Underlandet (Alice's Adventures in Wonderland)*, illus. Tove Jansson, Swedish trans. Åke Runnquist. Stockholm: Bonniers.

Carroll, Lewis. 1972. *Liisan seikkailut ihmemaassa (Alice's Adventures in Wonderland)*, illus. John Tenniel, Finnish trans. Kirsi Kunnas and Eeva-Liisa Manner. Jyväskylä: Gummerus.

Carroll, Lewis. 1981. *Alice's Adventures in Wonderland and Through the Looking-Glass*, illus. John Tenniel. New York: Bantam Books.

Carroll, Lewis. 1983. *Liisan seikkailut ihmemaassa (Alice's Adventures in Wonderland)*, illus. Tove Jansson, Finnish trans. Anni Swan, 1906. Leipzig: WSOY.

Carroll, Lewis. 1988. *Liisan seikkailut ihmemaassa (Alice's Adventures in Wonderland)*, illus. Anthony Browne, Finnish trans. Kirsi Kunnas and Eeva-Liisa Manner, 1972. Karkkila: Kustannus-Mäkelä Oy.

Chesterman, Andrew. 1997. *Memes of Translation: The Spread of Ideas in Translation Theory*. Amsterdam: John Benjamins.

Daly, Niki. 1999. *Jamela's Dress*. London: Frances Lincoln.

Daly, Niki. 2001. *Jamelan puku (Jamela's dress)*, Finnish trans. Riitta Oittinen. Kärkälä: Pieni Karhu.

Delabastita, Dirk. 1989. "Translation and Mass Communication: Film and TV Translation as Evidence of Cultural Dynamics." *Babel* 35 (4): 193–218.

Dillon, Leo, and Diane Dillon. 1998. *To Every Thing There Is a Season*. New York: The Blue Skye Press.

Gombrich, E. H. 1998. *The Sense of Order: A Study in the Psychology of Decorative Art*. New York: Phaidon.

Gorlée, Dinda L. 1987. "Firstness, Secondness, Thirdness, and Cha(u)nciness." *Semiotica* 65 (1/2): 45–55.

Gorlée, Dinda L. 1994. *Semiotics and the Problem of Translation: With Special Reference to the Semiotics of Charles S. Peirce*. Amsterdam: Rodopi.

Herkman, Juha. 1998. *Sarjakuvan kieli ja mieli (Comics)*. Tampere: Vastapaino.

Holy Bible, The. Authorized King James version. n.d. Canada: World Bible Publishers.

Jurvelin, Tuuli. 1990. "Aino lähtee Englantiin—kuinka suomalainen kuvakirja kääntyy englanniksi" (Translating Kristiina Louhi's picture books into English). Master's thesis. University of Tampere.

Kaindl, Klaus. 1999. "Thump, Whizz, Poom: A Framework for the Study of Comic under Translation." *Target* 11 (2): 263–88.

Kress, Gunther, and Theo Van Leeuwen. 2000. *Reading Images: The Grammar of Visual Design*. London: Routledge.

Lewis, David. 2001. *Reading Contemporary Picturebooks: Picturing Text*. New York: Routledge.

Morson, Gary Saul, and Caryl Emerson. 1990. *Mikhail Bakhtin: The Creation of a Prosaics*. Stanford: Stanford University Press.

Nodelman, Perry. 1988. *Words about Pictures: The Narrative Art of Children's Picture Books*. Athens: University of Georgia Press.

Nodelman, Perry. 1999. *Decoding the Images: Illustration and Picture Books in Understanding Children's Literature*, ed. Peter Hunt. London: Routledge.

Oittinen, Riitta. 1990. "The Dialogic of Text and Illustration: A Translatological Point of View." In *TextConText*. Translation. Didaktik. Praxis. Heidelberg. 1: 40–53.

Oittinen, Riitta. 1996. "Illustrated Stories: On the Dialogics and Carnivalism of Translating for Children." *Compar(a)ison*. Special Issue II/1995.

Oittinen, Riitta. 2000. *Translating for Children*. New York: Garland.

Oittinen, Riitta. 2004. *Kuvakirja kääntäjän kädessä (Translating picture books)*. Helsinki: Lasten Keskus.

O'Sullivan, Emer. 1999. "Translating Pictures." *Signal* 90: 167–75.

O'Sullivan, Emer. 2000. *Kinderliterarische Komparatistik*. Heidelberg: C. Winter.

Peirce, Charles S. 1932. *Collected Papers by Charles Sanders Peirce*. Cambridge: Harvard University Press.

Peirce, Charles S. 2001. *Johdatus tieteen logiikkaan ja muita kirjoituksia (Essays by Charles S. Peirce)*, Finnish trans. Markus Lång. Tampere: Vastapaino.

Pyhä Raamattu (The Holy Bible). 1975. Turku: Suomen Pipliaseura.

Raamattu (The Bible). 1993. Porvoo: WSOY.

Schwarcz, Joseph H. 1982. *Ways of the Illustrator: Visual Communication in Children's Literature*. Chicago: American Library Association.

Shulevitz, Uri. 1985. *Writing with Pictures: How to Write and Illustrate Children's Books*. New York: Watson Guptill Publications.

Spink, John. 1990. *Children as Readers: A Study*. London: Clive Bingley & Library Association.

Tabbert, Reinbert. 1991. *Kinderbuchanalysen II. Wirkung—kultureller Kontext—Unterricht*. Frankfurt: Dipa.

Venuti, Lawrence. 1995. *The Translator's Invisibility: A History of Translation*. London: Routledge.

Vermeer, Hans J. 1986. *Voraussetzungen für eine translationstheorie:—einige kapitel kultur und sprachtheorie*. Heidelberg: Vermeer.

Zitawi, Jehan. 2004. *The Translation of Disney Comics in the Arab World: A Pragmatic Perspective*. Manchester: University of Manchester, School of Modern Languages, CTIS.

CHAPTER 17

Change and Renewal of a Famous German Classic

Klaus Doderer

PERMANENT MODERNIZATION

Children's literature is involved in a continuing and irreversible process of change and modernization. It begins at the very moment in which a narrative comes into contact with one or more recipients. Each recipient will accept the forms, contents, and messages of the text in his or her own way. It is therefore not possible to present a children's story, poem, or play without giving a new version or sometimes a new interpretation of the original. This happens in simple oral retelling as well as in transforming classics into media such as film, theater, or radio. To present the version means to change the original.

Why is each presentation always an alteration, to a greater or lesser degree, of the original? Because the circumstances of the birth of a piece of fiction and the circumstances of its presentation and reception are always different. Such a thesis would seem to be self-evident, and it applies not only to children's literature, but to works of literature in general. Nevertheless, as the German proverb goes *"Der Teufel steckt im Detail!"* ("The devil is hidden in the details"). It reminds us that we have to differentiate between one situation and another, between one text and another, between one retelling and another, and between one audience and another. The interpretations and recipients are always different.

Some ideas expressed in *Retelling Stories, Framing Culture*, by John Stephens and Robyn McCallum (1998), relate to my theme. One sentence runs: "A reteller has to struggle with and overcome material which is always to some extent intractable because of its combination of strong, familiar story shapes with already legitimized values and ideas about the world" (x). I agree with this statement and I also share Stephens and McCallum's opinion that there is a trend in children's literature, especially in its traditional stories, "not just to preserve culture but to reproduce conservative outcomes" (ibid.). The question I ask is whether this thesis of reproducing conservative outcomes is also correct in relation to the text that I deal with in this chapter. I wish to analyze one story only, but nonetheless I have two subjects. The first is—in Stephens and McCallum's terms—"the material." It is the famous, and internationally well-known, German children's book by Erich Kästner: *Emil und die Detektive (Emil and the Detectives)*, which was first published in 1929. My second subject is—in Stephens and McCallum's terms—the "retelling"; that is, the film "*Emil und die Detektive*," which is based on the book and was produced in 2001. It has itself since become a bestseller.

THE ORIGINAL BOOK, ITS BIRTH, ITS AUTHOR, ITS RECEPTION

If we consider the "material"—that is, the original story—we can see that the plot is well structured. Emil, a schoolboy, is robbed of his money on a train to Berlin, where he is going to spend his holidays with his grandmother. In Berlin, Emil finds children—girls and boys of his own age—who form a group to help him. The main part of the story describes how Emil and his new friends search for the thief in Berlin. They are the detectives who hunt throughout the city, along the streets, and in the buildings, either running and walking or taking the tram. There is a happy end because Emil is able to prove, in a bank, that the thief's money was in fact originally his. The clever boy can show the adults pinhole marks he had made on the banknotes. The characters in the story are strong, and the relationship between them is based more on rational than on emotional criteria. First, there is Emil, a clever and obliging boy who arrives in the bustling capital from a small town. The other children are friends who spontaneously decide to help the strange newcomer. They are all involved in the task, but each member of the gang has a different function: one has to keep watch, another mans the telephone, and so on. They all come from different social backgrounds, but in this story they are equal, doing real teamwork. There is only one evil figure in the novel, and he is an adult; it is the thief, who appears in the book well dressed and wears a bowler hat.

The background and the setting are taken from an urban environment during the Golden Twenties of the last century in Berlin. Cars, trams, advertising pillars, hotels, and a bank provide the context of the story. The boys and girls are clever and self-confident members of this urban society. Such a special setting, such self-confident characters, and such a thrilling detective story in which boys and girls are triumphant—all told in realistic, contemporary language—combine to produce an atmosphere previously unknown in either German children's literature or in other children's literatures. That was the main reason for the enormous international success of the novel.

It was Erich Kästner's first novel for children. At that time, he was a rising star in the new generation of writers in Germany. When he wrote *Emil und die Detektive* he was 30, had previously published attacking poems on political and social issues, and was a pacifist and a democrat, fighting as a critic and essayist against the upcoming Nazis.

What kind of ideological issues can we find in *Emil und die Detektive?* First, children are participants in the social life of a modern urban and mobile society; second, children are confronted with the negative aspects of a modern lifestyle; third, human beings generally, and children especially, are strong if they work together and stick together; and fourth, children are able to solve a crime committed by an adult person on their own. Behind the fable, behind the characters, behind the setting and events of the original novel, and between the words and sentences of the text was a new philosophy of how children could live. It was the modern spirit of the Golden Twenties set against the fascinating backdrop of Berlin. It was the period before Hitler and before the Second World War.

Let me say something about the character Emil. He became an outstanding figure in the consciousness of many generations of children in German-speaking countries and beyond; the symbol of a clever, independent, open-minded boy who is also both brave and intelligent. He acquired an independent fictional identity outside the novel in the same way as did Heidi, Pippi Longstocking, Momo, Huckleberry Finn, Tom Sawyer, Peter Pan, Alice, and Harry Potter.

Widespread national and international reception followed shortly after publication in 1929. The text was translated into more than 50 languages and millions of copies were sold. A year after the novel was first published it was performed as a play, and a year later the first Emil film—in black and white—was screened in cinemas. In Hollywood, some suggested that the famous child star Shirley Temple should be offered the role of Emil. Films of Emil were made in the United States, England, Brazil, Japan (twice), and Germany (three times).

THE FILM OF 2001—A RETOLD AND CHANGED VERSION

Now, 72 years after the first edition of the novel, we are presented with an excellent cinematic renewal of Kästner's work (*Emil und die Detektive* 2001). The question is: is it a retelling with a tendency to cultivate conservative outcomes, or is it an example of the fact that an existing narrative nucleus, created in the head of an excellent writer and implanted into a children's novel of the early twentieth century, can become an essential part of a wonderful modernized version that is, in its own terms, likely to preserve modern culture?

First, we have to identify the characters, settings, and events in the film. The main character, Emil, has the same qualities as in the original narrative. His opponent, the thief, behaves in the same cunning way as in the book. The gang of children has the same function as in the original text. Berlin remains the place of action and the urban landscape is still full of busy traffic and crowds of people. Second, the nucleus of the story—or, to use my preferred term, the "fable"—has not changed: A boy, robbed in a railway compartment, follows the thief in an exciting pursuit through the streets, tunnels, parks, and buildings of Berlin, helped by a very active team of children. The clever gang manages to catch the thief, and there is a happy end. Third, the spirit of the text and its hidden messages remain in the film retelling: for example, it is a good thing to help others who are in need, especially other children; it is possible to make decisions and work independently, even as a child; if you share work with others you can be more effective; and if you use your brains then you will come out on top. Thus, there are many qualities that are "retold."

Nevertheless, the cinematic renewal of 2001 has many other aspects that are different and new, and have both changed and enriched the original narrative. They all follow the same tendency: to infuse the spirit of contemporary life into the story without changing the original fable. The social problems of our time and our society are transferred into the story. For instance, the leading role in the gang is now filled by a female character, a clever girl with an Italian background who works in a pizza restaurant in Berlin. So we are now confronted with two main actors, Emil and the girl called "Pony Hütchen," who are like a young couple (albeit without developing a love affair!). In addition, in this film version, the group of Berlin children are now multicultural, and include, among others, a gypsy boy and a Turkish break-dancer. The children from the slums mix with the son of the owner of a high-class restaurant. In addition, in this film version, Emil lives with his divorced father, who is out of work, whereas in the original book, Emil was the son of a hard-working widow. The boy's home is now located on the coast of the Baltic Sea in an impoverished area of Eastern Germany. The host in Berlin is no longer the boy's grandmother, but a young female vicar and her son. The settings, therefore, are the settings of our time. The children have mobile phones; the vicar's son uses his mother's computer; other children have skate-boards, kickboards, and in-line skates; and they read comics. The taxis look like taxis in any large contemporary city, and the emblems on the windscreen often indicate the country of origin of the drivers. The hotel in the film is a version of the famous "*Adlon*," well-known in Germany because many tele-vision programs have been broadcast from there. The thief is now dressed in a leather suit and has tattoos. These and many other minor changes abound.

It is important to remember that the original text's intention was to present the problems of the "modern era" of 1929 in a children's novel. This film version places the plot in contemporary Berlin and projects the social problems of today onto the basic story without destroying the original message.

CONCLUSION

My question at the outset was: What kind of changes and renewals took place in the film *Emil und die Detektive* (2001)? Is the result a new production with "conservative outcomes" or an appropriate and equivalent transformation with "cultural signification"?

In comparing Erich Kästner's famous classic published in 1929 with the film of 2001, we find that the fable of the original "material" and the nucleus in the retelling are identical. The story of the boy who is robbed, the pursuit of the thief in Berlin, the help offered by the group of children, and the happy ending all remain in the film. I would call this the fundamental fable. Around this fundamental narrative basis there are a number of components that can be found in the book as well as in the film: most of the characters have not been changed, the location of the main events is Berlin, and what is stolen is money.

However, there are also some differences. For instance, the female character—the girl with the little hat, "Pony Hütchen"—has a leading role and high moral status in the film, which she didn't have in the book. In addition, Emil's hometown is in a different part of Germany and Berlin is now the city of 2001 with the capital's landmarks occasionally shown in the background. Last but not least: in the 1929 book Emil was robbed of just 140 German marks; in the film it is 1,500. Obviously, the strategy of the reteller—in this case the highly talented theater director Franziska Buch, who also wrote the screenplay—was to modernize the story around the original fable. Why? Because the fable and its ethical content are still attractive in our current cultural context. The reteller therefore introduces some changed characters, settings, and events into the original fable. The point is, however, that the basic ethical quality, the open-minded spirit, and the fresh and optimistic feeling in the film have been taken from the book unaltered. The political and economic background of the contemporary German situation is referred to—problems such as unemployment, especially in Eastern Germany, or the multicultural structure of society. In addition, an up-to-date approach to sex education is apparent. Should we deny that kind of use of originals? Should we insist on an eternal copyright to protect the original? Should we declare that only the author's original is worthy of survival? Clearly stories should be updated, but we should try to retain their original message.

We now have more than one version of Emil, so we also have more than one way to become acquainted with this wonderful fable and its optimistic spirit. We can read, hear, and see the story of a boy who learns the hard facts of life and we can enjoy, in different media, a story filled with visions of hope, help, and solidarity.

BIBLIOGRAPHY

Emil und die Detektive. 2001. Filmstrip. Ed. Franziska Buch. Constantin Film, Munich.

Kästner, Erich. 1929. *Emil und die Detektive: ein Roman für Kinder (Emil and the Detectives).* Berlin-Grünewald: Williams & Co.

Stephens, John, and Robyn McCallum. 1998. *Retelling Stories, Framing Culture.* London: Garland Publishing.

CHAPTER 18

Too Many Elephants? Endangered Discourses in the Field of Children's Literature

Nancy Huse

This contribution originated in paradox when, wanting to be a genuinely international society, the International Research Society for Children's Literature (IRSCL) planned its biennial conference in South Africa (2001) and sought papers that would interpret the literatures of many nations. Thus began the paradox examined in this chapter.

Paradox is a useful metaphor to describe the complex speech and writing issues in an organization attempting to communicate across cultures about literary histories. However, an organization studying youth literature is particularly aware of, resistant to, and—perhaps—shaped by power/knowledge hierarchies. We analyze texts whose readers are not involved as authors; texts that often have relatively little fame, and which others in the scholarly group may not have read. Although none of these circumstances preclude our writing and giving papers at a conference, they do make such papers more than usually prone to unintelligibility when read aloud for and by critics using their second, third, or fourth language. Moreover, the struggle to achieve recognition for the study of youth literature as intellectual endeavor can dictate use of extremely standardized form and method. Hoped-for publication of conference papers exercises control over their writing and delivery, even though we may have earnest hope of oral discussion once the papers have been read aloud from a printed (typed) script.

A meeting of scholars in a new field—scholars from different continents as well as different language communities—requires not so much the tried and true tactics of the academy, but, as Walter Ong (1977) might agree, an oratory transformed by new media such as television. We need to speak publicly in a more private manner than print allows; we need to create face-to-face conversation. In addition to the changes in orality that Ong recommends, however, we also need changes in our writing practices. Several feminist critics, in particular, have urged that we scholars "get personal" in order to be effective as a social force (see, for example, Greene and Kahn 1993: 22). These considerations led me to shape a conference paper around the premise that a conversation requires a range of expressive possibilities, a certain lack of predictability too often missing from a set of scholarly papers.

Of course, I have had to face the paradox that a certain predictability is itself the essence of academic writing. Argumentation implies more standardization than does conversation. That results in papers that sound and look alike in print, and a vital part of a conference is lost in favor of the verifiability and details that the academy values. However, standardization weakens the IRSCL and similar organizations that must intervene dynamically in the processes of literacy and creativity represented by youth literature. Several examples of how standard expectations make us less effective as intellectuals comprised the speech I gave in South Africa in 2001, and in this chapter I elaborate on these examples in order to present my work as something of an argument while retaining a testimonial tone. I hope to show the political implications of aesthetic practices, so that our expectations will shift to allow experimentation and work in progress a more central place in our publications.

In a truly international conversation about youth literature, one might expect that regional patterns, various kinds of group diaspora, and the migrating identities of readers would produce a multiply intersecting set of discourses—splendid and intriguing, empowering and puzzling. Like the giraffes that move with zebras, like the mongoose and monkeys who play at the picnic tables in South Africa's national parks, our ways of talking, listening, and writing should open creation itself, so that scholars make it clear that our work is about generation, reproduction, the newness of cooperation, and community. Of course, I am far from alone in wondering how we can be more effective in articulating such urgent concerns.

These spirited words—generation, reproduction, and community—are frequent mantras in a recent book by Michael Hardt and Antonio Negri dealing with globalization and touted in *The New York Times Book Review* section as the "answer" to a moribund academic culture, a synthesis of political and literary theory. The work's central claim is that expansive networking—an exodus from closed systems, a migration away from dialectics and polarization, in which we learn to think globally and *act* globally too—is crucial to a decent world (Hardt and Negri 2000). Another critic, Isobel Armstrong, in *The Radical Aesthetic* (2000), argues that a decent world depends on play, because through its cognitive passion things lose their determining force and we become able to transform categories through a heightened sense of contradiction. Like the authors of *Empire*, who cite Charlie Chaplin and Saint Francis among their heroes, the author of *Radical Aesthetic* depends on cultural icons that many children's literature scholars know well: Vygotsky, Winnicott, and Dewey. Thus, if these two examples of what the world needs are any indication of the worth of our studies, we would seem far ahead in the game of change and renewal. Scholars of children's literature are forming vital networks about texts that the culture associates with play. For many of us, children's literature constitutes a cultural text that demonstrates the "work" of "play." However, that very paradox complicates the production of knowledge in the field.

Even though I would prefer to boast about the wisdom of the IRSCL, the sojourn in South Africa evoked a cautionary fable for critics. Visitors to this country delight in seeing storied animals in their habitats, yet the ingeniously devised parks cannot guarantee the animals' survival. Elephants, for example, abundant in the small territories available to them, are endangered. They need too many trees, too much space, and they forage until a landscape is barren. Rangers try various ways to thin the herds, but the gloomiest forecasters say that this species is already too genetically limited to survive. I think that academics resemble elephants, because once we pass over a trail, the force of our jargons, assumptions, and practices leaves a chewed-up sameness in its wake. Papers often sound exactly alike, making large claims about many narratives at once. Otherwise, the work is thought unscholarly and even kept from a hearing, or, if the paper giver is not part of a herd, he or she is not *heard*, even if permitted to speak. We are used to certain patterns; certain discourses are acceptable, and we had best not depart from them. My examples run the gamut from the introduction of new information to the politics of translation and publication, and from the limitations of conventional categories such as "nation" and "genre" to the possibilities that an author's transgressive texts can open for us. Think of this litany in the same the way that we think of sighting animals in their habitats: if we listen, if we watch, if we concede that multiple species determine a sound ecosystem, then my string of examples offers coherence of the kind that is obtained on safari rather than the kind that is obtained in detached and controlled argument.

My first example is drawn from a symposium at the University of South Africa, which the Board of the IRSCL took part in during a conference preparation meeting in August 2000. My paper tracing a mermaid story from Africa to America and back via the widely circulated work of Hans Christian Andersen awardee Virginia Hamilton (1936–2002) described how a wealthy white American anthropologist, Elsie Clews Parsons (1874–1941), had gathered nearly the entire canon of African American folktales we possess. Some of Hamilton's brilliance depends on the brilliance of that scholar as precursor. A scholar who believed passionately in multiculturalism early in the twentieth century, Parsons's pioneering anthropology stands as the foundation of many writers' work. Hamilton, like many of these writers, acknowledged Parsons as the source for her mermaid tale even while meticulously foregrounding the indigenous storyteller over the collector of folklore. The connection between Elsie Clews Parsons and Virginia Hamilton is a piece of women's intellectual history as well as an example of how youth literature draws from and even inspires cultural knowledge. As a major theorist of human community, Parsons is important to our scholarship. However, these claims seemed a deflection from, rather than an addition to, that scholarship; apparently, because a summary of my paper about Hamilton's mermaid tale included in the *IRSCL Newsletter* (Machet 2000) erased references to Elsie Clews Parsons. We are not used to crossing disciplinary boundaries, and when we make the attempt, we can lose our audience. Awareness of how difficult it is for literary critics to make new connections that defy our assumptions about power (for example, a white anthropologist effectively transmitting black folklore, a black writer acknowledging this process as part of her own genius) can signal us as to the importance of an aesthetic that values bird watching as well as big game viewing. Maybe bird watching, instead of elephant tracking, is a better global action, a more playful reality, and one that can make our work flourish. With that claim, I want to show several examples of endangered discourses—small creative creatures, not the mighty elephants we are used to tracking, reading, and publishing.

I carried books to the conference for discussion, in the spirit of intentional migratory labor that can transform *empire* and true to the notion of a radical aesthetic that closes the gap between language and objects. If the reason for measuring one another's scholarly achievements by volume and by analytic thoroughness is to prove that we belong to the academic world, then passing these volumes around in a print imitation of a speaker's props and hypothesizing about the discursive strategies we would need to understand them will have to be my proof strategy. I raise a series of questions about these books, based on examples of what is "out" as critical method. The idea is to open our ears to the sounds of the night, to the ideas that chirp and growl in the unexplored terrain of one another's experience.

My examples deal with three discourses: those of (1) dominant groups working with subaltern peoples, (2) activists assuming that childhood is not a separate sphere, and (3) writers who undergo significant cultural change well after reputations are established. For each of these discursive practices, there is a silencing scholarly paradigm. The language of colonizers is suspect; the agendas of activists self-interested; and writers survive because of patterns that critics approve of, not because the writers have authority. These discourses depend on unusual power dynamics to be heard, a willingness to suspend the disbelief our schooling teaches us as a major way of knowing. If we hear these discourses, it is because we are allowing one another to speak and be accepted in our differences.

I have already cited the work of Elsie Clews Parsons, the American anthropologist who gathered folktales from African American working people and thus is foundational to much subsequent literature. She also fostered the career of Zora Neale Hurston. Parsons was an elite with a dream, and it is not possible to talk about her work if we are reluctant to use the texts that missionaries and teachers have gathered. What will happen to folklore traditions that do not become codified in children's literature? Does it matter if tribal stories disappear? If we assume that all stories are alike, using an archetypal approach, then it may not matter. However, if we have resources such as Parsons's work, archives that preserve stories well, can we not at least inquire into what they hold? The example I want to discuss, one of the fearless encounters with elite culture by those of us searching for the lost stories, is from the work of the African American artist Faith Ringgold (b. 1930). Her story quilt *Dancing at the Louvre* (Cameron et al. 1998) shows art made from art and experience, a "radical aesthetic" dependent on a sense of play that transforms spaces. Readers of this article will have to imagine the two little girls dancing before the Mona Lisa, their braids flying, their artist mother flailing her arms; or, in the exploratory spirit of Louise Rosenblatt, whose transactional theory is widely circulated in the United States at least, readers will search out the work of Ringgold as an important part of evaluating the worth of my argument. (Reprinting Ringgold's pictures here would be best, of course, but costs are a barrier to inclusion in many scholarly books on children's literature.) Readers equipped with computers can, of course, view some of Ringgold's work on her Web site (www.faithringgold.com). As can be seen, our print limitations and expanded orality through the Internet are fully relevant to the notion that we need other activities besides the elephant watching that is common to our practice as published scholars.

The point of citing and showing Ringgold, then, is to manifest what could happen when artists transform traditional, patriarchal, racist practices via self-conscious metanarratives and other depictions of how various accounts must be juxtaposed, taken provisionally, and used merrily or wisely. We should be making books from records gathered by colonizers and transformed by our imaginative disobedience to official strictures. Bilingual or trilingual editions of Zulu stories should fill the bookstores, not just Harry Potter books. How many of our possibilities are daunted by avoidance and fear when we peruse archives or choose stories to retell? Ringgold herself had to find a way to use her painterly training to aid her development as a quilt artist, and then she resisted the art establishment in choosing to create children's books out of her profound aesthetic.

The second endangered discourse I ponder is that of activists writing for children as though young readers in fact are part of resistance to oppression or standardization. Normally, the work of activists in children's literature is unheralded, as though social change is unrelated to literary quality. Even when we know of writers' activism, those efforts are steadily seen as sidelines to the art; one example is Astrid Lindgren's work to provide humane conditions for animals in Sweden's food industries. Our strictures about narrative theory, the death of the author, or textual intricacies make it difficult to see this work as part of Lindgren's aesthetic impact, yet if we had ways to tell this story might we not realize what her books mean in deeper ways?

To reify my earlier point about drawing from intellectual predecessors in the ways in which Hamilton and Ringgold have done, I would like to refer to the work of a U.S. activist who influenced the more internationally known feminist writer for adults, Tillie Olsen. Meridel LeSueur, a feminist and communist, wrote lyrically and transformatively about the relationship of reproduction to production in *Nancy Hanks of Wilderness Road: A Story of Abraham Lincoln's Mother* ([1949] 1990). During a time when her work was blacklisted, LeSueur was able to publish children's books through Alfred Knopf. Until she died in 1999, LeSueur continued to view children as people with rights and power whom she could enlist in social change (LeSueur 1990). This view however is discouraged by our sense of children's vulnerability and by our fears of our own will to power. The question of whether LeSueur's editors at Knopf recognized her political creed as the basis of her children's books is still open. Were the books accepted because professional readers' responses did not pick up on the ways in which LeSueur imagined a changed world; or were they able to support a valued writer under attack by virtue of subterfuge, capitalizing on the "innocence" assumed in children's stories and in child readers? We do not know; records of editors' correspondence were destroyed when Knopf was bought by a large conglomerate. Like Ringgold, LeSueur herself believed that the realm of children's books offered more freedom in times of cultural conflict than did the world of adults' books (LeSueur 1990).

Such optimism from the writers is encouraging, but it seems to have become more difficult now to publish in English any children's books that argue unpopular political beliefs. One example, given to me in 1983 by an editor in Sweden, can illustrate the problem. Even though *Drakberget* (1981), written by Stefan Mahlqvist and illustrated by Tord Nygren, meets every standard of literary and artistic quality, this story of workers' rights and of the environment did not find an English language publisher. The assumption that children should not hear about Marx and the idea of workers of the world uniting blocked the circulation of the book to English language readers. The picture of child laborers underscores the irony of this marketing practice. How well do our ways of investigating texts allow us to hear the discourses of activism? Do children's books continue to present a smooth surface, like the controlled packaging of reality that Hardt and Negri (2000) name "Empire?" When books do unsettle the status quo, do we talk about them in ways that make this clear? Aren't there now controlling assumptions in the academy that culture determines us, without strong beliefs that we can change culture? Do such assumptions make powerful intellectuals and artists like Ringgold and LeSueur look naive and ineffectual in terms of their sociopolitical struggles? Many problematic literary issues are overlooked in the study of children's books because activism is assumed irrelevant to the work of the humanities and of the professional fields involved in discussing children's literature.

Intrinsic to an analysis of activism is artistic adaptation and appropriation. When IRSCL president Sandra Beckett asked each board member to pick out a book from his or her "home" country to take to the 2001 conference, I considered Nancy Willard's play, *East of the Sun & West of the Moon* (1989), a beautiful book I happened upon in my search for a suitable example of U.S. children's literature. Nancy Willard is one of the best writers in the United States, but I wondered if I could count this play as coming from "my" national literature. It crunches with English word play and child life that I recognize as "American," yet could I say that the book was "from" the United States at all? Wouldn't that deny the Norwegian origins of the story? I instead picked out a book of Seuss's artwork to bring, because I had less trouble seeing him in a national framework. I'm certain that if I really thought about Dr. Seuss as an artist, though, I would see a great deal more than American brush strokes. Thus, the academic impulse to be inclusive by encouraging us to select books from our own cultures is fraught with all kinds of difficulty, and that paradox is the point of my discussion. Each critical decision we make must be viewed in a wider context of global studies, and we must offer alternative critical paradigms as often as we can. Otherwise, our bonds with one another fall out of our memories and purposes. The elephant of nationalism is all too convenient in our categorizing.

A final example of endangered discourse in our field is an author's departure from her usual practice, and what happens when she shifts to use observations of children rather than allusions to classics to make her mark. Although Katherine Paterson has certainly made use of her knowledge of children to construct her books—the false dichotomy between observation and allusion must be qualified in her case above all—she has had a stunning ability to use references to other literary works to create her narratives. Easily noted are references to Narnia in *Bridge to Terabithia* (1977); allusions to Tolkien, Wordsworth, and folklore in the story of Gilly Hopkins (1978); and to the Parsifal structure of *Park's Quest* (1988). However, in a 1994 novel, *The Flip-Flop Girl*, Paterson departs from conscious use of written texts as muse for her own. This story does employ familiar Paterson word play—the title refers overtly to the orange sandals or flip-flops a girl in the story wears, and covertly to the protagonist herself, who is grounded in sturdier footwear but who finds herself unsteady nonetheless—but there are few references to literature, and Vinnie does not recover from the death of her father by reading books or imagining alternative worlds. The nonsense of ordinary life, in which a father can die of cancer and medical bills force a family to move in with a grandmother, sets the story in motion. The child who helps Vinnie is herself grieving a lost father, one incarcerated for murdering her mother. Paterson makes clear in her acknowledgement of the work of Virginia Fry, a teacher who works with disturbed children, that she is drawing on children's behavior and not—at least consciously—on mythic patterns to build a heroic tale. Although I am certain that an astute critic can show these operating in the text, it seems more important to note how the most bizarre elements of the story are the truest—the ones drawn from the kind of complex reality that will always be understood better if people's power to change their circumstances is acknowledged. Play is key to survival of the children—they each draw on games or songs they remember from their fathers, and the teacher they love is both playful and willing to cross boundaries. The teacher's presence evokes the girls' pain and healing in the absence of their fathers. The example is illustrative, however, of our practices in the academy. If I think that Paterson has done the impossible feat of moving outside of the monomyth, then I should explain, at great length, why and how this is so. However, I don't imagine Paterson "outside" of her storytelling history, even though this book seems different from many of her others. Instead, I believe there is a shift in her work that is important, even though it may be too soon to understand it. I need not understand it, I think, to recommend the book to you, but that is an unusual gesture in a published chapter. It reminds me of a story I heard about Eric Erickson, standing up after panels discussed "Ericksonian theory" and announcing that he was wrong, all wrong, when he thought those things, and they should no longer be described as "Ericksonian." Thus, this category of endangered discourse is the idea of change itself within a writer's subjectivity, and how readers produce meanings that can allow for authors who actually exist, struggle, and matter.

Literary life, then, must consist of listening to small variations, to heartbeats, to odd and unrealized insights as much as preferring grand schemata, stunning interpretations, and convincing arguments. The discourses I've described as "endangered" are the relatively unpopular ones of working across class, race, and gender lines; of advocating, with passion, alternative views of the world; and of noticing a writer's late work or aberrational moves as part of our descriptive and interpretive codes. The critical works I read as I prepared this chapter—*Empire* (Hardt and Negri 2000) and *The Radical Aesthetic* (Armstrong 2000)—are probably renewals rather than changes in literary studies, yet I hope that writing about children's books can sometimes be new; conceptions not heard, seen, or imagined before—children's literature as a source for theory building rather than a structure illustrative of known patterns. Although it might be too humble an example to startle us into actions that are global, Walt Whitman's poem "When I Heard the Learned Astronomer" can be instructive. It would not be much consolation to know about galaxies if the night skies were permanently darkened by pollution, and it is important to know the cost of keeping elephants in boundaries.

> When I heard the learn'd astronomer,
> When the proofs, the figures were ranged in columns before me,
> When I was shown the charts and diagrams, to add, divide, and measure
>   them,
> When I sitting heard the astronomer where he lectured with much applause
>   in the lecture room,
> How soon unaccountable I became tired and sick,
> Till rising and gliding out I wander'd off by myself,
> In the mystical moist night-air, and from time to time,
> Look'd up in perfect silence at the stars (see Van Doren 1945: 214–15).

BIBLIOGRAPHY

Armstrong, Isobel. 2000. *The Radical Aesthetic*. Oxford, U.K.: Blackwell Publishers.

Cameron, Dan, et al. 1998. *Faith Ringgold's French Collection and Other Story Quilts: Dancing at the Louvre*. Berkeley: University of California Press.

Greene, Gael, and Coppelia Kahn, ed. 1993. *Changing Subjects: The Making of Feminist Literary Criticism*. London: Routledge.

Hardt, Michael, and Antonio Negri. 2000. *Empire*. Cambridge, Mass.: Harvard University Press.

LeSueur, Meridel. [1949] 1990. *Nancy Hanks of Wilderness Road: A Story of Abraham Lincoln's Mother*. Reprint, New York: Knopf.

LeSueur, Meridel. 1990. Interview with author. Tape recording. Hudson, Minnesota, 12 May. See Nancy Huse, "Of Nancy Hanks Born: Meridel LeSueur's Abraham Lincoln." *ChLAQ* 18 (1), Spring 1993.

Machet, Myrna. 2000. "Children's Literature Symposium in South Africa." *IRSCL Newsletter*, no. 4.

Mahlqvist, Stefan. 1981. *Drakberget*, illus. Tord Nygren. Stockholm: Raben & Sjogren.

Ong, Walter. 1977. *Interfaces of the Word: Studies in the Evolution of Consciousness and Culture*. London: Cornell University Press.

Paterson, Katherine. 1978. *The Great Gilly Hopkins*. New York: Crowell.

Paterson, Katherine. 1988. *Park's Quest*. New York: Dutton.

Paterson, Katherine. 1994. *The Flip-Flop Girl*. New York: Lodestar.

Ringgold, Faith, Linda Freeman, and Nancy Roucher. 1996. *Talking to Faith Ringgold*. New York: Crown Publishers.

Rosenblatt, Louise. 1997. *Literature as Exploration*. 5th ed. New York: MLA.

Seuss, Dr. (Theodore Geisel). 1995. *The Secret Art of Dr. Seuss*. New York: Random House.

Van Doren, Mark, ed. 1945. *The Portable Walt Whitman*. New York: Penguin Books.

Willard, Nancy. 1989. *East of the Sun & West of the Moon*, illus. Barry Moser. New York: Harcourt.

Index

About the Contributors

CLARE BRADFORD teaches and carries out research at Deakin University in Melbourne. She is the editor of the journal *Papers: Explorations into Children's Literature*, and has published many journal articles and book chapters on aspects of children's literature, especially picture books and colonial and postcolonial literatures. Her most recent book is *Reading Race: Aboriginality in Australian Children's Literature* (2001). She is currently working on a comparative study of contemporary texts from settler societies.

KLAUS DODERER is professor (emeritus) of Literature at Frankfurt University. He was the director of the Institut für Jugendbuchforschung (Institute for Research in Children's Literature) at this university from 1963 to 1990. Doderer has analyzed literary genres, children's literature, and children's theater; has written about authors such as Hans Christian Andersen, W. Benjamin, Erich Kästner, Astrid Lindgren, Antoine de Saint-Exupéry, and Mark Twain; and has edited the first encyclopedia of children's literature, *Lexikon der Kinder und Jugendliteratur (Lexicon for children's and young adult literature)*, which was published in four volumes (1975–1982, reprinted in 1995). Professor Doderer was the first president of the International Research Society for Children's Literature (1970–1974) and the receiver of the International Brothers Grimm Award (Osaka, Japan) in 1987.

EILEEN DONALDSON is currently completing her master's degree in English Literature at the University of Pretoria. She is researching the role of the female hero in the genres of contemporary science fiction and science fantasy. Her fields of academic interest are fantasy and science fiction, and she is also involved in teaching English as a foreign language.

VICTORIA FLANAGAN is a Ph.D. candidate at Macquarie University, Sydney, Australia. She is working on her Ph.D. dissertation, "Cross-Dressing, Sex, and Gender in Children's Literature."

SIRKE HAPPONEN is preparing for her Ph.D. dissertation on Tove Jansson's Moomin books, texts, and illustrations, at the University of Helsinki, Finland. Her special focus is on movement implied by images and words. She has held positions as a research fellow and is currently a lecturer at the University of Helsinki. Her contribution to this volume was written during a research year at Macquarie University in Sydney, Australia. Her research interests include picture books and children's theatre.

MARGOT HILLEL is head of the School of Arts and Sciences (Victoria) at Australian Catholic University. She has published widely in the field of children's literature, both in scholarly and professional journals and in textbooks for teachers. She is president of the Australasian Children's Literature Association for Research.

HELENE HØYRUP is an associate professor at The Royal School of Library and Information Science, Denmark. She teaches children's literature and culture, and her work focuses on children's literature in a cultural perspective; that is, processes of canonization, mechanisms of defining taste, and aesthetics. Currently, she is doing research on Hans Christian Andersen and the shaping of the Danish field of children's literature in the nineteenth century.

NANCY HUSE is professor of English at Augustana College (Illinois), where she teaches youth literature, feminist theory, life writing, and other courses. She is a past president of ChLA (1995) and a former board member of the International Research Society for Children's Literature. Her books include *Noel Streatfeild*, a study of the British writer of children and adult's novels from a cultural feminist perspective. She has published articles in a number of journals on such writers as Katherine Paterson, Meridel LeSueur, Tove Jansson, and Louise Montgomery. Her current work in progress is an analysis of women's writing for children from the standpoint of various feminists.

JUDITH INGGS is a senior lecturer in Translation and Interpreting Studies in the School of Language and Literature at the University of the Witwatersrand. With a background in Russian and Linguistics, she completed her doctorate in 1997 on Soviet children's literature and poetry in translation, and South African youth literature. A more recent interest is in translations and adaptations of South African folk tales.

ROSEMARY JOHNSTON is the director of the Centre for Research and Education in the Arts at the University of Technology, Sydney, Australia. Her most recent publication is *Literacy: Reading, Writing and Children's Literature* (with other authors, 2001). She is a contributor to *Crossing the Boundaries* (2001), and has commissioned chapters appearing in two other books currently in production. She was secretary of the International Research Society for Children's Literature (1997–2001) and is associate secretary-general of the Federation Internationale des Langues et Litteratures Modernes (since 1997), an international board member of the Montgomery Institute (Canada), and a member of the International Committee of the Children's Literature Association. In 2000, she was H.W. Donner Guest Research Professor at Ebo Akademi University, Finland, working with a project funded by the Finnish Ministry of Education.

MARIA LASSÉN-SEGER holds a degree in English Language and Literature, Comparative Literature, Library Science, and Folkloristics from Åbo Akademi University. She is, at present, a junior research fellow in the English Department, on secondment from her post in the university library. She lectures on children's literature and is a regular reviewer of children's fiction. She began her doctoral studies within the ChiLPA project and is currently working on her Ph.D. dissertation "Metamorphoses of the Fictive Child in Late Twentieth Century English-Language Children's Literature."

DARJA MAZI-LESKOVAR is assistant professor at the Faculty of Electrical Engineering, Computer Science, and Media Communication and at the Faculty of Law at Maribor University, Slovenia. Her research interests are theory and poetics of children's literature, cross-culturalism and translations, young adult fiction, and fiction for dual audiences; as well as the history of children's literature. Her articles explore children's literature written in English and in Slovenian.

EVA-MARIA METCALF is Croft Assistant Professor of German at the University of Mississippi. A specialist on postwar Scandinavian, German, and Austrian children's literature, the major part of her work has been on Astrid Lindgren and Christine Nöstlinger. She studied at the University of Stockholm and received her Ph.D. from the University of Minnesota.

RIITTA OITTINEN holds a doctorate in literary translation and lectures in general translation studies at the Universities of Helsinki and Tampere. She is also a senior lecturer at the School of Modern Languages and Translation Studies of the University of Tampere. She is a scholar specializing in literary translation, text, and illustration (fiction and nonfiction), and translation theory. She is also a translator and illustrator. Oittinen is the author of the books *I Am Me—I Am Other: On the Dialogics of Translating for Children* (1993),

Kääntäjän Karnevaali (*Translator's Carnival*; 1995), *Liisa, Liisa ja Alice* (*Liisa, Liisa and Alice*; 1997), and *Translating for Children* (2000). Her new book, *Kuvakirja kääntäjän kädessä* (*Translating the picture books*) is due in 2004; she is writing an English-language book on the same topic.

ROLF ROMÖREN is a research fellow at the Institute of Norwegian Language, Literature and Media, Agder University College, Norway. His research interests include the history of children's literature, humor in children's literature, theory and poetics of children's literature, and boys' fiction. He is also a former vice president of the International Research Society for Children's Literature.

DAVID RUDD lectures in the Department of Cultural and Creative Studies, Bolton Institute, England, where he teaches courses on children's literature and critical theory. He has published articles in the fields of education, librarianship, media, and cultural studies, but mostly in children's literature, including a study of Roald Dahl's popularity with children (*A Communication Studies Approach to Children's Literature*, 1992) and *Enid Blyton and the Mystery of Children's Literature* (2000).

ANNA KARLSKOV SKYGGEBJERG is a Ph.D. student at the Centre for Children's Literature at The Danish University of Education, Copenhagen, working on the project "Fantasy Tales in Danish Children's Literature." She has published several articles about fantasy and children's literature in books and periodicals in Danish. She has worked with intertextuality in children's literature and the interplay between the romantic and the postmodern period.

THOMAS VAN DER WALT is a senior lecturer in the Department of Information Science at the University of South Africa in Pretoria. He is also the founder and chair of the Children's Literature Research Unit at the University of South Africa. He obtained his doctorate in Library and Information Science on the "Portrayal of the Boer War in South African Children's Literature" at the Rand Afrikaans University, Johannesburg, and also obtained postgraduate qualifications in History, Cultural History, Archival Science and Museum Science at the Universities of Pretoria, Potchefstroom, South Africa, and the Royal School of Archives, the Netherlands. He is the President of the African Research Society for Children's Literature and served three terms on the Board of the International Research Society for Children's Literature (IRSCL).

ANNE DE VRIES was curator for children's literature at the Dutch Literature Museum and the Dutch National Library, and part-time lecturer at the Free University of Amsterdam. Since his early retirement in 2002, he has been a freelance researcher and publicist. For more than 10 years, his research has concentrated on poetry for children.